This book is dedicated t
You were both out there

Published by BA Press 2021

Copyright © James Lee 2021

The moral right of the author has been asserted

ISBN No. 9798703160046

Typeset in Minion by Bus Stop Editorial Services

Cover and illustrations by Gary Bainbridge

LICKING
the TALIBAN'S
FLIP-FLOP

JAMES LEE

BA Press

KENT

Foreword

I AM OFTEN asked the same questions by friends and colleagues when they find out that I had served in Afghanistan. "Did you kill anyone, I bet you don't want to talk about it and what was it like?" My replies to them are "indirectly I suppose I did as I was part of a military force in a foreign country whose aim was fighting insurgents which would involve the loss of life, ask away, and it was just, well, a bit bizarre really."

I intended to make notes during my last tour of Afghanistan but in reality I made very few. Most of what has been written is from my memory and from speaking with those who served with me so there are gaps as most of it was quite mind numbingly boring. It's the story about the more mundane day-to-day experiences of someone who was part of the giant logistical machine and I hope that it enlightens you about the unnoticed work that makes the military function.

To the guys and girls who made my final operational tour an exhilarating experience or a challenge I have changed your names because I can't be doing with you bending my ear through your lawyer. I actually think you're all ace. To the Crabs[1] whom it may seem that I don't hold in high regard for their punctuality, I have nothing but the highest respect for the job you all do. It's just that one can't shake the inter-service rivalry and this Pongo[2] expects nothing less in return. To the Spams[3] who had to deal with me. Unlucky.

---

1 Derogative term used for the RAF by the other services. There are many theories on this but I like the one that whenever an unattractive task is announced in the office that requires a volunteer, the RAF will start walking slowly towards the door sideways.

2 Derogative term used for the Army by the other services. Everywhere the Army goes the pong goes, apparently.

3 Derogative term used for the Americans by the British.

Introduction

IT WAS THE Summer of 2011 and I had finally returned to the UK after serving overseas since 2006. It wasn't like the old days of Noel Coward and watching the Pathé news in the cinema whilst being separated from family for years as I had actually managed to get back to Dear Old Blighty a fair few times during my other adventures. Apart from two years in Cyprus when everyday was a holiday with the added benefit of going home every day as well, there was no real urge to return to the UK. I had been posted to 29 Regiment RLC[4] near the town of Cirencester in Gloucestershire. We in the RLC tended to get posted around the world as individuals and not as a whole unit such as infantry battalions.

I was a Movement Controller, known in the Army as a Mover, and my job was fairly wide and varied. Essentially the Movers would get anyone or anything military like from A to B and back again. There were two main Regiments for us Movers. The one here in Cirencester and 24 Regiment in Bielefeld, Germany. We shared both Regiments with the Postal and Courier boys and girls who were known as simply Posties or Stamplickers. Between these two Regiments there was a constant flow of Movers and Posties getting posted back and forth. You'd always know someone which meant the reality wasn't like the films when you turn up at your new unit and are given a hard time because you're the new guy. In fact, you could get posted to one and then come to the other three years later and someone would say "I've not seen you for a while, hope you had a good leave," or "that was a long course." I ar-

4   Royal Logistic Corps, or the Really Large Corps, as it was known, as it really was really really large.

rived at the Duke of Gloucester Barracks to find the majority of the Regimental inhabitants away enjoying their Summer Holidays, possibly in Cyprus. There was a skeletal staff left behind in case war was to break out, but this was more like a skeleton that was missing a couple of femurs, the skull, ribs and possibly the backbone. You wouldn't be able to get hold of the Operations Officer or possibly get your hands on some much-needed ammunition very quickly but you were guaranteed to be able to get a mattress from the bedding storeman or some bleach pretty schnellish. The use of this word may be alien to civilians but it's in the time-honoured tradition of British soldiers, wherever they have found themselves, they have gone on to adopt and, sometimes, butcher the local lingo. This particular one is derived from the German word 'schnell' meaning fast and has been passed down over the years from when the first soldiers arrived in Germany in 1945.

My new job at 29 Regiment was running the Operations desk in the JAMC.[5] Joint was one of the many words I heard during my career which seemed to come and go like fashions. Back in 1989 when I walked through the gates of Buller Barracks on day one of my Army career the word 'joint' meant something else. Proactive, niche and bespoke had all come and gone and I wonder which new fashionable words they are plagiarising now? Somewhere in the depths of the Ministry of Defence is an overcharging civilian consultant whose job it is to read the business news and pass these new words on to the chain of command to use to make the military sound like we are conducting war with degree of verbal modernity.

The constant whittling down of the three services meant that we all had to bunch together when it came to certain establishments. It couldn't be justified to have the Navy, Army

---

5   Joint Air Mounting Centre

and RAF doing the same job with different levels of comfort to suit the Pongos, Crabs and Fisheads.[6] Therefore, the AMC became the JAMC and could now process passengers from all three services. It was an airport terminal without the runway or the planes or the control tower anything that was involved in flying. But with superior military planning it was possibly for members of all three services to check in for a flight, put their bags on the scales, have their passport checked, buy a last-minute travel plug, move through to the departure lounge, get counted onto a bus that would then take them to the steps of their waiting aircraft. The only difference between a regular airport was that the distance from the gate to the bottom of the aircraft steps was about twenty miles, over at RAF Brize Norton.

Not long after my arrival and after a particularly hard military-style day which involved the old fashioned habit of trying to look busy while not actually being busy, I heard about the need of a volunteer to deploy with 80 Squadron to Afghanistan. I immediately thought:

Media version:

This is what I have been trained for, I've been waiting for this opportunity all my life, I will do my duty" blah blah blah!

My version:

Fuck it, at least I'll get some extra money and not have to pretend to work every day.

So off I popped to the Regimental Operations to see my friend Warrant Officer Louise Ballentore to announce that I was the man for the job.

Early in November I would deploy to Kandahar Airbase, commonly known as KAF, and told that I would be replacing Sergeant Beth Browning. She was in charge of the Air Trans-

---

6   Derogative term for the Royal Navy. I don't think I need to explain this one.

port Liaison Officer Detachment (ATLO). Beth was the head of the small detachment of two Lance Corporals. Their job was a sort of interface between the RAF and their passengers as the boys in blue just couldn't handle talking to the unwashed masses and referred to them as walking freight! We would be like the armed militia wing of the EasyJet check-in staff. I knew Beth as our paths had crossed several times in the past, but that's another story. These encounters had been by her previous name, Bev Hiscocks. I've no idea why she changed it. Maybe she was wanted by Interpol? In my eyes she was still Bev Hiscocks and much to her annoyance everyone still called her Bev. She was a woman a bit on the large side and I very much doubt if she could have passed a free lunch let alone her annual fitness test. She had some sort medical issue with her legs, which a medic friend told me that the medical term in question was lazyitis. Under the 'we can't recruit enough soldiers and certainly can't afford to lose anymore soldiers rule' she was exempt doing anything soldier-like which in turn meant she didn't look soldier like-either. She gave the impression that her uniform was a mould and that she had been poured in to it. As an afterthought it looked like a belt had been added afterwards to stop the middle bulging too far.

I contacted her by email and asked some general questions regarding the nature of the job and the first line of her reply announced that due to the recently publicised Canadian Forces withdrawal, Tim Hortons, the doughnut chain, was closing down! This personal disastrous fact was included in all further correspondence and would be the main talking point when I arrived. To this day and no matter how hard I try to remember what she told me about the job I all I can recall that if you went to KAF after November 2011 and you wanted a Tim Hortons Donut you'd be bitterly disappointed.

1

NOVEMBER 2011

Tuesday 1st

AS I DRAG my gorilla box down the stairs it makes a considerable thump on every step. This is amplified by the all-metal construction of the stairwell, and even more so by the cheap flimsy walls that make up the Sergeants' Mess accommodation block. The block is quite new and could be described as an ambitious building project that had to make some serious savings a few months before completion. It's just before midnight and I could have been dragging a dead body out to a shallow grave, but I know nobody will complain about the noise as this is considered normal.

The make-up of this block is typically a 50/50 split between Movers and Stamplickers. The Movers would be off to work a late shift at Brize Norton or watch a shipping container being loaded at 3am. I presume the Stamplickers will be off to issue a book of stamps or reject some mail because it won't fit through that plastic letterbox tool that they need to tell the difference between a letter and a parcel. Some of them would escort official sensitive mail around the world. I knew one guy who spent six months flying to and from Afghanistan and he'd boasted that he had watched every film ever made, even the French Noir ones. I had no reason to doubt him.

I immediately feel the light rain on the back of my neck as I continue to shuffle backwards out of the door, scraping the big plastic gorilla box across the coarse brick paving. My new uniform feels strange on me as it's the first time I have worn it.

I had been on the usual few weeks of pre-deployment leave, spending time with the family and saying goodbye to my two children. As I am not a fisherman, a hunter, or into paintballing, my brand-spanking-new camouflaged kit remained in its plastic wrapping for the duration. It's always the same feeling though when you put your uniform on for the first time after a long period wearing civvies. The boots have a heavy feel to them and the beret an alien sensation as the cold leather banding comes into contact with your forehead. The trousers feel a bit tighter too, but this is normal due to my lack of interest in physical exercise while on leave, and an increased interest in indulging in some extra culinary and alcoholic delights like a condemned man.

I've gone through all the kit I had been issued for this deployment and I will be taking about one-third of it. The remaining stuff will remain in the box in my room in South Cerney, only to be given straight back to the Quartermaster upon my return still in its original packaging. I presume he would then issue it to the next person to store in their room for six months. Since the bad press the Army had received about not issuing either the right, appropriate or enough kit to their soldiers, they had come up with a novel solution. Simply issue everyone deploying the entire clothing stock held on the MOD clothing inventory. They'd even issued you stuff that you weren't allowed to wear. Somewhere in the UK, a company was awarded a substantial contract to produce thousands upon thousands of camouflage forage caps. Someone military had then decided that they basically looked crap, therefore they would never grace the head of anyone. The Army was ordered not to wear them within the known universe. I would love to know who made this decision so that I can send him or her a written demand to pay back the proportion of my taxes that contributed to our defence budget.

I knew this Tuesday would be a drag. I dislike this moment just prior to deployment. It was a strange situation and I had experienced it so many times before. If I had received a call saying I could go right now I would. The night before I had a few beers in the Mess bar with some friends and I awoke before the sun rose, with a mild hangover. My hangover, that is, and not the sun's, because that would be just preposterous. I vaguely remember Carl Sagan once saying the sun was not a big drinker. I try my hardest to stay in bed in the vain hope that my full bladder and now-drier-than-a-Taliban's-flip-flop mouth might somehow go away and let me go back to the Land of Nod. I eventually realise I am not going to win this war of attrition, so I throw in the towel and get up to release and replace liquids as required.

I breakfast alone in the Mess tucking into my usual order of scrambled eggs on toast with an insane amount of pepper. After a morning of reading nothing in the papers and drinking too much coffee I head off into a grey, damp Cirencester for reasons unknown. I wander aimlessly around town watching daily life go on around me knowing that it will continue after I depart and everything will be the same on my return. I decide to have some lunch in a bistro on Cricklade Street. I have a couple of salmon fish cakes with a sweet chilli sauce and the usual salad that accompanies these dishes to make you feel you're getting your money's' worth. I also have a glass of Peroni, knowing that this will be my last beer for quite a while. I'm sure I feel my liver give a sigh of relief.

You might like to hear I spend the rest of the afternoon checking, re-checking and re-re-checking my kit, but this is the real world and I spend it doing modern life stuff. I park my car up in the designated car park for people going away

14

on tour. I cancel the insurance and pop the SORN declaration in the post with the tax disc in an attempt to claw a few quid back from the DVLA. I attempt to track down the Mess Manager, who must be related to Lord Lucan. She has the ability to seem to be about while simultaneously not being about. The desk in her office always has a steaming brew on it which, when added to her unique ability to remain hidden, gives it a Mary Celeste feel. She also has a child gate across the door to keep in the three awful tiny yapping dog rats, that are possibly her surrogate children. They are vicious little buggers. It's a pity they never disappeared. On this day I don't require the help of an aboriginal tracker as I find her in the kitchen chatting to the massive Fijian military chef. She is telling him off for giving out generous portions which were eating into the company profits. Gone are the days of the Messes being run by the Army Catering Corps. They are all run now by companies with names like Sodemexo or Eliorsawyoucoming with a view to making profits at the expense of taste. This is unlike the era of the Slop Jockey[7] which adopted the more simple approach of making food at the expense of taste.

In the good old days - this term is questionable, as I remember canvas webbing, plastic waterproofs and vague health & safety policies - every soldier who lived on the camp paid a flat monthly rate for food and was entitled to three meals a day. This included as many seconds, thirds, fourths, and sometimes fifths as they could physically put away. The married soldiers were also entitled to as much food when they were on duty, and I had heard instances of them bringing their kids in to fill up on grub. This practise was commonly known as 'beanstealing,' and the new system stopped all of the above dead in its tracks. My perception of how this devastat-

---

7   Polite name for an Army chef

ing change came about was that a minority group of soldiers, who were technically living on camp but, in reality, lived off camp with their girlfriends, would whinge about this flat rate. In 1997 I think it was about £60 a month. Their argument was why should that have to pay it when they don't eat on camp or that they should only pay for what they eat as they were all still stuffing their faces at lunchtimes. I still remember them popping in for quite a few dinner times, breakfast times and most times. Something had to be done, as the voice of nutritional dissent was becoming louder, and in the good old British tradition, when our military are in times of need, we promptly looked across the pond to the US for ideas. We adopted their 'Pay as You Dine,' idea, where you simply pay for the food there and then, like a restaurant, but just without the waiters or tips. Straight away we renamed it according to what it would actually achieve, which was 'Save as You Starve.'

It nearly didn't happen, as there were some experts somewhere who worried about the soldiers who'd spend all their wages in the first couple of days on prostitution, drink or PlayStations. How would they eat? Malnutrition would be rife and next they would be selling their uniforms to pay for food. So, a system was put in place where a soldier who had no cash could basically get a meal and it would be deducted out of his next month's pay. Almost full circle. The peculiar anomaly also meant that they could still use military chefs to prepare meals. I never found out whether they were getting free labour or they were paying his wages of which the MOD probably took a share and passed what was left to Mr S. Jockey.

Back to the undercover Mess Manager and the generous massive Fijian chef with his 'stuff your profit margin' attitude. In his defence, I suspect a normal portion would have looked unimpressively small in his huge bucket hands. I just want to check a few things with her, such as that she would be aware that I was going away, so that hopefully upon my return I wouldn't be presented with the following:

1. Someone living in my room.
2. A bill for £300 worth of champagne dated 31st December from a drinks chit with my name and an X for a signature.
3. Several random bills for food because one of the Mess staff thought Sergeant Lee Mulligan was me.

Once I ensure that most of the above would not happen in my absence I sign the Warning In and Out book situated in the foyer of the Mess. The fact that we have to warn them that we were going to be out of the Mess must have meant we were pretty important. I would 'warn back in' six months later but it isn't much of a warning if I have already arrived. Maybe it should have been named the 'Hi, honey, I've been home for hours, what's for dinner,' book?

The minibus turns up so I chuck my kit in the back, climbed on board, and think, "Well, here we go." Fifteen seconds later we arrive at the armoury and I climb out again. Here is most of the team that are to deploy, it consists of about 20 soldiers all looking busy doing a job that could be done by one. All the weapons are laid out on the floor in their padded bags that we use for transport, and serial numbers are being checked, cross-checked and polka-dot checked. Staff Sergeant Nick Richardson stands leaning against the outside wall with a bit of paper in his hand, practising the art of looking busy A4-style.

Nick and I first met back in 2001 when we were both serving with 2 Close Support Regiment in Gutersloh, Germany.

We were both Corporals at the time and he was a Blanket Stacker[8] in the stores section and I was a driver looking after their vehicles. That February we had both found ourselves on exercise in Poland. We were living in a tent on an old Soviet training area, freezing our arses off with a Private Formby, whom we called George for obvious reasons, who, whenever he came back from taking a crap, stank of shit.

"Is he keeping a warm turd in his pants to stave off the cold?" said Nick, pulling a face as if he'd just licked a lemon.

As we sat on the frozen ground with the aroma of George's latest chocolate log assaulting our noses, eyes, and ears, we discussed the topic that there had to be better jobs elsewhere in the Army. Possibly ones that didn't involve sitting in a tent somewhere in Poland during the wintertime trying to work out if a Private soldier had shat himself.

"What about those lazy Mover cunts in the hotel down the road?" said Nick.

He still calls them that to this day even though he is now one of them and a high-ranking one too.

"We could do that job, lad," he said, poking me in the chest with his northern accent.

I could see him getting excited. "How fucking hard can it be? All those bastards do is sleep in a nice warm hotel and once a day knock up a bit of twatting paperwork for anyone who needs to piss off back over the border to Germany."

So, upon on our glorious return to Germany several weeks later, we informed the Chain of Command that we wanted to change jobs and become Movers. When asked why we explained that we thrived on new challenges and wished to develop our potential to the maximum so that we would be an asset to the Army.

---

8   Storeman.

Finally all the pretend work is done, the weapons and personal kit have been checked and loaded on to the baggage truck, its shutter noisily pulled down, and sent ahead. I climb back onto the minibus with all the others for the drive over to Brize Norton. It was a cold wet night, and, once we left the dimly lit camp, the back of the minibus was plunged into near darkness. Everyone is pretty quiet during the 40-minute drive, sitting in their own thoughts, feeling sad after saying goodbye to their loved ones, contemplating what was ahead. Anyone who does talk does so in a hushed voice, just enough to hear them speak but not what they are saying, like a subconscious mark of respect. I sit in my own thoughts, looking outside as the water droplets on the window distort the lights from far-off lonely farms as we travel down the empty country lanes of Gloucestershire and Oxfordshire. I recognise this point from before and even though I know the emotions are familiar it's still not the best of experiences. I am about to enter a system from which there will be no escape for six months unless I am injured or worse.

I descend into thoughts of whether I would make it back to see my children again or to finally live life without this devotion to the Army. I always felt that I was going away to a sort of prison for six months as, yet again, my normal life was to be put on hold until my return. However, this time I know that this will be the last one, the last tour, the final push, but I don't know whether to feel glad about it. My thoughts turn to the unluckiness that materialises in life, and if anything happens to me on this last tour I will be mildly annoyed.

Wednesday 2nd

As soon as we enter Brize Norton we can feel the sombre mood ebb away as life comes back to the bus. Talking becomes louder, the sleeping ones wake up and stretch, and the smell of a fart makes everyone moan and blame someone else.

The RAF has arranged a special treat for us. We are to fly to Camp Bastion on an antique. Some people pay good money to fly on vintage aircraft but here we are getting it for free. Our aircraft of choice is the BA and Pan Am hand-me-down, with several other not so careful owners and high mileage on the clock, Lockheed TriStar. Ironically, it will transport us in 1970s comfort to a country that used to be great in the 1970s. These aircraft were past their sell-by date in the 1980s when the RAF bought them and God only knows how the technicians manage to keep them flying. Probably Black Nasty?[9]

Apart from witnessing some Special Forces blokes getting caught trying to smuggle bottles of spirits and the usual two-hour stopover in Cyprus to look at the duty-free we weren't allowed to buy, it's an uneventful journey. It's pretty much the same as flying on a budget airline: uncomfortable seats, crap food, and landing with the lights off and blinds down while wearing helmets and body armour. Thankfully the Tri-Star is fitted with some electronic stuff which would hopefully stop a missile fired by a goat herder from permanently grounding it, therefore we are able to fly direct into Camp Bastion.

The RAFs ageing fleet of Tri-Stars and the even older VC10s couldn't cope with the task of moving hundreds of personnel every day, so the RAF relied on civilian charter aircraft. These operators didn't see a need to fit any missile-defeating kit for flying into Schiphol so Camp Bastion or KAF were off-limits. This made the route to Afghanistan painful and a test of en-

---

9 An industrial strength black tape that can remove eyebrows. It's also rumoured to have prevented plane accidents and the falling of nations.

durance by making you fly via Cyprus as normal, then on to Al Minhad airbase in the United Arab Emirates, hang about for hours waiting to be squeezed, and I mean squeezed, into a C-17 cargo aircraft. The seats were bolted to the aluminium pallets that would normally carry the cargo. The pallets would be loaded onto the rear of the aircraft and would move along on rollers, eventually being locked in place in their desired location. The seats were fitted so tightly onto these pallets that you'd have the legroom that all airlines could only dream of could they get away with it. I flew this route previously a few times and I remember fondly the pain in my knees and the efforts of the crew pulling on my arms and legs trying to straighten me out like a piece of plywood that had been warped due to prolonged water immersion.

It's late when we arrive and the air is still and pleasantly warm. Once I am away from the smell of the aviation fuel, the other smells kick in. They are a combination of diesel fumes and burning plastic with a slight hint of shit. We are bussed to a tent that serves as the arrivals lounge on an old cast-off German bus still with the tour company's name and contact details written down the side of it. Assman Reisen of Aachen. I can't imagine I'll ever forget that name. In the tent we are one part briefed and two parts shouted at by a female Lance Corporal who welcomes us to Camp Bastion but somehow makes me feel like I was in deep trouble for coming here. The next few hours are a sleep-deprived haze of which I can remember little other than collecting my bags from the baggage reclaim carousel, which was a patch of dirt outside the tent. Carrying my ops bag over my right shoulder and dragging my gorilla box with the other free hand. We are led to a tented city the size of a small town, our accommodation for the next few days, where I finally crash onto a cot longing for sleep.

Thursday 3rd

It's four in the morning and I am still wide awake. The heaters keep switching on when their thermostats reach a chilly 25°C. It is a Baltic 18°C outside. The heaters are the extra noisy type designed not to be used within a mile's radius of anyone trying to sleep, think, or have a conversation without shouting. I am lying on my sleeping bag with a constant trickle of sweat running off my forehead and down the back of my neck. My T-shirt is damp and my pillow, which was one of my towels, had compressed so much it's like laying my head on a brick. Sleep eventually comes but I wake without the feeling of having slept at all and with the same symptoms of a hangover. Today will be a day of trying to keep awake during the numerous briefings that lay ahead.

After some breakfast we move to the tent that was used for briefing incoming troops. It is like a circus tent but with only the dull colours of a faded green covered in years' worth of brown dust. You could say it's possibly full of clowns though. At the front are several whiteboards still marked with the wiped-out briefing notes from the last load of troops to arrive, along with posters about stuff that was really important. They are so important that three seconds after looking away from them I have forgotten their important messages.

I do remember that they were in the old World War Two style though, and I am expecting to see one of Hitler and Goering sitting behind two ladies on a bus with the caption 'Careless talk costs lives.'

At the back there's a long line of the standard six-foot wooden tables loaded with several shiny silver water boilers, a Styrofoam cup mountain, sugar in brown paper bags, the entire world's production of plastic spoons, and the best South American coffee that money could buy. Only the best for our brave troops. It's a make I had never heard of and will most likely never come across again. It tastes like a mixture of Tesco's own brand coffee, which had failed the quality test, and dirt. At least it gives us the impression that it will assist us in the next few days of sleep deprived torture. The seating is benches, lots of wooden slatted benches so that by the end of the first hour we will all be slouching and not in the required posture to avoid long-term back pains.

And so it begins. Briefs about the current situation, new tactics and weapons used by the enemy, Health & Safety briefs, personal health briefs, disease briefs, briefs about our ace kit, briefs about the colour of the General's new car, briefs about briefs, etc. It isn't really sinking in as I am sitting there thinking that if I put two big bright yellow Post-it notes over each of my eyes, I could draw a wide-open eye on each one of them with a Biro, so it would it give the desired illusion that I was wide awake and showing interest.

The only bit of information I will ever recall from all this is the tip from the medics about soldiers' tendencies to play with the local wildlife when they should not be playing with the local wildlife. Their tip is worthy of a prize awarded from the Royal Society of Preventative Medicine.

"If it's got more or less legs than you, don't fucking touch it," shouts the MO.[10]

The day finally finishes at about eight in the evening and we all march back with stooped backs to our noisy tented city for an evening of more sweating and sleep deprivation.

Friday 4th
Again, I wake with hangover symptoms. I think my body is just a bit confused at this point. Later, as we are drinking our

------

10   Medical Officer.

first cup of brown water in the circus tent, the briefing bods say that they have a treat for us. Some of the briefs will be held outside. There is a massive outbreak of silence, not quite the reaction I suspect they were hoping for.

One of today's briefs is from a young Captain, who is an Operational Lawyer from the Army Legal Services, about issues that might arise for some on their tour. He tells us that he doesn't care if we fall asleep or don't listen but he has to tick the box on the back of his fag packet that says that he'd briefed us.[11]

Judge:	Did the accused attend the said brief?
Defence:	Your honour, he was so tired that he slept through it.
Judge:	But the back of the fag packet says otherwise. Take him away!

Saturday 5th

It is an early start as we have to finish the day zeroing our weapons on the ranges. This is a normal requirement, which involves firing the weapon to see where the bullets hit the wooden target. It's normally either too high or off to one side. Then, by adjusting the sights, up, down, left, and right as required, you should ensure the bullets eventually hit where you are actually aiming at on the unlucky target. It's normal procedure to fire five rounds, check, fire another five, check, and finish off with a few more rounds to ensure all is good and that if you actually need to shoot someone then you won't shoot the guy to left or right or above or below him.

After another morning of sitting in a mildly uncomfortable

---

11   I looked in my notebook years later to see if I had taken any notes on the briefs but all I found was that I'd drawn a picture of a motorbike with square wheels with the caption underneath 'Army, be the Best!'

stress position, we finally head off to the ranges on a coach which was kindly supplied by Hans Grubenschnitzel Tours of Regensburg.

We have been given brown paper bags with our economy lunches in. These are commonly known as horror bags for the untold disappointment and misery that they contain:

> ▶ Cornish pasty or cats arse[12] from an unheard-of company that, without the military contract, would have gone bust in the 1960s; *or*
> A selection of white bread sandwiches with egg mayonnaise, grated cheese, or pink death;[13]
> ▶ A packet of crisps from a company that again you'd never heard of but with a design that looked awfully familiar that made you suspicious that they were imported counterfeits from Eastern Europe;
> ▶ A Wagon Wheel or Blue Riband;
> ▶ A heavily bruised apple or black banana;
> ▶ A bottle of Panda Cola.

Prior to a previous tour of Iraq, I was undergoing the pre-deployment training down at Lydd ranges. The military chose this area near to Dungeness in Kent as it's the closest you can get to recreating some of the armpits to which the Army deploys while staying on the mainland UK. In fact if you have ever seen a budget sci-fi programme in which some intrepid space travellers have found themselves stuck on an inhospitable planet, it will probably have been filmed at

---

12   Look at the end of a sausage roll and then at your cat's bumhole. See what I mean?

13   Cheap ham

Dungeness. It was again several days of briefs that were identical to the ones that we had been subjected over the last few days. I swear all they had done was change the word Iraq for Afghanistan.

It was the middle of January and we were being treated to an outside brief in minus five degrees. We all opened our horror bags to discover frozen Cornish pasties and cats' arses. The Slop Jockeys had triumphed again as there was disappointment and misery all round that day as we tried to defrost them under our armpits. Frozen foodstuffs wouldn't be a problem today in the warm Afghani Autumn but the Slop Jockeys had really used their heads to go one step further on how to administer an extra twist to today's dose of disappointment and misery. Because we were nice and far away from the civilization with all its rules and regulations, almost everything in the horror bag, the pasties, cats' arses, Wagon Wheels, and Panda Cola were months past their best-by date. With this overwhelming sense of feeling valued by my masters and a bellyful of horror I lay myself down to zero my rifle and proceed to shoot in the unique style of being visually impaired. After several trips to the target to look at the bullet holes all around the edge of the target, the Infantry instructor looked at my RLC cap badge in my beret and says.

"What job are you doing out here?"

"I'm the Mover up in KAF," I reply.

"You'll be fine," he pats me on the back.

So, I am now ready to take on the Taliban. At least if I can't shoot them then I could bore them to death with all the information that has passed through my half-dazed head during the last few days. To assist me in my task I have Lance Corporals Joe Parkes and Paul Seckerson to keep me company for the next six months.

Joe is about 24 and wanting to get on with his career in the Army. He has done the rigorous P Company,[14] as he wants to eventually serve with an airborne unit. He'd already passed the "running about with a big rucksack on" stuff, but when he came to start his actual parachute training there weren't any planes available. He was told to come back in a year because the RAF didn't have any spare planes as they were all tied up doing operational stuff such as moving us bunch of idiots around Afghanistan.

He has a long-term girlfriend and is in the process of buying a house with her. There's nothing like making one of the most stressful things in your life even more stressful by doing it from thousands of miles away while serving. I bought a house while in Iraq in 2009, and buying them as a civilian is a piece of piss.[15]

Paul is over 30, married with a young family and had been in the Army for a while. Before becoming a Mover he had been a medic for a number of years and now seems comfortable with his lot. He was happy not to cause a fuss but just do his job and take the wage. Paul has a wonderful talent for looking grumpy all of the time. I imagine he'd keep his grumpy face on even if he'd just won a million pounds on the lottery. I am yet to become aware that he was a Mormon, and, to be honest, I don't know much about his religion but he will be more than happy to answer questions later on. He

14   P Company is an extremely tough course for Parachute Regiment recruits. It is also open to other trades within the Army, both regular and reserve personnel who volunteer to serve in an Air Assault unit.

15   He was planning on getting married some time during his return so I dropped a hint every week for an invitation. I'm still waiting for the invitation, Joe...

does eventually tell me that he doesn't drink coffee because of his belief that he should avoid substances that were harmful to his health. However Coke would be deemed to be OK and he would quaff it like it was water. He would also come to have an uncanny knack for getting close to incoming 120mm Chinese rockets of the extremely unhealthy variety.

I would put him on the night shift as per his request as he has a lot of DVDs to watch. He would always be trading kit with the Spams and would hold the indisputable title of First British Soldier to Own a Pair of MTP[16] Shorts. I'm guessing they are still being worn to this day during summer barbecues in his back garden.

The night shift was never going to be really busy, and a few months into the tour he would start looking bored. He'd have watched all of his DVDs and would turn up for his shift looking like he was about to go on a mission behind enemy lines. One evening he would be especially bored and make a low-slung holster for his weapon magazine. After laughing my head off for 10 minutes I would tell him to get rid of it as he looked like a twat and would get the piss ripped out of him by everyone including the Taliban.

But that's all in the future. Right now Paul, Joe, and I are all sweating on the bus back to the main part of Camp Bastion, a bus supplied by Bratwurst Reisen of Arsewinkle. We are looking forward to a rest from being soldiers for a couple of hours. As we step off the bus we are greeted with the news that we are all booked on the next plane to KAF and have to be at the departure terminal - another tent - in 30 minutes.

So begins a mad dash to get back to the accommodation, pack, accept leaving gifts, attend leaving drinks, give a leaving speech, and write my own obituary:

---

16   Multi Terrain Pattern. It was the new camouflage we'd been issued for this tour.

Recently posted back from serving in Germany,
Staff Sergeant Lee, liked going for lone walks,
booking tables for one at restaurants, and playing in
a one-man-band. His family will be none the wiser,
while women worldwide will be at a loss at his
demise during a rocket attack while he was heroically
trying to fill out a workspace risk assessment for his
Display Screen Equipment laptop.

We all squeeze into an ancient white Tata pick-up that makes a loud metal clang every time the driver steps on or off the accelerator. I imagine the one bolt holding the engine in place is working overtime. I'm sure that I had been in this same jeep before on a previous tour and it was making the same noise a few years back. Pity the defence budget couldn't stretch to a spot of basic maintenance.

The three of us sit on the back seat with various bits of luggage on our laps and our weapons stuffed into the foot-well, with their sharp sticky out metallic parts digging into the fleshy backs of our calves. It's too hot to keep the windows up, but when Paul winds the window down we are all treated to a triple surprise of the winder actually working, that it doesn't come off in his hand, and by how quickly the cab fills up with dust. He winds it up again, and again we let out another "Oooh!" of surprise as it works flawlessly in the opposite direction. We continue to sweat in the now dust-filled cab.

Upon our arrival at the departure tent it's a mad scramble to get all the kit inside and checked-in before the RAF close the check-in wooden table. I ask a bored-looking RAF policeman if he has change for the baggage trolley and he gives me a look that tells me his 43rd tour has just started. We present our IDs and our motley collection of belongings, check them in, and move through the security checks, which involve putting our weapons through the X-ray scanner. I'm not too sure what they are expecting to see. We finally make it through to the departure lounge, which is just the other side of the check-in tent. We could have saved everybody a lot of effort by just walking around the back to it. It's another tent with some benches and several industrial-sized rusty looking tins of baked beans that are full of black water and a month's worth of cigarette butts. Waiting for the flight is a mixture of British, American, and Afghani soldiers, and some civilian contractors. Everyone ignores us, apart from the Afghans who just stare at us. I can only presume that there is nothing in the Pashto or Dari vocabulary that their mothers could use to say it was rude to stare. If there were any free spaces on the benches to sit on we still wouldn't bother because any minute now we are going to board our flight...

Three hours later, with sore feet, we are still standing in that tent, waiting for the glorious RAF.

The plane that will take us to KAF is the C-130 Hercules, commonly known as the Herc. It's been the main tactical transport aircraft of the RAF and almost every other air force since I can remember. I have spent so many hours cramped in the back of so many Hercs over the years. Anyone who has flown in a Herc more than once will know that it's not really anything to brag about. You sit shoulder to shoulder, either with your back to the fuselage facing in towards the aircraft or in the middle facing outwards. The seats are a fabric web mesh that is comfortable for at most 15 minutes. The Hercs are noisy with lots of vibration and with no real windows to look out of. When the plane accelerates for take-off everyone slides to the rear a little in unison as the mesh seating is rather slippy. This is repeated the other way when the pilot stamps on the brakes during touch down.

We land at KAF late on that Saturday night and as the Herc is still moving the Loadmaster opens up the rear ramp. Everyone on the flight instinctively looks down the fuselage of the aircraft to take in the restricted view out of the back which is one of a huge plane parking lot. Everything is bathed in the sodium lights that turn the night into a yellow day. The lights and concrete stretch off into the distance, showing a scattering of aircraft of all shapes and sizes. It's a real plane spotters' paradise that has to be kept secret for fear that they might pass out should they be exposed to such a sight. The Herc finally parks up at its stand and the engines start winding down, which means one thing for the crew. It's the end of their shift and they have to get going otherwise they won't be late for tomorrow's flight. Right now I'm imagining the film version as I step off the ramp of the Herc. I take my helmet off, put it under my arm, like a General. I start surveying my new home for the next six months through my tired eyes and I take a deep breath while looking quite militaristic and soldier-like. The reality is that both nostrils are assaulted with the smell of shit. I gag and then stumble as I misjudge the drop off the ramp. As soon as I regain my dignity, I see a chubby Bev Hiscocks wobbling towards me rapidly. We shake hands and she says, "Timmy Horton's shuts tomorrow."

After the full debrief about Timmy Horton's impending closure due to the Canadian military's impending departure from

Afghanistan, I sit against a blast wall alone. Joe and Paul have met their clones from whom they would be taking over and disappeared off on the bus, which was predictably the 34 to Koln Zentrum. Bev excitedly speaks to a new Herc crew, who have come on duty and are busy trying to ready their aircraft in time so that they could be late. She talks to them like she was their awkward best friend, even laughing at her own jokes when they don't respond. One of the crew looks at me and rolls his eyes. I know the relationship they have had to endure since being in KAF and I give him the 'I know your pain' look. The boys in blue manage to get their Herc fired up and taxiing for their sortie in record time. I'm sure they will make down the time at some point so as not to disappoint their waiting freight. We hang about to watch the Herc take off so that Bev can call ahead to its destination to let the Movers know that it is inbound. She then blows it a kiss, and says bye-bye. I roll my eyes but there is nobody about to see my embarrassment. I'm going to be in for a few days of this during our handover/takeover and I am contemplating an excuse I could use to get her out of KAF possibly by tomorrow evening. To hell with the handover, I'll just work it all out as I go along.

Bev is all finished for the evening, so we depart Whiskey Ramp in the duty wheels, which is a fairly new white Nissan pick-up. It thankfully isn't fitted with the "loud clang when you put your foot on the accelerator" option. Whiskey Ramp is over the Northside of KAF and this is where most of the plane things happen. The accommodation and offices are across the runway on the Southside which means it is a 20-minute drive on the only road that also runs all the way around the entire airbase. I am in such a sleep-deprived state that she could do some stunts in the pick-up, crash out through the main gate, drive into Kandahar for a kebab, and drop me back at the accommodation and I wouldn't notice. When we get there she guides me to a room like a drunk and says, "See you tomorrow."

A Very Brief History of Kandahar Airfield

Kandahar Airfield was built by the Americans in the mid-50s as a stop-off refuelling point for their piston-powered aircraft just as their Air Force were starting to enter the jet age, thus giving it the impression of a complete waste of time, effort and dollars. This was the Cold War era so it's highly probable that there were some intentions to use it in a bust-up with the USSR. The Soviets were also investing in an airbase to the north of Kabul called Bagram.

The Soviets used KAF during their little 10-year skirmish from 1979 to 1989 and, upon their departure, it was under the control of the Soviet Russian-backed government until its downfall in 1992. The next owners were the Taliban who ran the gaff until the Americans came back in 2001 on Operation Enduring Freedom and promptly evicted them with several tonnes of heavy ordnance.

As operations increased, more and more NATO members moved in including the Brits who used it as our main base until Camp Bastion was up and running with its own runway. Now the focus was on Camp Bastion and KAF had been relegated to an outpost where they parked the Hercs.

Sunday 6th

I peel my eyes apart about sevenish and straight away regret the night before. My head feels like it's full of molten lead and my vision is blurry. I unstick my tongue from the top of my mouth with a little help from some water from the bottle that

I have kept with me since leaving Bastion last night. My vision clears just in time to notice, swirling around in the bottom of the cheap plastic bottle adorned with its unfathomable foreign text, little bits of yesterday's sandwich. My mind starts trying to recall the night before and how many beers I had sunk and where I had ended up. As my mind starts up like a knackered old laptop, with a cracked screen, the previous day's memories begin to appear in my head and I pull a face to match that cracked screen. I am back in Afghanistan. Again.

Immediately I get the odour of faeces transiting up my nostrils. The source of the offending smell comes from a big lake of sewage, that has been fittingly named the Poo Pond, and is the size of a couple of football pitches. The engineers had created a miracle when constructing the camp because, judging by the constant offensive bouquet, it always seems to be located upwind regardless of the wind direction. It is surrounded by a big red and white plastic chain supported on wooden stakes that must have been put in by someone in a rush as they are pointing to the sky at different angles like a hedgehog having a bad hair day. Hanging from the chain at random intervals, probably also placed on there by the same hasty man, are more bio-hazard warning signs than I have ever seen or am ever likely to see again. Some joker, obviously with more time on his hands than Mr Hasty and probably access to a gas mask, had painted a very professional sign warning people not to eat the brown carp. Nice to see war bringing out the comedian in people, I think.

I have spent the night in the bed from the film *Bedknobs And Broomsticks*. Another item that I will spend time thinking about how it found its way to KAF. Maybe a mistake was made when ordering some really essential supplies. The only conclusion I came to was someone asked for 'More firepower and a shed' and understood 'a metal bedstead instead.'

I go in search of the bogs which, as always, are normally only a few doors down the corridor. After entering several rooms with people in various states of waking or going to bed and apologising I am finally successful on my fourth attempt. I am greeted with the familiar sight of the usual row of sinks and showers, all done in a tastefully beige plastic with years of stains that could be a map of the local area. The toilets are at least porcelain, but the cubicles are made from plywood. Obviously, an afterthought job done by the engineers as I guess the Spams were in here at one point and they are not shy when it comes to curling one off in full view of their comrades. The cubicles are so tiny that when you sit on the bog your knees are pressed against the door putting the ornamental lock under undue pressure. Again, after a month of racking my brains, I will come to the following conclusions as to why they were so small:

1. All the engineers on the task were themselves small;
2. That was the biggest cut of wood that they had;
3. They were taking the piss.

The accommodation block is a prefab building about 30 metres long, with a corridor through the middle and a door at either end. The rooms can comfortably accommodate at least four soldiers. I reckon that they could have accommodated the same amount of airmen or sailors as they generally tend to be about the same size. All the blocks are laid out in neat rows with the thinnest of concrete walls in between them running the entire length. This wall is the blast wall and it is there to offer protection from the shrapnel of an exploding rocket or mortar round that the locals will send us every couple of days. They look so thin that they would struggle to stop the blast from the siren, and there is nothing to protect the ends of the blocks. It will transpire that I'll give a cheer the day when the new blast walls, at least two feet thick, are placed at the ends, finally offering us some real protection. I will leave for home a few days later.

The next bit is Bev's favourite part of her handover, showing me the DFAC.[17] In the days before we became reliant on the Spams we used to call them simply 'the cookhouse' or in some cases of below minimum culinary acceptable standards 'the shithouse'. Our use of these terms would have caused confusion with our Allies so we adopted US term DFAC. Thankfully this was open to military abuse and everyone agreed that it now stood for 'Deep Fried American Crap'.

The DFACs, like most of the civilian organisations in theatre who had won contracts, were run by companies from the US. The senior managers are mostly American, the junior managers from Eastern Europe, and the workers from Asia or India and are known as TCNs[18]. These TCNs fulfil numerous mundane tasks around the base. With their population of somewhere in the region of 10,000 just in KAF alone they are the unsung heroes doing the crap jobs that we didn't want to do and facing the same dangers for just a few dollars a day. There are several DFACs situated around the airbase feeding the entire population throughout the day. Each one has a sort of gastronomic speciality. The one in the TCN part of camp does mainly Asian grub, the one in the British compound is obviously curry-based, and the American one served up good ol' garbage.

The queues for the food are Biblically long and I have a

17   Dining facility.

18   Third Country Nationals.

theory that this is where the culture of soldiers growing beards when on tour originated from. As you enter you have to scan your meal card or, if you have forgotten it, sign your name, which would be the name of someone else or a fictional character. It had become my standard practice when signing for something from someone who didn't know you and there was a chance of a bill. I was just making sure that I wouldn't be presented with an invoice for six months' worth of food when I tried to depart. The desk where you carry out the above transaction is staffed by at least three bored-looking TCNs, watching the never-ending queue of military personnel slowly shuffle along. The next part is the compulsory washing of hands to keep the dreaded DV virus at bay. There are long communal troughs with push-button taps and disinfectant dispensers. The drying of one's hands is taken care of by Mr Dyson's super-efficient air blade hand dryers of which there are 20 to choose from. He must be so proud of his part in the fight against the Taliban.

Over our first breakfast of powdered eggs - I thought only people during World War Two ate powdered eggs - cheap white Sunblest-type unbendable cardboard bread and a *cofftea*,[19] Bev mentions that there had been a rocket attack in the night. I thought it had been a dream that the rocket attack alarm had gone off during the night. Thankfully my training kicked in and I took immediate action by rolling over onto my left side, plumping up my pillow, and going straight back to sleep.

Upon venturing outside we are all instantly blinded by the bright sun. This is magnified by the very fine and light dust on the ground. Hands over our eyes, we newbies stumble and trip and bump into things as we fumble for our issued sun-

---

19   It's neither coffee nor tea, but is also both coffee and tea.

glasses. The entrance to the office is about 10 metres away, which turns out to be just the distance it takes to fish a pair of issued sunglasses out of your pocket and put them on while stumbling, tripping and bumping into things. As I go through the door I'm now blinded by the darkness as I have just managed to get my sunglasses onto my head.

We are shown by Bev into the office, in reality is a posh cupboard. We file into the beating heart of the passenger air movements office in KAF and I am already planning the Christmas party games of squash or hide-and-seek. We share the limited space with the RAF Police who thankfully aren't averse to burning the midnight, afternoon, or morning oil in the office. It has one small sliding window about chest height, which gives a lovely view of the mountains. Well it would if it weren't for the blast wall, so what we have in place is a featureless grey view of nothing that the eyes struggle to focus on. There is a net to keep the bugs out, which can also be slid open. The space in between the building and the blast wall is littered with years' worth of plastic bottles, bits of ripped hessian, and other objects of an unknown nature. All of this is covered in the familiar light grey dust. I presume the wind put a lot of the garbage there, with a nice top-up helping from soldiers throwing their empty bottles over the wall. The office is decked out with two big desks and, around the side, a mixture of filing cabinets, a secure locker, small tables, and a couple of military-issue armchairs. The material that they are made out of probably breaks the fire safety rules and would have been very unfashionable in 1967. I wonder if the pilots and drivers were aware of the essential cargo for which they were risking their lives when hauling these essential supplies into KAF during the early days. In the corner is the MMARS[20]

---

20 Movement Management Air Reservation System

machine. Again, the British Military is at the cutting edge of technology here. It is an online seat booking and reservation system. British Airways had used something similar and the Military, being quite forward-thinking for once, had copied it and rolled in out in 1984. However, BA had stopped using it a long time ago, because it was shite. How could we take on the enemy with a computer that had a green screen with the homepage text permanently burnt into it, and a dot-matrix printer that reminded me of Saturday afternoons watching the football results come in on *Grandstand?*

The printer would become so annoying that we would normally switch it off, because anything of interest would be either over the phone or by email and not on the printer. It will end up being off for weeks at a time. Now during the weeks it was offline we would be sent every passenger manifest of every RAF aircraft departing to or from theatre. These manifests would be held in an electronic queue somewhere on an antiquated server, possibly on an island in the middle of the Indian Ocean, just waiting for the moment when we would switch it on again. After a couple of minutes, it would start printing off 300 metres of backlogged passenger manifests. We would leave it off for the last two months of the tour, only switching it on again just as we left the office for the last time for my replacement to discover. At least they will have enough paper should the bog roll supplies not get through.

Bev occupies the main desk. I am not allowed to occupy it until she has handed over her empire and departed. She has that air of someone who can't wait to get out of there but is worried that the whole system and war would come to a grinding halt as soon as she walked out of the door. The process of her handing over to me starts with her showing me files, where I could find documents, get access to email accounts, and how to put the laundry in. It's all so interesting and I'm sure I will remember absolutely none of it.

Joe and Paul go about with their counterparts learning the ropes and I won't see much of them for the first few days. We have to hand in our weapons to the armoury within the RAF compound on the other side of the airfield, as being on KAF was deemed safe enough not to warrant being armed. I hope that in the case of an outbreak of severe fisticuffs that the opposition will give us some notice of their intentions, thus enabling us to travel the two miles, form an orderly queue, sign for our weapons one at a time, and be handed them through the microscopic hatch at the armoury.

The actual job that we have all been sent here to do is cover the post of ATLO. Hercs will fly from KAF to Camp Bastion then on to Kabul and eventually back to KAF several times a day. It's a green version of Ryanair, just with less hassle, with our highly trained pilots flying in big circles around Afghanistan, transporting anyone in theatre who had a reason to be there. In simple terms, we are there to count passengers on and off aircraft, produce a passenger manifest, and do any other jobs deemed fit by the chain of command that may require the attention of three idiots. I have done this job before in various locations and the normal thing is to do everything yourself. Due to Afghanistan being fairly fashionable at this time in its history, the budget is matched to the political interest, thus it is currently a bottomless purse. I would soon find out there were plenty of opportunities to have two or three people doing the same job, both civilian and military, to ensure next year's budget will be even bigger.

Our neighbours in the office block on one side are part of what I guess to be some sort of private security company that occupies several offices. They only wear civilian clothes, albeit the same light-coloured cargo pants and polo tops. I will speak to some of them infrequently over the next few months and they are all either ex-military or ex-Royal Ulster Constabulary.

The room on the other side is lived in by someone. There would always be loud TV or music coming from it and the odd female TCN from Thailand sneaking in and out during the evenings. We never will work out who was in there.

The block adjacent to us houses the admin staff, such as the Posties, RAF admin clerks, the Padre, the Station Commander, and Base Warrant Officer.

The courtyard in between is taken up with a long green canvas military tent in which the Afghani barber and his son work. He had been there when I had passed through KAF on a previous tour several years earlier and he offered his one style of haircut and tailoring services to the troops. He had decked the floor out with wooden pallets covered with a carpet to keep his customers' feet dry during the floods. The sofas on which the troops sat and read the same FHM magazines from years ago are still there, still decorated in their unidentified stains of possible biological origin.

One of the first things we will all do will be to get him to tailor our bush hats. These hats had been designed with a wide brim to keep the sun off the wearer's face. Somehow the fashionable thing to do is to have the brim cut down to about half its size as soon as you arrive in theatre. I have no idea why we do this, other than being blind followers of fashion and not wanting to look like we had just stepped off the plane. I'm sure there has been no attempt to stamp the practice out as I can only imagine the difficulty in policing it when all 10,000 have already done it and you don't want to be the only one looking like a rouge derrière.[21] A couple of weeks from now, it turns out, the barber will disappear, never to return. The tent would be taken down and returned to its rightful owner who had probably claimed it on their insurance ten years ago. The pallets would be put to good use by sorting them into something that resembled a pile of crap, the carpet would sold as an antique Persian rug, the sofas burnt, and the FHM mags donated to the NAAFI to sell back to us for £5 each. The word on the street will be that he had been passing information to the Taliban.

The barber, AKA 'The Barber,' meets his handler in the downtown Kandahar Shisha Hookah Lounge just before our arrival.

Handler: "What intel do you have for us this week on the British infidels?"

Barber: "They still like their hair cut short."

Handler: "What else?"

Barber: "They also still like the brim of their bush hats cut short."

Handler: "Tell me something I don't know?"

Barber: "I heard that 29 Regiment's finest are arriving next week."

The handler puts his head in his hands and weeps.

Eventually Bev takes me down to the air terminal. Don't think Heathrow, think large corrugated iron warehouse with bits missing, held together with string and surrounded outside by sleeping soldiers in various states of dustiness.

It's owned, run and manned by a company called CATO,[22]

---

21   Poor military French for red arse, which means "the new guy".

22   Combined Air Transport Operations

which is part of the KBR[23] empire. It's run by a rather rotund Ex-Territorial Army Brit called Micky Afendoulis who was christened by the RAF coppers as Fatendoulis. His deputy is Keith, who is ex-RAF and due to his odd style of management towards the TCNs I initially think had been an Air Vice Marshall. It later turns out he had only been a Corporal. He is probably making up for his frustration of his lack of promotion while serving. The middle management are Romanians and the workers the usual TCNs from Sri Lanka, Bangladesh and India, etc. They also have an RAF Warrant Officer, who has an office in the freight warehouse. His name is Mark Wright and he is a right bastard, by all accounts, but I get on with him like a freight warehouse on fire for some reason. They also have a Romanian Warrant Officer working for them who seems to be the handyman as he is always busy sawing bits of wood or painting walls. I'm not too sure that this was what he wants to do or just Mark telling him that's what Warrant Officers did on tour. You've got to remember that the Romanian Army are still fairly new to this war-fighting stuff and would probably believe anything we'd told them.

The air terminal is used by all participating nations in the War of Terror for the movement of their troops and civilians. These flights can also be used by participating troops and civilians in the War of Terror for wherever they need to go in theatre to continue their War of Terror. The troops and civilians are waiting for flights to wherever they needed to be in the great outdoors. It's comforting to see a level playing field, in that all are treated with the same amount of contempt usually reserved for the serving military. There is the luxury of

---

23 A rather large American company that provide the military with a wide range of contracts for the more mundane services required in conflicts such as waste disposal, catering, construction, etc. Morris Woodruff Kellogg, inventor of the cornflake, is the K in KBR.

one dusty tent held down with sandbags, with a scant offering of broken plastic matting which means a couple of lucky sods don't have to lie in the mud during the winter. The luxury of more tents hasn't yet reached this far but CATO will eventually manage to acquire some second-hand benches with 'Do not remove from Kabul Airport' stamped on them.

I am now about to experience the well-oiled machine that is the processing of passengers by Bev's team. One of her Lance Corporals goes outside and, at the top of his voice, requests that anyone booked onto the next Thumper flight to wherever should congregate around the terminal entrance for their brief. Thumper is the codeword for the RAF flights, which I'm sure confuses the Taliban's intelligence cell for about three seconds. One month later, when we suspect that they had broken the code, the codeword would be changed to Ramp. It's hardly Bletchley Park.

The bulk of our passengers are our own troops as booked on by the movement's cell down in Camp Bastion. The smiling ones are either off on their R&R[24] or are finishing their tour. The unsmiling ones are not. The remaining seats are offered up as 'Space-A' to anyone hanging about like a bad smell, which is pretty much everyone else outside. I presume it's short for Space Available, and it will always be on my list of things to ask an adult what it stood for, although I'll never get round to it.

Before the Lance Corporal can start his pre-flight brief he is customarily asked by almost everyone if this is the briefing for the Thumper flight to wherever it is going that day. He eventually starts reading from a clipboard in a very military manner. Most of it is of a negative nature such as 'Do not,' or 'You can't,' or 'You will be removed from the flight.'

---

24   Rest & Recuperation

I am already planning to replace some of it with 'You'll get a slap,' for reasons soon to be revealed. The main area of concern is making sure that weapons are unloaded prior to entering the building, as the CATO staff are not fond of being accidentally shot and that they remain unloaded until they have got to wherever they were going because, by coincidence, the RAF crews are also not fond of being accidentally shot. Just to clarify what unloaded means. For those of you not overly familiar with a bullet chucker, it's when the magazine, the bit that holds all the bullets, is removed from the bullet chucker and is kept removed from the bullet chucker. Any bullets in the spout, the barrel, are also removed thus leaving it in, what is colloquially known in military circles as, a safe unloaded state. Fortunately for us there is one nation who, prior to flying, are constantly wanting to put their magazines back on their bullet chucker, cock it, thus putting one up the spout, with the safety catch being the only thing stopping a 5.56mm hole or 30 appearing in the aircraft's fuselage or someone's body. Ladies and gentlemen, I give you the Americans. What is it with their *laissez-faire* attitude towards weapons? Is it the watching of too many crap films with lots of guns, or was it their belief that everyone who was not American was potentially a Taliban fighter? I don't know, but I do know I lost count of the times I caught them loading up and cocking their M16 bullet chuckers just as they were getting on the aircraft. At least we knew who to keep an eye on.

Once the briefing has concluded the passengers, avec bags, shuffle through the metal door carrying, dragging and kicking their bags into the terminal. Don't imagine the glass-fronted grandeur that is Gatwick Airport, picture an abandoned cattle shed. They then start queuing up in front of the check-in desk. Don't imagine a British Airways check-in desk, picture a grotty wooden desk. This is the point at which we really start earning our money. The Spams enter as always with a comical amount of bags. I hear that they had to deploy with every bit of kit they had ever been issued including all their white socks and pairs of oversized shorts, which probably have a label in them with the following description: Shorts, Men's, Silly, for the use of being ridiculed by the British Army.

There are two TCNs on the desk, one armed with a passenger manifest, and Bev standing behind them both. The one without the manifest asks the passenger for his ID. Upon gaining it he passes it to his colleague with the manifest who then looks for his name on the list and highlights it once it's found. Our job is to ensure this is carried out correctly. It's going to be a long six months. The TCN in charge of ID passage will then ask, "How many bags, sir?" in perfectly understandable English but with a slight accent of his country of origin. In time I'll come to realise that if the passenger wasn't American he would reply that he had two or three bags, upon which he would be handed two or three baggage labels. If they were an American then it would go more like this...

TCN:	"How many bags, sir?"
American:	"Pardon?"
TCN:	*(louder)* "How many bags, sir?"
American:	"Say again?"
TCN:	"Hoow maaany baaagsss, sirrr?"
American:	"Sorry, I can't understand you"
Me:	"How many bags, sir?"
American:	"Forty-seven."
TCN:	*(sarcastically)* "Sorry, sir, but I cannot understand you."
American:	"Foooorty Sevennnnn."

Me: "Oh, dear God."
American: "Watch your tongue, young man."

Once the passengers' bags have gone through the X-ray machine they then disappear through a hole in the wall, never to be seen again. Sometimes they will turn up at a destination, and sometimes they will turn up at the same destination as the passenger.

The passengers, now only sporting their carry-on luggage and their gun, will go forward to RAF Police, which is the empire of our resident RAF coppers. They are now instructed to put their bags, weapons, and everything metal they have on their bodies through the X-ray scanner.

"What about this?" they say as they pull something metallic out of one of their many pockets.

"Through the scanner, please, sir," says the copper.

The usual procedure becomes a game in which the passenger will produce varying metallic objects such as coins, a phone, dog tags, watches, or knives, one at a time and ask the coppers if it should also go through the scanner until the queue behind them goes out the door and all the way back into downtown Kandahar. I will never be able to shake the feeling of how wrong it looks putting a gun through an X-ray scanner and nobody batting an eyelid. They are looking to see if he is hiding any weapons in his luggage or maybe luggage in his weapons. They then walk through the metal detector, which will invariably go beep and the game will start all over again. Once the game is finally concluded they are reunited with their metallic possessions and wished a very unpleasant trip.

It's then off upstairs to the departure lounge. Don't imagine anything other than a large square room made from breeze blocks with an extra thick layer of beige paint, no windows, strip lights that buzz, and rows of metal seats that have been polished to perfection over the years with the constant flow of soldier's bums. The backs of these seats are angled a little too ambitiously in trying to meet the needs of the sitters' comfort. This, combined with the highly polished surface, means that whenever you sit back to relax you slide off like a piece of paper coming out of a printer. They then wait here for at least a couple of hours with only the strip lights for entertainment.

Check-in is finally closed about two hours before the flight is due to depart. After finding several remaining passengers, who have been well hidden, and listening to music on their headphones, the check-in is re-opened and finally closed a second time and sometimes re-opened and finally closed again depending on how well hidden the passengers are or how loud they have their music.

While the waiting crowd of travellers is upstairs and wondering how to stop sliding off the seats, it is a hive of activity downstairs in the CATO office. Bev is handed several copies of the passenger manifest. The guys in the freight hall have loaded the baggage onto aircraft pallets and strapped it down. Complete with passenger numbers and baggage weights we phone this info through to the RAF. We have a critical time of one hour and fifty-nine minutes to get the paperwork to the Herc crew. The first couple of times, being keen, I will rush off in the pick-up on the two-mile drive around to Whiskey Ramp to find the Herc earmarked for that day's flight to be sitting in its parking slot in a complete state of not-an-awful-lot-happening. Later on in the tour, I will consider just taking the paperwork straight to the crew's accommodation and passing it to the Loadmaster while he is dozing in his bed.

The passengers are called forward from their holding cell

of a departure lounge back downstairs to a fenced-off area outside that resembled a prison exercise yard. If you don't incarcerate passengers they will make a break for it and it buggers the numbers up. This is their last chance to use the facilities that are a long line of portable toilets which give off a constant aroma of generic cleaning chemicals and stale piss. Once final relief has been taken care of, they are counted and herded on to the bendy bus that once was the 154 to Hamburg Hauptbahnhof, complete with missing side panels and both wing mirrors shattered.

Bev and I drive ahead so that we will be there to meet the bus at the back of the Herc. At the Herc, the Loadmaster, who is responsible for the back of the aircraft, asks us again how many passengers. He instructs us to send the passengers over in groups of 10. When the passengers finally arrive we pass this request to our guy on the bus while all of us keep an eye out for an American who will inevitably try to load and cock his bullet chucker before getting on the aircraft. Does he think Bin Laden is piloting this particular one today?

There is one last final count of bodies as they file onto the Herc. Once they are all sitting uncomfortably, the baggage on the pallet, which arrived a few minutes ago is ready for loading. The rear ramp of the Herc is raised so that it's now horizontal to the ground. The forklift loader-type machine is always driven by a pimply and bored 12-year-old-looking RAF bod, as they would never trust a TCN with a machine anywhere near this expensive plane. He manoeuvres in close to the Herc and lines it up with the back ramp with skill. The forklift loader and the entire floor of the plane all have miniature rollers fitted so that, once correctly aligned, the pallets float effortlessly from the vehicle into the plane with a mere token shove. It's now time to wait as the crew do their piloty things prior to take-off. We have to ensure that the thing actually takes off and doesn't just go for a taxi around the airfield. It's always a bit of a problem trying to identify ours, as the Herc is a very popular aircraft with the military and there will be one taking off every two minutes. Once we are sure it's ours disappearing off into the sunset, we then call Bastion on an old Nokia mobile phone to let them know it has departed and with how many passengers in the back.

The handover is unremarkable. I nod in agreement while getting dragged around the place waiting for Bev to go home. I am shown around a strange-looking building that is where passengers are dumped off the incoming flights so that they won't get mixed up with any outgoing passengers. It's an unremarkable looking, very old, yellow-coloured building, probably built way before the US or the Soviets had even thought about building airbases in the region. It has high walls and was rectangular with a few arches in the walls that have newer-looking plywood doors fitted. Inside, larger arches run the length of the building. It's decked out with a variety of desks, tables, uncomfortable steel benches and leather sofas.

The walls are several feet thick which gives it the feeling of a bunker and there is a massive hole in the ceiling that has been patched up with a concoction of metal scaffolding, wood and bits of tarpaulin. It's called the TLS, which stands for the 'Taliban's Last Stand'. The story that I am told is that it was here that the Taliban found themselves holed up during the Battle for Kandahar Airport back in 2001, as it all started unravelling for them. As the name suggests it was the place of their last stand here on the airport, but I have no idea if the hole in the roof was linked to their final demise.

There is an air of excitement due to the completion of our predecessors' tour. It feels like they are really trying hard not to be too happy about it in front of us condemned souls. Our turn will come in a lifetime of six months and I will happily rub my replacement's face in it. Eventually, Bev and her team disappear off home on a Tri-Star that came direct to KAF. I'm sure she's pulled in a favour because she can't be arsed going down to Bastion, as it will turn out to be the only time a Tri-Star comes into KAF during my time there.

The next few days we spend settling into our roles and getting lost while driving around KAF. I put Paul on nights at his request as he wasn't much of a sun god, while Joe and I cover the days. We have the NOS[25] white pick-up truck for us to use at our leisure, and it is in a lot better condition than the one down in Bastion. It could be just a shell with square wheels that was pulled by an asthmatic donkey and it would be in better condition.

Thankfully, I don't have to sign for it as it is owned by KBR, who now and again will take it away and return it a day later saying it had been serviced. We won't exactly be high-mileage commuters. In fact, we won't be high-speed commuters either, as the speed limit around most of the camp is 20mph and the place is crawling with bored American and Bulgarian Military Police just itching to give you a ticket. I hope, when they come to sell the pick-up, they'll put down that the third, fourth and fifth gears were unused.

Wednesday 9th
As I come out of the accommodation that morning on my way to the DFAC for some breakfast disappointment, someone shouts "Scouse," in a high-pitched excited tone. This was the name by which I was known when I first joined up, as I had a slight Liverpudlian accent. I am from the Wirral and am not

---

25   Not Otherwise Specified – Generally something that's a bit of everything.

from Liverpool or a Scouse, but soldiers don't let these facts get in the way when it comes to a nickname.

I turn around to see a skinhead in uniform. It's Brendon Horsfall, otherwise known to me simply as Ned, due to a near-sounding equine-type surname. I never let spelling get in the way of a nickname. He was a good friend from my time in Germany during the early 90s when we were drivers together in 8 Regiment of the Royal Corps of Transport.

We spent our free time travelling around Europe or across the recently-removed Iron Curtain. We even made it as far as Siberia and China. The rest of our time was spent explaining to our Troop Commanders that just because we travelled to strange places that we weren't unhinged or communist sympathisers

We had bumped into one another over the years in different countries and had kept in loose contact, as soldiers do, with years between any correspondences. I knew he was already in theatre somewhere as he had contacted me over the phone about a year ago to sign some paperwork saying that I had known him for a while and he was of sound mind.

Lies of course, he's a fucking fruitcake. He had applied for a job with the pixelated face brigade[26] therefore I had visions of him with a massive beard sitting down to lunch with some Afghani village elders to discuss security issues. The reality was that he was making sure all their vehicles passed their MOT and were serviced on time. Oh, the kudos!

He heard I had arrived in Kandahar, probably from the barber, and he thought that if he hung around the Brit compound long enough that he would either get arrested for being creepy or bump into moi.

We shake hands.

---

26   Special Air Service – Their faces are always pixelated in pictures.

"How's it going," he says.

"You still owe me a fiver," I point out without any hesitation.

"Fuck off," he says as he bursts out laughing.

"Can I book flights through you to get to Bastion?" he adds, still giggling.

"Yeah, I'm good, thanks. It's only been, what, five years since we last met up?" I say sarcastically, in response to his forwardness in seeing me as his personal booking clerk.

"Yeah, yeah, whatever, can you book me a flight or what?"

"Of course, but what's it worth?"

He pauses.

"Ow," I shout, as he reaches out quickly and suddenly flicks my ear.

"You're a fucking retard," I say with the pain still burning on my ear.

"I'll promise not to beat you up every day."

"When do you need to fly?"

"Next week."

"Oh, do you now?" I put on my James Bond villain voice and rub my hands together, trying to look and sound menacing, "it'll be my pleasure to book you a fight."

"If you stitch me up, I'm gonna rip your fucking head off," his voice goes an octave higher.

My head is buzzing with plans.

Thursday 10th

It's dhobi[27] day and I offer to take all the guys' bogging kit to the laundry. Our dhobi is taken care of by, wait for it, KBR and they are staffed by, you'll never guess who, the TCNs.

We are issued hand-me-down grey oblong cloth mesh bags

---

27   Washing - Another word used by the Army from way back when we were in India.

and I guess they had once been white. Our stinking, smelly, dusty kit goes inside, and the top is tied off with a drawstring. We can present them at one of the many facilities, whereupon a TCN will attach a tag with a number on it so that we can retrieve it 24 hours later. Everything is boiled, washed, and dried together in big industrial machines, but, as I don't have any whites, this isn't a problem.

However, down the line, after six months of this aggressive washing style, I will come to note that my uniform was slowly shrinking. I will lose 10 kilos during my tour but my uniform will shrink faster than I will losing weight and, over time, my sleeves will gradually move further up my arms and I will have to let the trousers out.

"I see you're nearly at the end of your tour, Staff," an Officer will say to me one day. Under normal conditions he would have said, "Staff, I think you'd better give the pies a miss." But conditions won't have been normal... I return over an hour later after driving in circles around KAF completely lost. The dhobi place is only 200 metres away from our office.

Friday 11th
The last flight of the day has departed and Joe and I give the usual nod to the departing Herc that, as usual, we thought was one of ours but probably wasn't. In the RAF engineers' building there seems to be a little bit of excitement in the air. Is it possibly because it was Friday? I doubt that it's this, as a Friday in KAF is just like any other day. We eventually find out from the crabs that in the Yankee DFAC it was Surf and Turf night so we head over there to see if the excitement will match the food quality. Joe parks the pick-up in a massive puddle that could have been a lake. I open the door and look down at deep brown wet stuff that could be anything from rainwater

to raw sewage to hydrochloric acid.

"I forgot to pack the lifeboat," I say, "any chance of sailing to the nearest island?"

"Aye aye, Staff, full steam ahead to DFAC Island, Captain Staff," replies Joe.

"You're such an anchor," is all I can come up with.

We aren't to be disappointed by the disappointment of being moderately disappointed. The steaks are meat-flavoured rubber and the lobster is just a seafood mush NOS. In time I eventually realise that the buzz came from eating a different type of disappointment in a different location, so that it felt a bit exciting.

We are the only Brits in the DFAC and, while we are queuing, the rocket attack alarm sounds. Some Spams immediately get on the floor with their hands over their heads, and we decide that we would like to join them down there. Some, with their empty trays in hand, get on one knee so as not to lose their place in the queue, and some just carry on as if nothing is happening. I see one of the TCN chefs crapping himself trying to half hide behind the hotplate while reaching across it to continue serving up the food to a Yank who isn't taking any notice of the alarm or the chef. I hope he gets a medal for not spilling his chow and eating it in the face of hostile enemy action with complete disregard for his own safety or trouser size.

Saturday 12th
We get notification from Camp Bastion when they send that day's manifest through that there will be two prisoners on the

evening's flight. This will become quite a common occurrence but this first experience will stuck in my head. The guards call to check on the flight timings and see what time we want them to report directly to the back of the Herc. We do this, as having potential enemy combatants checking in with the normal passengers would be just weird. When the Spams move prisoners around the camp they have a big truck or a van, sometimes armoured and not too dissimilar from the G4S ones you would see moving prisoners back in the UK. When we move them, it's done for comedy value. I have no idea why, but the vehicle of choice is a Suzuki minivan. This is the type of vehicle used in the UK by self-employed plumbers who don't have a lot of tools. It's like a Dinky toy but a little bit bigger. The windows are blacked out with bits of cardboard stuck onto the windows by Black Nasty. This may be to save the embarrassment of the driver. I wonder if they ever thought about putting cardboard across the front windscreen, with a little letterbox out of which the driver could look. It would be like training to drive a tank Heath Robinson-style.

The guards meet us by the back of the aircraft at a prearranged time while the prisoners are kept in the minivan until all the other passengers are loaded. I've used the term loaded and not boarded because the RAF refer to passengers as 'walking freight.' We have to brief the passengers that there will be prisoners on the flight with them, and, under the rules of the Geneva Convention the taking of pictures of prisoners is forbidden. Later on in the tour we would normally do this brief right in front of any Americans who happened to be on the flight while looking them directly in the eye and giving them enough body language hints that it was them that this brief was aimed at. All other nations on the flight didn't seem to care less that the bad guys were on board. On the other hand, the Spams would always act excitedly as if we had some celebrity on board. They would always attempt to get a picture, even better a selfie with the poor prisoner to send home to Mom to prove that her tax dollars weren't being wasted.

Once the Loadmaster has done his safety brief through a megaphone, because Hercs are not the quiet planes as depicted in the films, where you can have a normal conversation even on the ground, he gives us the thumbs up to bring them over. The side door on the minivan slides back and out pops two of our enemies. They are tiny and I think for a minute that they are possibly children. They are wearing our desert camouflage body armour and helmets. This again is a requirement under the Geneva Convention that we offer them the same protection that we had ourselves and the above attire was a standard requirement on all flights. Their guards lead them out of the tiny van by their hands, which are bound together in front of them with plastic cuffs that are really oversized cable ties. Another guard guides their feet onto the tarmac because they are blindfolded.

They don't have the usual blindfold that a magician would use or a bit of cloth tied behind their head, no, they have a pair of plastic safety goggles. The type you may use when using an angle grinder that also have the elastic that goes around the back of your head to hold them in place. They have been covered in Black Nasty to restrict their view totally and possibly give their eyebrows a bit of a trim. Their long shirts flap about in the wind from underneath the bottom of their body armour. Their helmets are on the massive side of one-size-fits-all-known-fat-knappers[28] and hang off at an angle. The chin straps are done up to keep them on their heads, even if they are hanging off to one side. The whole prisoner look is fin-

---

28 Fat knapper: military slang for "head"

ished off by pairs of baggy trousers and leather flip flops.

I am getting bored so I try to initiate some discussion.

"Would you lick a Taliban prisoner's flip flop for £5?" I ask.

"No way, you sicko," replies Joe.

"Would you lick a Taliban prisoner's flip flop for £500?"

"Stop it, you're making me feel ill."

"Would you lick a Taliban prisoner's flip flop for £5000?"

"Which side?"

"You're so cheap."

Over the tour, I'd find the prisoners were mostly always of very small stature. Ned will tell me at some point he'd come across one who was over six foot tall. He must have been the main lookout guy or in maybe in charge of replacing the light bulbs. Seeing these two waif-like men shuffling across the apron being led by their armed guards, restrained and blindfolded gives them a sense of very real vulnerability. Yes, they were potential enemy combatants, but I can't help but feel some humanity for them. That empathic feeling probably would disappear pretty quickly should I end up with one of them holding a rusty kitchen knife to my throat.

Sunday 13th

Sundays are normally relatively quiet due to the RAF not having the drive to do a Sunday morning flight. The good news for us is that because of this we don't have anything to do either. As we are still new in KAF we think it would be good to impress someone by going into the office at the normal time to show a sense of keenness. We are the only two moving about the compound. The admin office is locked up including the Padre's office. Because he's RAF he too probably had a dislike for working Sunday mornings. We tread quietly down the corridor to our office whereupon we open the door as quickly as we can hoping to scare the shit out of Paul. The coiled spring that is a sleeping Paul springs into life with the energy of a water droplet. He's sitting in the only comfy chair, with his legs splayed out, an arm on each rest and his head fully back. As he wakes with a noise that is half snore and half choke, he tilts his head forward and stares at us through one eye that looks like a pisshole in the snow

"Oh, it's you," he remarks, with the unpretentiousness of someone who was already bored with the tour.

"Fucking hell, it's Sleeping Beauty," says Joe. "Rushed off your feet last night, then?"

"There was fuck all happeninggggggggggggaaaaaawwww," as a yawn comes out mid-sentence.

He arches his back while still in the chair and starts a stretch while holding his arms in the same direction of his legs, which makes him look like he is making an attempt to stand to attention whilst not getting out of the chair.

"As you were, killer," I add.

"I think," he says, around another yawn, "that on that bombshell I'll be off to my scratcher," and with those fine words of wisdom he is up and gone, not to be seen again for the next 10 or so hours. Joe and I sit in the office for nearly two hours discussing the merits of shaving foam against shaving gel while the phone doesn't ring and zero emails turn up. We just can't take the pressure anymore so we decide to go and take the pick-up to the wash-down point as it is starting to look a bit dusty.

I get Joe to drive so that I will feel more important being chauffeured around. He tunes the radio to BFBS[29] and I immediately turn it off again as no doubt there would be utter shite on and a presenter telling us how great BFBS are.

---

29   British Forces Broadcasting Service

This claim isn't hard when your only competition is the even shitter American Forces Network with its dullard presenters. Later on I will tune it into the local Afghan station so at least when I am driving about I can imagine that I was on holiday. But, principally, it will be because Joe can't stand the wailing Arab music and annoying him makes the days pass by just that bit quicker. The local car and truck wash is another KBR-run facility manned by the familiar TCNs with Spam overseers. There are several lanes to choose from when approaching wash-down and our human nature is to choose the one with the fewest vehicles waiting in line, but, as we have all day to kill, we choose the line with the most vehicles. The queue gives us ample time to read the numerous signs warning us about the unspeakable dangers that come with cleaning a vehicle. The Yanks had a canny ability to take the 'It's elf and safety gurn maaad,' to another level, putting the UK in the second division of PC league tables.

As we wait for the guys in front of us to finish their dangerous vehicular washing activity, the sun shines through the open side window and I start to doze. I drift in and out of consciousness for a few minutes. I then have a bit of a rollercoaster of emotions while coming round.

"Fucking hell, I'm in Afghanistan," I think with a minor shock.

"Oh bollocks, I'm here for the next six months as well," as it turns to disappointment. "I'll get £5000 extra for this though," as I go back to happiness.

My sunglasses are on so I'm able to keep an air of looking soldier-like, which is 'in control and fully alert in a slumped position.'

My eyes open and I gaze on the mountains in the distance under the clear blue sky. I start to try to determine the different sounds produced by the airbase. There is a constant background buzz of generators all running at a high RPM, while every minute there is a departing aircraft on full power with an added throaty grumble crescendo as a convoy of large armoured vehicles raced by. I notice some small birds perched on the warning signs looking nervous. All of a sudden I can hear them making their busy chirping sounds above the general din.

The vehicle in front starts up and moves forward 10 feet to the washing point and the fat bearded Spam civilian contractor behind us starts on his horn because we don't immediately pull forward. "Fuck off," yells Joe towards his open window.

"It's only been a week and they are getting on my tits already," he says, slightly quieter.

"That long?" I reply, with an overacted look of surprise, "I was attached to them in Kabul for five months on my last tour."

"They must have driven you up the wall?"

"We used to have morning briefs, afternoon briefs, evening briefs and night briefs. The funny thing was I was never wearing any briefs for any of them."

"Living on the edge, eh?"

"Not by choice, some nobchops walked off with my bag at Bastion when we arrived thinking it was his."

"Aha, never put all your undercrackers in one basket, you should know that by now, Staff."

"I eventually liked living on the edge."

"Did you get your bag back?"

"The unidentified lost bag procedure sprang into life and achieved nothing. Three weeks later, when I was at the air terminal in Bastion I just casually mentioned to some Private Mover if they had a bag knocking about?

"He pulls a bag out from under a desk and says in a thick Scouse accent, 'Errr... like dis one, Staff?' It was an award-winning impression.

"Turned out that nobchops brought my bag back the next morning after realising it wasn't his but no one thought to tell me. At least I was reunited with my shreddies."

"Bet you never made that mistake again?" laughs Joe.

"Now you mention it, I put something in your bag before we left."

The vehicle in front finishes so Joe starts up and moves forward to the washing bay. The fat Spam behind us must have heard Joe earlier, as he's deadly quiet now. We put our windows up and wait. We wait a bit more. We carry on waiting until we notice a TNC looking at us through the side window. He's holding the long pressure washer wand and is thrusting it in our direction with both his hands again and again. We continue to watch him from inside the pick-up and don't react one bit, which makes his thrusting motions accelerate. Scared that he is going to pass out, Joe eventually puts the window down and says, "Just a rinse please."

The TCN, who looks like he'd been sent to KAF by a popular vote in his village to get rid of him, shouts aggressively at us, "YOU CLEAN, YOU CLEAN, YOU CLEAN."

"Alright, mate, calm down," says Joe as he opens his door.

"Looks like we," he emphasised the 'we' bit, "are washing the pick-up."

"We?" I say in a monotone fashion and with the air of a higher rank than Joe, while not moving a muscle.

As he slams the door shut, he grabs the pressure washer from the TCN, and points it at the windscreen. It blasts into life for all of two seconds. As the now brown water starts sliding down the window in silence, I can make out the blurred outline of the TCN dancing about and I can hear his muffled screaming, which is obviously aimed at Joe. He's going off his head at 1,000mph but I do pick up him saying something about safety glasses and signing paperwork. Probably a waiver saying we won't take KBR to court in five years when our eyeballs fall out.

"Of course we read the fucking signs, for fuck's sake," replies Joe, clear as crystal.

Tuesday 15th

It was late in the evening and I was in my room writing a letter to my kids under a single light bulb when the wailing rocket alarm sounded. I quickly got on the floor face down and covered my head with my hands as per the Immediate Action drill. I then realised that my helmet was just in front of me so I reached out and quickly put it on. As the wailing alarm faded the monotone electronic voice started to announce: "Rocket attack, rocket attack, rocket attack." There was a pause in-between the words "rocket" and "attack "and you could hear the words echoing across KAF. As I waited with a slight feeling of dread for the incoming bangs, my door suddenly swung open and I heard the voice of Ned. "What are you doing down there, you big girl's blouse?"

Wednesday 16th

Wednesdays are SITREP[30] day. Once a week I have to put together an email of the weekly shenanigans that were happening in KAF. I send the report to Second Lieutenant Evans, commonly known as Troopy, who is based down Bastion. Troopy is in charge of the air terminal tent along with Nick.

In keeping with the archetypal military hierarchy style, be-

---

30   Situation Report.

cause she is only a lowly Second Lieutenant and straight out of Sandhurst, Nick is really running the show. She's on hand as his officer voice when other officers couldn't or wouldn't want to take advice from a lowly Staff Sergeant with 16 years' experience. She has a surprisingly strong Welsh accent for an officer, which had probably already set her career ceiling.

The SITREP is primarily to highlight any problems with the processing of passengers for the Thumper flights to and from KAF. Secondly, it's to keep the chain-of-command informed of any external problems that may affect us as a detachment, which in turn could affect the Thumper flights. Lastly, it's to tick the box that the military were fulfilling their obligations of keeping the families back in Cirencester officially informed of what their loved ones are up to. In this modern-day of emails it was pretty much redundant as, by the time it reaches the families, it's second-hand information.

The report writing would become one of the aspects of the tour that, as time went by, would make me struggle to find stuff that was remotely relevant or interesting. Systems and procedures had been in place for years now and therefore everything tended to run pretty smoothly.

KAF ATLO SITREP
week ending 16/11/2011

▶ Timmy Hortons have now withdrawn from KAF. The last doughnut sold is already on eBay for $500. The inferior NAAFI donuts have increased in price from their already extortionate prices due to a rise in demand. One NAAFI donut is worth a ride in the jump seat in the cockpit of a Herc.

- ▶ Hand over from 24 Regt detachment now completed.
- ▶ Ramp flight passenger processing running smoothly with CATO assistance.
- ▶ Airside passes now obtained from US Air Force Military Police.
- ▶ Two IDF[31] attacks. No casualties reported.

I liked to list them in order of importance.

Saturday 19th

We are working the afternoon flight, and during the lull, as we make the passengers wait unnecessarily in the holding cell upstairs, I pop over to see Mark Wright in the CATO freight terminal. His office is on the other side of the warehouse and, as I walk in-between the pallets of essential supplies piled high, I pass a Spam who is brushing the warehouse floor with the smallest of brushes grumbling to himself. I knock on Steve's door, pop my head around the door and say. "Aye up, Sir."

He's on the phone and beckons me to come in and take a seat on his big leather sofa as he carries on his conversation.

"The package will be on tomorrow's flight," he says in his northern accent. "I'll make sure it's in good condition when it arrives with you."

I can just make out the voice on the other end but not what they are saying.

"Just make sure it doesn't come back here again," he adds with a hint of intimidation. "Yeah, it's breathable packaging so it shouldn't sweat too much."

---

31   Indirect Fire – When the bad guys just fire their munitions in the general direction of us without any precision.

I'm starting to wonder what type of conversation I am now privy to. Some cheese he didn't like? Maybe someone had asked him to make someone disappear Mafia-style?

The pace at which he is talking speeds up a little. "Yeah, yeah, yeah, no worries... will do, will do, yeah, yeah, speak to you later, bye, bye, bye."

He is obviously losing interest in speaking to the other party any more.

"Fucking hell," he says, as he puts the phone down, "you getting to grips with everything?"

"Yeah," I shrug my shoulders and pulled a face. "You know how it is, same crappy job, just a different location."

"Well, it pays the mortgage, I suppose," he replies.

"What's with the Spam cleaning the hangar floor with the tiny brush?" I enquire.

"Ah, Sergeant Bellend was late for work again," smiling, as if he was going to enjoy telling me about Sergeant Bellend.

"Sergeant Bellend is called Sergeant Bellend, not because it is his name but because he is a complete bellend," he says, still smiling.

"God knows who in the Spam military decided to promote him to Sergeant? He's a fucking retard with the organisational skills of a handcuffed crab," he says, now giggling.

"He couldn't work out how to open a plastic water bottle the other day, so he..." with his hands on the desk he paused, leaned forward and looked me in the eye, "so he bit the top of the bottle clean off."

Steve now bursts into a loud bout of laughter.

"I mean if this is the level of the Spam NCOs, then we are all really fucked here."

Laughing with him I can't help but wonder if he is going to make him disappear too.

Monday 21st

I am very bored this morning, so I find the National Lottery terms and conditions online and I print them off, all 40 pages, and put them in an internal mail envelope to SSM Kiwi Copperwaite back at South Cerney with a yellow Post-it note.

'SSM,' I start with his title so it will give the impression that it is from an officer. 'Could you please have a look at these and let me know what your thoughts are? We need to make sure all our ducks are in a row before going ahead.'

I sign it off with some scribbly initials to complete the confusion. I then put the internal envelope in a proper envelope and send it to Sgt Mike Birbeck, with a little note asking to put the internal envelope in the South Cerney internal mail for me so that the BFPO post stamp wouldn't give me away.

Kiwi is on the Sergeants' Mess committee and I know this will confuse him. Being a top soldier, he will take the time to read it all, and I can see him in his office, scratching his head, wondering who the sender is and how he should go about this extremely vague task.

Morning japes complete, I set off for a day at work for Queen and Country, just via the laundry and coffee shop...

The Boardwalk

Situated in KAF is the Boardwalk, which is infamous as well as it is famous, as well as being welcomed by the troops and despised by others. At the centre is a small Astroturf football field which, in turn, is encircled by a dusty running track. There is always a chubby Spam doing a spot of running in the midday sun, wearing his issued oversized shorts, a hi-vis belt, white socks pulled right up to their knees and a grey issued tracksuit top emblazoned with the words 'US ARMY. I assume it was in case they pass out in the heat and whoever finds them to knows who they are and where to send them.

Surrounding the recreational facility was an excess of shops, coffee shops, and restaurants that are made from old shipping containers, bits of corrugated iron, and wood, which gives the whole place a shanty town feel. In front of these and going all the way round is the actual boardwalk, which can accommodate at least eight large soldiers walking abreast. The entire pedestrian area is raised and under cover so that the potential customers can enjoy their shopping experience out of the winter mud or undercover from the scorching summer sun. You can see the various architectural skills that are present or not, as some places are glass-fronted classy looking establishments that wouldn't look out of place on a UK high street and some have a small hatch type sliding window cut into the side of a shipping container. Some of the shops are run by locals and sell Afghani goods such as rugs, clothing, fags, pictures, musical instruments, bicycles and Rolex watches. The ones run by Americans and Europeans sell military-style equipment, from bags to knives to truncheons to crossbows. I'm not too sure who would find themselves in the position that they needed to buy any of the above.

There is an abundance of places that specialised only in the production of embroidered Velcro badges. Inside, their walls are adorned with thousands of examples badges, with unit names, positions, nicknames and national flags. This emblem economy must have contributed for at least 50% of the country's GDP as it seems as soon as someone gets into theatre they suddenly stop being rational and get caught up in the emblem craze. Some of the other nations' soldiers were like Boy Scouts with their badge collecting.

'This one is for map reading, this one is for first aid and

this one is for killing the enemy.' They have so much Velcro on their uniform that the risk of a spark from the massive build-up of static electricity meant they should have been banned from partaking in any re-fuelling tasks.

The coffee shop popularity was mainly down to the lack of alcohol and one gaff in particular was the Green Bean, which, luckily for me, had a promotion in place called 'Buy a Cup of Joe for a GI.'

It worked by you signing up online and someone back in the US could buy a GI a cup of Joe. As far as I was concerned we were on the same side and as I had been attached to the US Army in Kabul I consider myself an honorary GI and fully entitled to misleading the American population. Every day I'd receive an email with a code and short personal message from a civilian wishing me a safe tour or insisting I kill everyone I met who was not a freedom-loving American citizen. I'd present myself at their establishment and redeem the code for a free cup of Joe, thus giving me the satisfaction of saving me in total a whopping $271.79 during my time in KAF.

> Cost of 1 Green Bean cup of Joe $2;
> Tour length 6 months/182.5 days;
> Can't be arsed going to the Boardwalk
> days 25% = 46.62 days
> 46.62 – 182.5 = 135.88 days @ $2 per day = $271.79

After a couple of weeks, I worked out that if I put a random six-figure number on a yellow Post-it note I'd still get a free cup of Joe. If the CEO of Green Bean should just happen to read this then as an admission of my guilt I'll happily send you a cheque to cover the cost of my fraudulent ways, plus a goodwill gesture. The restaurants ranged from a TGI Friday, where you could go and sit down in with a waiter service, to takeaways from chains that you had heard of, may have heard of, and had never heard of. Not once had I the courage to sample these delights as there were rumours of dodgy cooking practices and stories of soldiers suffering from life-threatening cases of the shits. I presume someone in charge was monitoring these places, as now and again one would disappear, and I mean disappear Afghani-style, as in the shipping container doubling as the kitchen would be almost surgically removed leaving a 20-foot gap. I'm sure this gastronomic justice wasn't doled out for minor indiscretions, but the extreme cases such as trying to pass dog off as deep-fried chicken.

The football pitch was also used for the many visiting artists that came to theatre to entertain the troops. When the celebrities came to entertain the UK forces it was open to everyone in KAF, which would lead to all the other NATO nations personnel scratching their heads at the knob jokes. When the Spams got someone to entertain them, nobody else was invited. All the roads to the boardwalk were closed off with armoured vehicles and soldiers in full kit denying anyone other than the US military access to their brand of entertainment. Looking back now, maybe it was for our own good. The first time I came across this I thought I had become distracted and accidentally walked off KAF into the middle of a big operation in downtown Kandahar city.

KAF ATLO SITREP
week ending 23/11/2011

▶ Dunkin Donuts have opened a shop on the Boardwalk. NAAFI donut sales have plummeted overnight causing hyperinflation of the value of their doughnuts. A three week-old newspaper is now worth five NAAFI donuts.

▶ Three IDF attacks. No casualties reported but the scrapyard took a direct hit which tidied it up a bit.

Friday 25th

I get a text from Sergeant Dave Davidson down at Bastion asking me to price up some fags as he had heard they were quite cheap in KAF. After a quick recce in one of the many Afghani shops that were dotted around the boardwalk, I find a premium establishment that does 200 of the finest imitation Benson & Hedges for the extortionate price of $2. They also do original Mont Blanc pens for under $10, which is a steal.

I give him a call on the landline.

"Dave, it's $2 for 200 tabs."

"Get me 5,000," he replies instantly, sounding quite desperate. "I'll have the cash on the next flight."

"Mate, for $2 they're probably full of radioactive shit at best."

"Hopefully the best radioactive shit," the reply comes again, rather too quickly, "just get 'em on the next flight down here."

Over the next six months I will send thousands of fags down to him and I believe he's miraculously still alive at the time of writing.

Sunday 27th

It's Sunday night and I pass over the reins of power to Paul who settles down for a busy night of watching DVDs. He has a Herc due in later that night with three passengers on it.

"Will you be able to cope with tonight's passenger numbers?" I ask him.

"I dunno, depends on their nationality. Three Spams is equal to dealing with 50 Brit troops."

"Well, you know, I'm the hands-on type of SNCO who's not afraid to muck in, so if you're feeling the pressure, give me a call and I'll send Joe down to help you."

"Eh, you what?" says Joe as he looks over the top of a FHM mag from 2003 that he is reading for the sixth time today.

We're on our way to the DFAC for some evening disappointment, and I'm talking to Joe about the merits of buying a decent watch and not the crap that Ratner's used to sell when the rocket alarm sounds its wailing siren. Now armed with the information that inbound to us on a low trajectory are one or possibly several Chinese-made 120mm rockets travelling at a great speed that will impact indiscriminately and explode into a thousand jagged sharp bits of hot metal shrapnel, we nonchalantly lie down on the ground while continuing the conversation.

Joe, being a bit younger than me, says, "Ratner's, never heard of 'em," as he snuggles up to the base of a concrete blast wall.

"The owner, Gerald Ratner, thought that his stuff was crap and made this known during a speech," I'm now shifting myself towards the same blast wall while still facing him. "These remarks went public and nearly ruined his company."

BOOM.

We both flinch and try to make ourselves smaller.

"So now, when a company director or chairman doesn't think about what he's saying and similarly commits corporate suicide..."

BOOM.

That one is a bit nearer and we both flinch again as we feel the shockwave through the ground.

"For fuck's sake," I say.

I make this comment towards the explosions getting closer and not Gerald Ratner's monumental fuck-up.

"...It's known as doing a Ratner," I carry on.

"What an utter bellend," says Joe with his hands over his head and face in the dusty stony ground. "Is his business still going?"

"I'm not sure, to be honest, I think he changed the name of his company and it hung on by the skin of his teeth," I say muffled, as I'm now pushing my face into the base of the blast wall.

The all-clear siren sings its relieving tune and we both stand up covered in white dust that makes us look like ghosts.

"Fucking hell," says Joe, trying to brush away the dust, "these were clean on this morning."

We make our way to the DFAC and I notice that in the queue for the evening meal every fourth person has the dusty ghost look.

Halfway through my bowl of dhal, one of our medics suddenly appears in front of me and sits down.

"Alright, Staff, how's it going?" he says in such a manner that he didn't really have my personal wellbeing in mind but his own well-being that was directly linked to something he wanted from me.

"Not too bad thanks," I reply with suspicion.

"What are the chances on getting on tomorrow morning's

Thumper flight to Bastion?" he enquires.

"No problem," I say, while blowing on my latest spoonful of steaming hot dhal "there's plenty of seats available. Just be at the terminal about nineish and I'll get you on it."

I then put the spoon of hot dhal in my mouth.

"It's really important that I get down there in the morning." he replies, as if I hadn't said anything.

"Owl gef oo un," I say, with a mouth full of rcd hot dhal.

"You see, if I don't get down there before 12 it's going to cause some problems."

"Owl gef oo un, don urry abouf if," I say, with a mouthful of now very slowly cooling dhal. I just give him the thumbs up to try and persuade him that it isn't a problem.

"I'll catch you later, Staff," says Joe standing up, obviously bored by what is unfolding in front of him. With the guilt-free luxury that he is not involved in the conversation he promptly buggers off. I'm left to try and finish off my dinner while trying to explain to Dr Kildare that I don't personally own the aircraft or have the final say on who may or may not travel on them, and my ability to get him a seat on a Thumper flight would make no difference to me financially, physically or mentally whatsoever.

After dinner I make my way towards the exit while carrying my plastic trays. I brush off the paper plates and plastic cutlery that are mixed in with food into one of the big bins. The trays are piled up into a square-looking plastic skyscraper waiting for the TNC to take them away to the industrial dishwasher. As soon as I go from the bright lights of the DFAC to the dark outside, my night vision is kaput and I start to walk blindly in the direction of the accommodation. I know that in about ten paces there's a small sharp rise in the ground and I anticipate my toes kicking it as I get closer. I slow down as I know I am now getting near to it. The front of my right boot feels the incline and makes contact. If anyone were watching me through some night vision goggles they would see me walking like a drunk trying to negotiate a small mound as if it were Glastonbury Tor. I attempt to climb in the style of a drunk and predictably fall forward onto my knees and swear. I begin crawling on my hands and knees up the tiny embankment. At the top I get to my feet again and brush off the grit that has stuck to my palms. I see the dim lights that illuminate the accommodation not too far away and again set off blindly in its direction, knowing that there are no more obstacles to navigate. Ten seconds later I am face down on the ground again after bumping into something that should not have been on my planned track. I roll over onto my back, my feet still stuck in the unknown obstacle, I feel for what had caused this latest fall. My hands reach down towards it and touch a thin cold metal tube and some rough plastic which I instantly recognise as a ploy prop chair.

"For the love of God," I mutter, "who, what, why?" I say in desperation, as my mind tries to fathom why there is a randomly placed chair out here.

I'm then aware of someone approaching with a torch while I'm getting myself to my feet for the second time that evening.

"You alright, Staff?" says the familiar voice of Joe.

"I've fallen over twice in the last two minutes and I'm not even pissed."

He shines the torch on the poly prop chair which, in the light, we can now see is knackered.

"My theory is that It probably belonged to one of the Crabs, and the route of least resistance is to just throw it out here because taking it to the bin is too much like hard work for the sideways-walking bottom-feeder."

"You are probably right, Mr CSI Kandahar."

I enter my room and put the light on and it instantly goes off. I do the usual on and off a few times and then stick my head out into the corridor to learn two new things that evening:

1. It is also now dark in the corridor. It was light when I was walking down it about four seconds ago.

2. Everyone else is now looking out of their rooms.

"Fucking hell," says someone, which grabs everyone's attention, "we're on fire."

An electrical junction box on the ceiling is starting to produce smoke.

"Where's the isolator switch?" another voice calls out.

"I think it's here in the fuse box," says Joe, pointing at a small white metal hatch on the wall with a padlock on it.

As we all look at the hatch helplessly, the smoke continues to fill the corridor. Jamie Savage, the RAF Warrant Officer Mover, steps forward and starts trying to get a grip on the corner of the hatch as it's not quite sitting flush to the wall. He's Scottish, so as he fights for a grip on the corner his attempts are accompanied by grunts and unintelligible mutterings which are no doubt a series of profanities. He eventually gets his fingers in and, with a bang, he pulls the entire thing clean off its hinges. The first thing we notice is the big red isolator switch with the words 'Isolator Switch' written beneath it. Jamie flicks it off and the smoke stops. The hatch is still attached to the wall by the latch and padlock and on the inside of the bent and broken hatch is a sticker informing us of the number to call in an emergency.

Someone calls the number saying it's an emergency and 30 minutes later an Indian TCN arrives, whom we all presume to be an electrician. Initially he goes off his head wanting to know who has vandalised the door to the fuse box.

"You can't be ripping doors off just because the fuse has popped," he says in his heavily accented Indian voice.

Jamie, also in a heavily accented voice, taps him on the arm and says, "Look at that, pal," gesturing upwards towards to the melted lump of grey plastic on the ceiling. "Can ye ney smell the burnin?"

"Oooooh," says the sparky, in an accent which could have been Indian or Scottish.

With a look of confusion Jamie asks him, "Why is the fuse box door locked? It strikes me as a bit dangerous, pal."

"Because when fuses keep blowing, soldiers replace with nails or tin foil. Verrrry dangerous."

"Aye, fair one, pal, but the fuse didn't blow in this case while we were burnin' down."

The Indian sparky is silent for a minute while he thinks.

"I'll have to get an electrician in the morning to come and fix it, so you'll have no electricity tonight I'm afraid."

Jamie, looking slightly surprised, says, "Are you not a sparky, pal?" then adding "I mean electrician," realising he probably wouldn't know what a sparky was.

"No, sir, I am a plumber.

British casualties for the month of November
7 killed & 17 wounded.

2

DECEMBER 2011

Thursday 1st

I AM BRUSHING my teeth when the attack alarm goes off. It's pretty unusual for it to go off in the morning. They must have cut the fuse too short on the rocket.

I look at myself in the mirror, the toothpaste all around my mouth and running down my chin making me look slightly rabid. I raise my eyebrows in mild surprise, make an "ooh" sound, and promptly carry on. I stop again briefly as I hear a couple of thuds in the distance, look myself in the eyes, and think, "I really should get on the floor." But, due to the minging state of the floor, I carry on scrubbing my gnashers.

By the time I finish my morning routine the all-clear is sounding. I check the Nokia phone just in case and see that I have a new text.

It's from Paul. "Plane has just been hit by shrapnel and ain't going anywhere."

My immediate reaction is, "Bollocks," which I say out loud, immediately thinking that we now have to take care of 50 passengers who should have been on their way to Camp Bastion.

As an afterthought, I reply, "Any dead or mangled? :("

"Nope, all alive :)," comes the instant reply.

"I presume you didn't lose your thumbs, LOL?"

I had jokingly instructed Paul and Joe that if they ever got injured when out and about they were never to call me, only to text me. As they stood in front of me looking confused, I had to explain that I couldn't do with all the screaming from the phone down my lughole. It would be too much like getting a massive bollocking from a shouty person. Whereas "aaaaaaaaargh" in a text message would be a lot easier to understand and less distressing for moi, thus having an overall calming effect on the situation for all, but mainly for me.

The rockets had come in from the Northwest on a low trajectory. One came down about 150 metres from the Herc that was already loaded up with all the passengers and waiting to be late. Paul had just passed the paperwork to the loadmaster and was just about to jump off the back ramp when an ear-deafening boom and instantaneous blast wave rocked the aircraft on its undercarriage. He instinctively threw himself onto the floor of the Herc to reduce his profile as the shrapnel tends to travel outwards and upwards.

There were only two small problems with his cat-like reaction. One being that in the aircraft he was several feet above the ground and in line with the trajectory of the shrapnel and the shrapnel had already whizzed past at several hundreds of miles an hour. The passengers were even more exposed, as they were strapped in higher up on the netted seats down each side of the aircraft. They, at least, had a smidgen of protection as they were ready for the flight, with their body armour and helmets already donned. The only part of the Herc that had the luxury of armour was the cockpit keeping the drivers safe. Paul was the only one not wearing anything and the wafer-thin aluminium fuselage could only offer the supersonic flying chunks of sharp metal a resistance equivalent to butter. His kit was currently two miles away doing something far more useful which was holding the door open to air the office. He said later that he had a similar feeling to that of being the only one naked at a party. I never asked him how he came to that conclusion. As he lay on the floor and the aircraft stopped rocking, it filled up with what he initially thought to be dust. This was a sound thought as it is the main commodity in Afghanistan. It later turned out to be fibres from the sheets of insulation that line the inside of the fuselage. They were falling from somewhere in the ceiling area, as a piece of shrapnel had torn a 10in gash through the top of the fuselage near the tail end. Through the network of pipes and cables above their heads, the sun started to shine through where it wasn't meant to shine through. Two bits of shrapnel had hit the aircraft, the other one making a fist-sized hole in the left aileron. The aileron would be replaced that day, but after inspection of the hole in the fuselage, it would emerge that one of the main spars had been damaged. This will be enough to ground the aircraft until they can get some engineers from the UK to fly out to carry out the repairs.

In a few days' time, while we are mooching about on Whiskey Ramp waiting for that day's Herc to bugger off, we will go to look at a shipping container that was closer to the impact. It was peppered with about 15 holes. The metal of the container wall was a lot thicker and stronger than the aircraft or our flesh and it had been sliced through with ease by the fragments of the rocket. The entry holes are smooth around the edges as the metal had been bent inwards out of sight. The exit holes look like they had had a more violent experience, as the shattered rocket casing had ripped through the metal, leaving sharp torn twisted strips pointing out in the direction of the shrapnel's journey. The bits of exposed steel that had been shredded open are still shiny and unblemished as if it had just come out of the factory. It won't show any signs of corrosion just yet due to the dry atmosphere. All the holes are from waist height upwards, which was a sobering reminder as to why we should get on the floor when the alarm sounds. Paul, the passengers, and the crew were all in a very perilous position this morning, and it was by sheer luck that nobody had a medium-sized hole somewhere in their body. I will point this out to Joe and he will take a sharp breath and make a sound that really should be texted to me.

Whiskey Ramp, where all the aircraft park and where we do the majority of our hanging about talking bollocks, is very open and very exposed. This rocket had reminded us that you could still get killed or horribly mangled while even a good distance from the impact. The RAF, being a bit more on-the-ball, would manage to get some blast walls positioned between each of the aircraft within a couple of weeks. It's $60million a pop for a replacement Herc, and I suspect this would probably be the main driving force towards getting the blast walls acquired so quickly. This would at least give us something solid to hide behind other than our pick-up with its Play-doh-like aluminium hull.

Monday 5th

The highlight of the day is a Romanian soldier who turns up for the flight looking slightly out of it, which grabs everyone's attention. The sniffer dog understandably takes an instant attentiveness to him and he is hauled to one side by the RAF Coppers who pat him down. Turns out he has quite a lot of hashish hidden in his weapon and magazines. It is in small cling film wrappers and moulded to fit in the various empty bits of his AK-47 including the barrel. Most of his magazines are full of the stuff and he doesn't seem to have any ammunition on him. This is irrelevant as there's no way he could cock his AK-47 drug-filled weapon anyway without smoking it all and by then he would probably just want to have a chat with the enemy. The Romanian guys working at CATO are called to assist and are clearly embarrassed by one of their countrymen trying to smuggle drugs onto an RAF plane. The Romanian military police are summoned and turn up within two minutes. I've been here about a month and it's the first time I've seen the Romanian MPs. It turns out I won't see them again until April next year when they'll come out of hiding for a football match. I wonder if they moonlight as kitchen staff. They handcuff him and roughly push him out of the terminal while speaking in Romanian with a 'you're in deep shit' tone. I half suspect that once they were out of sight that they are all mates. They'll apologise to him for the rough handling but explain that they have to keep appearances up, give him his gear back, shake hands and say, "See you next week, Andrei."

Tuesday 6th
In an email from Bastion we are instructed to use the word 'Ramp' instead of 'Thumper' for the RAF flights. The Taliban Bletchley Park department must have finally cracked code for the flights. This change should confuse them for a few months until they crack the new code word and work out what we idiots are on about now.

Wednesday 7th
I arrive in the office after a spot of lunch which involved eating something new. Not new as in by choice but new as in I thought it was something else. Ned is sitting in the only comfy chair flicking through an FHM magazine from 1999 and, without looking up, he says, "Can you get me on tonight's flight to Bastion, you Scouse git?"

"Charming," I reply. "Kiss your mother with that mouth, do you?"

"Nope, just your mother," which he says far too quickly.

"You need to grease my palm if you want to get on one of our flights." "Grease your what?" he says looking up, breaking into a laugh. "You filthy animal."

"You know it's gonna cost you," I say, pulling up a seat in front of the computer. "They're going pretty quickly to the highest bidders."

Pretending to look at the manifest on the screen I start to shake my head and make sucking noises through my teeth.

"Oh, dearie, dearie me, there's only one seat left and I see that the Deputy Chief of Staff from Joint Force Support has made an offer of $3.76, the remaining credit on his welfare telephone card and a half-eaten mouldy Timmy Hortons doughnut. You're gonna have to come up with something special to get that seat."

His counter offer, "How about a flat-screen telly?"

"Sold to the idiot in the chair," I shout, and I bang my hand on the desk to seal the deal.

"When do you want to pick up the telly?" says Ned, "We'll have to steal it, of course."

"Eh," I say. "I was only kidding, you don't have to bribe your way onto the flights."

"I can get you one if you want, but we'll have to steal it from the pixelated face guys."

"Result," I say, feeling happy at the prospect of not stealing but borrowing a telly indefinitely from the steely-eyed killers. "This tour just gets better every day."

"They never watch it," he adds. "They are always far too busy on killing duties all the time so it just sits there gathering dust. I don't even know if it works, to be honest."

Being a good friend, and having a talent for not following procedures, I don't put Ned through the waiting upstairs in the holding cell or on the MOT failure 66 bus to Aachen process. I do have to make him check-in like all the others, though. There's only so far my talent will go. He checks in his bag and after it disappears through the hole in the wall I follow it through. I open it up and fill it with as many water bottles I can physically fit in there. It's a lot as it's a rather large bag.

The bag upon check-in weighed a puny 15lbs. Now, it weighs closer to 150lbs. The Albanian TCN curses something filthy in Albanian as he nearly breaks his back lifting it onto the aircraft pallet. I pop back through the hole in the wall and carry on as if I had just had to deal with a minor problem. Job done.

Once the check-in is complete Ned, Joe and I all jump in the pick-up and drive over to Whiskey Ramp to wait by the Herc and talk bollocks for an hour.

I put the question of boredom to Ned.

"Would you lick a Taliban's flip flop for £5?"

"Probably," comes the reply from the back seat in a manner suggesting that I had just posed a normal question. "Which side?"

"Does it matter?" I say.

"Of course," he says, leaning forward in between Joe and myself, "the unlucky bloke might have stood in goat shit."

"He could have been really unlucky and stood in goat shit, taken it off and stood in it with his barefoot and then put it back on," I say, playing devil's advocate.

"Well, in that case, I'd probably want a bit more."

"£50 is my final offer."

"I'd try and eat it for £50, as long as I can scrape off the shit with a twig."

Joe, unable to hide his disgust, asks, "Were you two dropped as babies by any chance?"

"Yeah," we reply in unison.

Eventually, the Herc is ready for the passengers and I put Ned on first, giving him the illusion of Royal treatment. The loadmaster guides him to the front of the plane and seats him right next to the urinal so that he'll have the faint aroma of piss for the duration of the flight. Before he can protest, the rest of the passengers start walking onboard and are ushered to fill up from the front thus squashing him in and blocking his escape routes.

As I wave goodbye he mouths back what I think is "tour ducking bed." I smile, turn, and flee off the back ramp of the Herc.

Later that night I receive a text on the duty phone from an unknown number informing me that they were going to rip my head off when they saw me again. I have an inkling who it might have been from.

KAF ATLO SITREP
week ending 07/12/2011

▶ NAAFI has introduced a "buy three coffees and get a free stale doughnut" promotion. Uptake is slow.

▶ The RAF Police prevented a Romanian soldier with drugs hidden in his weapon trying to board Monday's afternoon Ramp Flight. Handed over to the Romanian MPs for a minor beating up.

▶ Only one IDF attack this week. No casualties. C-130 hit by shrapnel prior to taxing and is now undergoing long term repairs. Remaining fleet is sufficient to cover and the extra crew means flights are now running on time for the first time in the history of the RAF.

Friday 9th

Ned is back from Bastion and had a hellish time down south carrying a rather heavy bag and ensuring all the SF[32] vehicles are sort of legal concerning their documentation. After getting me in a headlock for at least five minutes, and finally realising no matter how much he pulls and twists my head it's firmly staying put, I manage to get a swift knee to the balls, bringing the hostilities to a conclusion.

Gasping for breath, he starts telling me, "You sit me next to the bog, you twat, then when I get down there I can hardly pick up my bag. To save the embarrassment in front of all of the other passengers by not unpacking 300 water bottles I decided to swallow my pride and carry it to the transit accommodation."

A smile appears on my face.

"Which was fucking miles away."

I start to giggle.

"I was pissing sweat everywhere, carrying the equivalent of a washing machine. I thought I was going to pass out."

More laughter exits my mouth.

"Eventually, as there's no one about, I decided to start dumping the bottles in a ditch," he mimes emptying his bag, "when some dickhead shouty bloke turns up in a jeep accusing me of fly-tipping. He's going on about water being a scarce commodity and how I should be ashamed of myself."

I'm now in uncontrollable fits of laughter.

"He then promptly drives off without offering me a lift, the git."

"Oh I wish I'd been there," I say, between bouts of laughter.

"Just you wait, you fucking knob," he scowls at me.

Being military-like we decide to give the job in hand a

---

32   Special Forces

name. OPERATION TELLY SAVALAS is what we come up with and it is on tonight. We get the kit that's required ready, which is just the pick-up, and we head over to the SF compound where Ned lives and where the TV is located. The place is quite deserted as the SF boys are not ones for sitting around twiddling their thumbs.

The telly is to be found in their upstairs welfare room, which is made out of several Portakabins stacked up and bolted together with the interior walls removed, thus making the upstairs room about the size of a small classroom. Around the walls are shelves full of books donated by well-wishers and more than likely unread. In the middle is a ping pong table with a pair of bats left at each end upon conclusion of the last game. It must have been a tough game as they have bits of red rubber missing revealing the wood. In the corner are some moderately comfy military issue chairs surrounding the prized telly.

We get distracted and have a few games of ping pong to pass the time and to make sure that there was nobody about. The telly is a make I'd never heard of and, to be honest, the name on the front is a collection of letters that would have been a bad hand at Scrabble.

It is a fair old size and we struggle to get a decent grip of the smooth black plastic glossy edges. We struggle initially to carry it upright as our sweaty mitts just slide over the smooth surface. We get a good grip underneath it and, looking like two men about to pick up a very expensive painting, we count, "one and a two and a three."

The first attempt nearly ends in disaster as we don't realise it is still attached by a cable which was wrapped around the cabinet a few times before disappearing into the back of a DVD player. Unaware of the cable, we are stopped in our tracks immediately, with the effect of the telly suddenly being almost yanked out of our hands. We fumble and momentarily lose our balance as it crashes back onto its cabinet. We unplug the offending cable, thus making the second attempt silently successful, unlike the first raucous attempt.

Once it's up, we flip it over so that we are now carrying it like a mini stretcher. Squeezing out the door and down the stairs to the sounds of "Ooh, ah, hang on, wait a mo, bit more, and that's it" we finally make it to the pick-up only for me to realise the keys are in my pocket and we have no hands free between us. We balance one end of it on the edge of the side of the pick-up's cargo area and as I am hunting around my pockets for the keys Ned just pushes it so that it topples over the edge and crashes into the back.

"Well if it wasn't fucked, it is now," I say, stating the obvious.

"Nah, these crappy foreign TVs are built to take some punishment," he says, like an expert on crappy foreign TVs.

We don't hang about and hot-foot it back to my accommodation. Still under the cover of darkness, we again manhandle the beast from the pick-up to the accommodation. Once inside the corridor, we pass one of the Crabs who has just come off shift and looks half asleep. He doesn't react as he makes way for us to squeeze past. I'm more than certain that the next day he'll be wondering about the strange dream he had of meeting two Pongos carrying a massive TV down the corridor and what it all essentially meant.

With my back to my door I use my elbow to push the handle down and then my spare leg to kick the door open. I have already made space on the table in the corner for it and we gingerly place it down so as not to damage it any more. I excitedly plug it in and the red standby light comes instantly to life. We both afford a smile of a job well done we look at one another as we realise that the remote control is still back at the SF compound.

"You tit," says Ned.

Monday 12th

I arrive in the office in the morning to find Paul sitting in his armchair munching on a big box of doughnuts.

"Where did you get them?" I enquire.

"Bastion sent them up on last night flight," he says, tucking into another one, "I didn't want to eat them in the early hours as you know it's bad to eat too late."

"I think they have the same health benefits any time of the day," I point out as I take a seat, still looking at him with an air of suspicion, "that's why they are so popular."

"Any idea what Bastion are after by sending us gifts?" I ask, trying to confirm my suspicions.

"Nowt, Staff, it's my birthday."

I immediately sit up and say, "Thank God," then, remembering that Paul is a Mormon and that I'm clueless when it comes to religion, change it to, "Fuck, I mean thank fuck. No shit, I mean shit, aw, sorry, Paul, I didn't realise it was your birthday."

"Don't worry about it, Staff," he says, with a face full of icing sugar making him look like a celeb on a night out who'd just come out of the toilet cubicle with his mates. "Nothing to report from last night so I'm off to my scratcher. See you later, night night."

During a window in my busy morning schedule, I think hard as to what to get him as a token to show him that I do have a heart. I think about popping down to the Boardwalk for a browse as I have three Green Bean tokens that required drinking. I am not convinced he needs a Rolex watch or a crossbow, although they could come in handy for realising he should have been somewhere 20 minutes earlier and sorting out unruly passengers.

I wander outside to sit in the morning sun and then I see it, the present that you could only get in KAF, unique to that part of the world and unavailable anywhere else outside of Afghanistan.

KAF ATLO SITREP
week ending 14/12/2011

▶ Due to poor sales with the last NAAFI promotion last week, the manager has now been replaced by Sandra from Kabul.
▶ No IDF attacks this week. The damp must be getting into the fuses.

Monday 19th

We have a visit from Prince Edward and Sophie Rhys-Jones. Well, I say "we," but they are coming to meet the Tornado pilots and not us as we aren't interesting or sexy enough for them. Jamie Savage calls me up, gives me the details for the RAF Learjet that will be arriving with them that evening, and asks us to attend to make sure things go smoothly. I'm not too sure what he means by 'make' as I have no information regarding their visit other than a time and place. Who, how and where they were going once they arrived is someone else's problem that I am, thankfully, not privy to.

I have to admit that I am a little excited at finally meeting a member of the Royal Family, as all my other potential encounters with them while serving have been thwarted by circumstances out of my control such as diarrhoea or a deployment to Iraq. Everyone I ever spoke to during my time in the Army seemed to have met at least one of the Royals. When I was in Iraq, with 20 Brigade, the officers and NCOs even managed to rub it in when I mentioned that I was missing an encounter with Princess Margaret back in Germany. They'd all tell me in a blasé manner how they had met most of them and even worked in certain jobs which entailed dealing with some Royals week in week out. I'm sure it was a conspiracy.

They are due to arrive early in the evening so once Paul appears in the office from his day of sleeping I say to him, "Prince Edward and his missus are flying in tonight so can you cover the normal flight? Joe and me will deal with our Royal guests."

"Yeah, no worries, Staff," he calmly replies, "I've met him a few times before anyway."

"You as well?" I express, in a somehow stunned and yet not-stunned manner.

I turn to Joe, "You've only been in the Army five minutes, you can't have met him too?" I say in desperation expecting him to say yes.

"Nope," he says while shaking his head, "I've not met Prince Edward."

"At last someone who hasn't met a member of the Royal Family apart from me," I say with a slight degree of delight.

"Just Prince Charles and the Duke of Windsor."

"What, eh, where, how the holy fuck?" I struggle to get the words out and eventually just resort with a "fuck off."

"I've met the Queen," adds Hamish, who is sitting quietly in the corner reading a 2008 copy of Country Living. Without

93

raising his eyes from the pictures of perfect country lifestyles he adds, just to make sure I am demoralised just that bit further, "twice even."

The door squeaks open as one of the private security guards we know, who works a few doors down, comes into the office on the scrounge for some batteries for his GPS.

"Fucking hell, does your $5,000-a-week salary not stretch enough to buy some AA batteries, you tight bastard?" I ask him.

He laughs, "I wish," then his face suddenly turns to one of anger and in a thick Geordie accent, "It all goes to the bastard ex-wife, like."

Seeing his stress levels suddenly head towards the roof I quickly change the conversation with, "I presume you were in the Army before you were a private sponger, I mean security guard?"

"Sure, did three years in the Light Infantry," his face turns back into a smile as I can see him remembering better times.

"And did you meet any Royals?"

"Most of them, like."

I passed him a pack of batteries. "I hope they are all flat, leak all over your GPS and you get lost in the desert on a Thursday afternoon."[33]

"Charming," he replies, leaving the office in a state of confusion.

I get Joe to drive over to the area where the Learjet should be parked. However, it is not there as described by Jamie Savage so I naturally presume that it is late. It is the RAF after all so this is a fairly sound assumption.

After 30 minutes of sitting in the pick-up talking about licking Taliban flip flops, Royal Family conspiracies, and

33 It was rumoured that the local men would partake in something called Man Love Thursday. No idea if there was any truth in it.

watching taxing planes we get bored so I call Jamie to find out where it is. He tells me that it landed on time and should be there. We start to drive around in circles looking for the plane. After 10 minutes we finally spot it hiding behind a huge cargo plane. I tell Joe to keep the engine running as I jump out of the pick-up. Walking up to the plane I can see the two pilots in the dim electronic glow of the cockpit. They don't see me as I walk past their window because they both have their heads down and are concentrating on something on the dashboard. Probably busy setting the clock.

I climb up the steps and pop my head inside, very hesitantly expecting to meet the Prince and his wife, and say, "Hello," in the direction of the cockpit.

"Hello," comes a reply from the back of the plane, "come on in."

I take the last step into the plane and am met by a female steward in a light brown flying suit as she gets up from an extremely comfy-looking brown leather seat. I introduce myself "I'm Staff Sergeant Lee, the Kandahar ATLO."

"I'm Katie," comes her reply, as we shake hands.

"I'm just here to see if there's anything that you need?" I add, looking nervously over her shoulder for the Prince and his wife.

She laughs sensing my hesitation and says, "Don't worry, they've gone."

"I don't fucking believe it," I mutter under my breath.

"Sorry?" she says, looking confused.

"Aw, nothing, it's a long story. Too much sun and dust. Plays havoc with your mind, you know."

I was quite disappointed, as this was possibly my last chance of meeting a member of the Royal Family.

"I'm just here to see if you need anything while you're waiting?" The reality is that all I can do for them is take them to the NAAFI for an overpriced stale doughnut and a manky coffee.

"No, I don't think so," she says, pretending to think. "I think we are all good, fuelled up and ready to go later on tonight."

"Would you like to have a look around the plane while you're here?" she offers. It's about the size of a large Transit van, but without the plywood walls, selection of tools, dirt and gobby driver.

"Er, OK," I say, while simultaneously thinking I could see all the plane from where I am standing.

"Can I get my colleague?" suddenly thinking of my troops and how Joe might like to see on-board a small jet.

I call Joe over and ask him if he wants to have a look around the plane.

"Fuck, yeah," is his intelligent and childlike excited reply.

Katie the steward shows us towards the cockpit, in which we have to take turns to squeeze down the narrow aisle, and introduces us to the pilots. They are busy playing a game on an iPad, passing it between themselves, but briefly look up and say "Hi," before being drawn back into their game. I am looking at the mass of buttons and switches when the game evidently comes to an abrupt end. The pilot in the right-hand seat gives out a little cheer while the pilot in the left-hand seat gives out a little whimper.

"Three-nil," says the champion pilot.

Turning to me he says, "So, have you been here long?"

"Couple of months," I say, while still looking at the complicated dashboard.

"Six-month tour, I presume?" says the loser pilot.

"Yeah, I should be out of here in May."

"That's a long stint," he replies.

"Normal for us pongos," I say and then add, "but I can't complain as all I'm doing is counting people on and off planes. I could be counting how many Taliban I have stabbed in the face every day."

They both laughed and I bid them both farewell. They wish me all the best and tell me to stay safe. I shuffle backwards down the tiny aisle to let Joe go and bore the pilots. Katie then shows me around the back of the plane, which is where the toilet is located. It's a proper toilet and not the bucket that we were used to on the Herc, which, understandably, we are highly encouraged by the crew not to use. She lets me try one of the extremely comfy leather-bound seats, in which I adopt a very lazy-looking slouched position.

"I miss slouching," says Joe as he returns from the cockpit, "we don't have anything as comfy to slouch on here."

She then proudly shows us the fridge and straight away I notice a plastic bottle of fresh milk. Fresh milk in KAF is as rare as rocking horse shit. Since a series of attacks on the over-land supply route, they had to start flying provisions in and fresh milk wasn't at the top of that priority list so we had been on the powdered and UHT stuff since we'd arrived in theatre.

I gesture to Joe and straight away he knows what I am getting at. I manage to keep Katie talking to distract her while Joe does the dirty deed of relieving the milk from its rack in the fridge door.

With the reallocated goods safely stuffed in Joe's jacket somewhere, we know it's time to beat a hasty retreat. We both thank her for taking the time to show us around, shout bye down the tiny aisle towards the pilots, and retreat down the steps.

We don't say a word as we walk back towards the pick-up. I

feel I am now somehow giving off an impression of guilt. We continue to stay silent just in case the pilots are now watching us through binoculars trying to lip-read a conversation that would incriminate us.

Joe starts the vehicle up and we drive off. Only when we are out of sight of the plane does he pull the plastic bottle containing the white gold from the inside of his jacket. We burst out laughing and continue for about five minutes.

"In time," I am able to say, "we'll both get 20 years for this, you know."

"I hope Edward and Sophie like black coffee," says Joe, laughing so hard that he nearly crashes into a ditch.

We were both still laughing as we get back to the office for our coffteas with fresh milk.

Tuesday 20th

The day starts off well as I wake *sans* phantom hangover and I have a clean uniform. As soon as I open the door to go outside I know it's going to be a long and shitty day. On first glance, it looks like a case of very dense fog but it turns out to be a dust storm, only without the storm part, which means it's just dust hanging about in the air and which won't bugger off because of the lack of wind associated with a storm. I've experienced these before and know it could possibly hang about for days. On my way to the office, I know that Paul will be on permanent send at 300 words a minute as soon as I go through the door.

I arrive at the office and pause in front of the door. I look at the patterns made by the paint on the door and fleetingly wonder who painted this door and where they are right now. I put my hand on its cold metal surface and drop my head to look at the floor. I take a deep breath and push. As soon as the door opens a millimetre Paul says, "Staff."

I continue to enter the office and I raise my hand to indicate silence, saying, "I know, I know." I don't actually know the details but I know the crux of what the problem will be and that it is going to be a long shit of a day.

After his 'not so very brief' brief I become aware that we have a sizeable number of passengers in the CATO terminal who are supposed to be in Bastion at this point. They include the usual varying NATO nationalities going about their business around Afghanistan, our own personnel, of whom the majority are either going on R&R or have finished their tour, and a large contingent of Afghani workers from Kabul.

I give the RAF at Bastion a call and the picture that emerges is that the dust storm is far worse down south and is causing chaos theatre-wide. Nothing is moving at Bastion but KAF are still somehow operating. My main concern is the R&R and the end-of-tour bunch as I know they will be eager to get home, especially as it's a few days before Christmas. The normal procedure is that the big planes bring all the soldiers to and from Brize Norton and the Hercs bring them to and from Bastion. If the big plane is a commercial charter one from the likes of Flybe or Air Moldova then these are not normally fitted with missile defeating gizmos and it will have to land as close as possible to Bastion, such as two hours away in the United Arab Emirates. The plan then is that a C-17 will ferry the soldiers to and from Bastion a few times, thus making the trip to and from theatre as long as physically possible whilst at the same time making it look fairly efficient. If the plane is an RAF one with all the missile defeating gizmos fitted then it could fly direct into Bastion safely, making the whole process a whole lot shorter and simpler. The only minor problem is that the RAF ones consist of museum pieces that break down upon landing. I suspect that the RAF engineers would then have to visit numerous museums looking to scavenge spare parts from the display aircraft. With the cost of paying for five engineers to get into the museum, given that they don't work weekends, it isn't a very efficient way of supporting the running of a war.

I ask the question of what plane we were expecting and the unsurprising reply is that it's an RAF one. I immediately propose the idea of the flight from the UK coming direct to KAF and I can almost smell the MBE. Of course we would have to deal with several hundred soldiers who arrived on the flight, and it wouldn't be me personally, but at least we can get the 10 or so poor sods stuck here home in time for Christmas. The policymakers and planners wouldn't put a plane into KAF for fewer than 35 passengers. I fucking bet they would if they were here themselves looking at the prospect of eating a lump of white processed crap pretending to be one of Bernard Matthews' finest turkeys on the 25th. In an offhand remark, I am also informed that the Prime Minister is visiting troops in theatre and he is now at KAF due to the dust. I hang up and immediately forget the remark as an awful RAF attempt at humour. Joe and I make our way to the terminal in the pick-up and everything looks yellow. Even our white pick-up has a yellow tint to it. The sky is yellow and the normally yellow sandy coloured armoured vehicles we pass look even yellower. We arrive at the terminal and there is a biblical amount of yellow-coloured troops sitting outside. Some are on the few benches provided by CATO, but the majority are on the hard, dry - now yellow - mud floor, also provided by CATO. Some sit in small groups, some on their own, and some are curled up sleeping, using their pile of kit as an improvised oversized pillow. They have their arms wrapped around their weapons, making them look like they were hugging them with a degree of intimacy. One guy is playing Somewhere Over The Rainbow on his ukulele while everyone else ignores him. It's a strange scene so I stop and observe for a bit.

I turn to Joe and say, "Any minute now I am expecting a Yank general in a Stetson hat to appear and say, 'I love the smell of napalm in the morning."

"Why would you expect that?" Comes the reply of someone who has obviously never seen Apocalypse Now.

Again I take a deep breath just before I enter the CATO office door, expecting a bombardment of issues and problems. I am greeted by the sight of Bogdan, one of the Romanian staff, sitting at a desk, with his feet up, watching the news on the computer. "Morning, Bogdan," I say.

"Oh, hi," came the startled reply, "you've a few passengers upstairs all looking a bit bored and your David Cameron landed an hour ago."

Hearing this news for the second time started to get my interest. "Where is he? Down the NAAFI, I suppose, getting the coffees and doughnuts in for the entire British contingent?"

"Probably," was his reply. I notice that Bogdan didn't taken his eyes off the telly while telling me this. After a long pause, I say, "Are you shitting me or what?"

He turns to me, looks me in the eyes, and says in his thick generic East European accent, "I am not shitting you. Why would I make up a story about your leader coming to see you at Christmas time? If you don't believe me take a look outside. There's one of your brand-new shiny C-17s parked up."

After a quick shufti outside to see a not-very-common-to-KAF gleaming C-17 adorned with the words Royal Air Force on the fuselage parked on the apron I finally concur that it isn't a wind-up.

The morning is spent dealing with frustrated soldiers and confused Afghani labourers. I am informed by Bastion that they are going to have to remain here until the dust clears, which could be a few days. I have to break the news to the ones who had finished their tour that they are more than likely not going to be home for Christmas.

The rank and file troops groan while an old RE[34] officer who looks like he has had an extremely hard tour because his face is like a weathered prune swears profusely. I notice a young female RAF officer is holding back the tears. I feel completely helpless and very sorry for them. We pack everyone off to the transit accommodation in the British compound so at least they don't have to endure the horrendous CATO metal chairs. I have to arrange for an escort for the Afghani contingent as we have no idea who they are and can't have them wandering around KAF. I try calling the RAF Base Warrant Officer, as he is responsible for security, but he is up to his eyes in looking after the Prime Minister and his massive press entourage, so he tells me to sort it out. None of them speak English, and they are starting to look confused and a tadge worried. I need to get hold of someone who speaks Dari to tell them what is going on so hopefully they wouldn't be wondering why they are not currently building walls in Helmand but rather having to endure an idiot speaking loudly to them. I put this task down on my list of priorities. How hard can it be to find someone who speaks the local lingo?

While dealing with the other 100 problems and fending off angry armed passengers with my military training I get a call from Jamie Savage requesting I go and meet the British Ambassador for Afghanistan who will be touching down in 10 minutes. The gods are looking out for me as the Herc parks

---

34 Royal Engineer

outside the CATO terminal and not the four-mile drive away on Whiskey Ramp so I can deal with him quite quickly.

As the engines shut down, the back ramp opens, I nod to the loadmaster to approach the aircraft. He hands me the passenger manifest with three names on it and I see three elderly gentlemen in suits sitting towards the front of the aircraft. With my analytical brain, I assume that these are my passengers. I introduced myself, welcome them to KAF, and request that they follow me. I take them through the terminal to a waiting Major, who greets them and asks them to follow him to a waiting vehicle. Not once during my brief meeting with Sir William Patey — as I will later discover him to be — does he or the others acknowledge my presence. I say, "Goodbye, sir," as they turn away from me to follow the Major, and, not too quietly, I add, "I hope you all get the fucking shits." For a brief second, I wish I hadn't said it that loud, as one of them glances back with a slight look of disbelief. As soon as he turns back around I'm immediately glad that I did say it.

By lunchtime, we have most things under control but we're still trying to find a Dari speaker to tell the labourers what was happening. Finding a Dari speaker is now my top priority as they are the only ones left in the terminal and are starting to look in a mild state of panic. How hard can it be to find a Dari speaker in Afghanistan, I think to myself again? Even though KAF is in Afghanistan, and surrounded by Dari speakers outside the wire, I'd have more chance of meeting the Prime Minister than finding someone who spoke Dari.

The word on the street is that David Cameron is only visiting the Tornado Pilots because he thinks everyone else is quite boring. A couple of hours later I get a call from Sergeant Sidney Lazenby at the postal detachment telling me that the Prime Minister will be visiting us mere mortals just after lunch. He must have finally got bored of speaking to the four Pilots and decided to go and have a mooch about somewhere else. Joe and I decide to drive over there after lunch to have a look.

I am standing at the back door of the postal detachment, chatting with Sidney about the finer details of how a dust storm cannot be a storm without any wind when we see a cloud of even more dust with people in it walking across the compound towards us. Somewhere in the scrum is the Prime Minister. They stop short of the building while someone, evidently not very bright, explains that this is the post office where the soldiers get their letters and parcels from home. They then approach the back door where we are standing. We all brace up looking somewhat uncomfortable at being in the presence of someone who was not in the military but a high-ranking civvy and famous.

One of the Gurkha posties asks for a picture with the Prime Minister. Joe and I decide to muscle in on this opportunity and we photobomb the picture as another postie takes it. Straight after the shutter closes, the Prime Minister turns to the Gurkha postie and says, "So you're a Gurkha?" The Gurkha postie answers his question with a look of utter embarrassment, confusion and mostly silence. After slightly too long of a pause, the Prime Minister turns to Joe, shakes his hand and thanks him. Next is my turn and, before he could get any words out, I ask, "Any chance of a pay rise, sir?"

He looks me in the eye and laughs.

As soon as he lets go of my hand he is hurriedly approached by one of his staff who looks at me with a scowl and ushers him away. I turn to Joe, laugh, and say, "I presume that's a big fat fuck off, no, then?"

As the rabble depart to go and look at something more

interesting than our bunch of idiots, Joe continues to laugh out loud, while the Gurkha postie continues to look shell-shocked. We agree to head back down to the terminal to continue our impossible search for a Dari speaker.

Late afternoon and I am still in the CATO terminal. Finally, I find someone who speak enough Dari that they are able to explain the situation to the labourers that they are not going to be arrested and sent to Guantanamo Bay by the Spams. From their smiles, I guess that they were mildly relieved.

We start the check-in process for the Prime Minister's flight and I receive a phone call from an angry-sounding official person. "Is that Staff Sergeant Lee?" he bellows down the phone.

I automatically say, "Yes, sir," as I have no idea to whom I am talking, so I presume it's the highest of all the ranks.

"The Prime Minister and his sycophants will not be checking in as he's the fucking Prime Minister and will be reporting to the aircraft directly."

"Yes, sir," I say, without an ounce of hesitation, as you can't argue with a voice that both sounds confrontational and also gives the impression of a colossal quantity of unquestionable authority. The mystery caller of authority hangs up just as I was pronouncing the "i" in 'sir'. I am genuinely disappointed as I was looking forward to asking the Prime Minister if he had packed his own bags and if he would be putting his aides through the X-Ray machine head first.

I manage to get 10 minutes to myself so I pick a desk to sit at whilst looking subconsciously professional with my feet on it. I am starting to feel mentally tired after a whole day of dealing with problems. It was just by chance that this break gives me a bit of space to think, which results in a mini-brainwave. Outside is the Prime Minister's C-17, sitting on the apron.

His party consists of a dozen aides and a couple of security henchmen. The journalists who are travelling with him I reckon consist of about 40 or so. This means that there are free seats on it for me to get at least some of the stranded passengers back to the UK for Christmas. I can almost smell the MBE again. I make a call to Bastion and put my plan across to them, which they think is a marvellous idea. I just have to navigate the bureaucracy to make it happen. The aircraft was booked by PJHQ,[35] therefore the seats are controlled by them. Seats on RAF aircraft are controlled by someone, normally the organisation or person who has booked the plane. This is to stop anyone with access to a MMARs machine from just putting their mates on it because it just happens to be going somewhere they need to get to. Twenty minutes later I get a call from Bastion saying that PJHQ are happy for us to fill the extra seats with the stranded. The C-17 is able to carry a certain number of passengers, but, with the agreement of the Captain, they are authorised to take a few more onboard. I already have the passenger manifest with passenger number one being a certain Mr D. Cameron, therefore I can work out how many extra I can squeeze on. I send Joe off to round them up from the transit accommodation with the message that they had 30 minutes to get their shit together if they want to get home for Christmas. I take a walk to the plane to speak to the Captain about his extra passengers. I walk up the steps into the plane looking for someone in a flight suit. The first person I see is the Prime Minister, who is surrounded by a few of his staff. He is looking at the floor, nodding his head with his arms folded but one hand on his chin. I pause briefly to look at him. He raises his eyes from the floor, looks at me, smiles and winks. I smile and nod back to acknowledge his

35   Permanent Joint Headquarters. It's a big gaff somewhere in London which doesn't move, hence the "permanent".

gesture as if we have always been best mates.

"I bet you're not mulling over that fucking pay rise, are you?" I think to myself.

I find the loadmaster and tell him of my plan. He toddles off up the stairs to the flight deck to speak to the Captain and I am left waiting. As I stand there, tapping my foot on the aluminium floor, I look around the aircraft. I have flown several times on the C-17 but it's always impressive as to how cavernous they are. They have seating down the sides similar to the C-130, but it's a padded seat and not made from the bum-numbing web material. The padding is on the thin side so as to ensure a bum-numbing ride even on this modern aircraft. More seats can be added in the main load area by adding adapted aircraft cargo pallets, which have seats bolted to them. I notice that each of the seats on this particular flight had a fluffy white pillow. They wouldn't look out of place on the Singapore Airlines flight to London, but, onboard the C-17, with its minimalistic fixtures, shiny aluminium flooring, lack of windows, and exposed cables, they looked entirely alien.

The loadmaster comes back with the reply from the Captain, "He's not too sure about letting soldiers on the Prime Minister's flight."

I take a second to process what I have just heard and add, "You have to be kidding me?"

As I get that sinking feeling, I plead, "You have extra seats, I'm trying to get people home for Christmas and PJHQ have authorised it," I say it with a hint of "go and tell the Captain to stop being a knob."

From somewhere in my normally empty head comes, "I'm sure they won't be encouraged by someone to write to their MPs about empty seats on a departing plane that they could

107

have sat on to get them home in time for Christmas." I managed not to do a "wink wink" motion to him.

I can see him now thinking deeply and go in for the kill.

"I can see a media shit storm happening, with a high chance of heavy shit showers at our level if it doesn't happen."

He pauses to think, "I'll go and speak to him again."

"Correct answer," I say to myself.

I make my way back to the terminal to break the good news to the stranded souls. The rank and file troops cheer and the Royal Engineer officer doesn't swear profusely but slaps me on my back and then swears, "Fucking well done, Staff." The female RAF officer has tears in her eyes again but this time of happiness and I feel an overwhelming sense of achievement.

I pop out to the check-in area to see how it was going with all the journalists and I hear a raised female voice. One of the journalists obviously isn't a happy bunny. I have no idea who this person is so I wander over to get a handle on what is going on. She is a middle-aged lady who is evidently not over the moon about having to check-in for some reason and seems to think this is below her. I check the manifest for her name, I find it and I have no idea who she is.

She doesn't seem happy about a few things, such as getting her gear checked, having to wait before getting on the plane, and the fact that we didn't know who she was. I give her the option of getting the civil flight to Dubai in two days' time if she doesn't like how we run things. She eventually calms down as we pack her off to the holding cell upstairs. I am tempted for a minute to throw her bags in the bin.

As Joe and I watch the C-17 disappear into the haze of the not-so-stormy dust we are finally able to head back to the office. It was late in the evening and we don't talk at all on the 30-second drive back to the office. We must be tired.

We are greeted by Paul, who is sitting in his chair like a grandad. He's reading a six-month-old copy of the News of the World and is only missing the slippers and pipe.

As I take off my dusty jacket I announce, "What a pain in the arse couple of days that was. I'm glad to see the back of the milk-providing Royals, the tight-wad Prime Minster, the chatty Ambassador, and that gaggle of fucking whining annoying media bellends."

With well-thought-out words, Paul says, "Long day then?"

"Paul Seckerson," says Joe with a sudden burst of energy, "your chosen subject on tonight's episode of Mastermind is stating the bleeding obvious."

We all burst out laughing.

"What's my starter for 10?" says Paul through the laughter.

"That's University Challenge, you throbber," I point out.

Joe-remy Paxman holds up the plastic bottle of white gold, "Name the member of the Royal Family who's currently on a plane back to the UK and is drinking black coffee?"

Paul puts his hand up and I say, "Seckerson, Kandahar Polytechnic."

"Would that be Prince Edward?"

"Correct, and, for a bonus, how much in US dollars did Micky Fatendoulis offer me for it?"

"$20?" he says without hesitation.

"You said $20," I add a bit of a pause to enhance the tension, "but our survey said," I pause again.

Joe waits, then loudly makes the sound of the big red cross from Family Fortunes, "Uhh urrr!"

"It was $40," I shout, and, with an afterthought, I say quietly, "you know that it's quite possibly the only bottle of fresh milk on the entire base so guard it with your fucking life, Paul."

Wednesday 21st

I start the day with fresh milk in my cofftea while reading the online news about the Prime Minister's visit to Afghanistan as reported by a certain journalist whose name jumps out at me. There are a few pictures within the article and unfortunately not the one of me asking him for a pay rise or of her tantrum in the terminal.

There is no mention of the extra passengers I managed to get on the flight and I can feel the MBE slipping away. I also read the piece on Prince Edward and Sophie's visit and, although I didn't expect to read about some missing milk, I am somewhat pleased not to see the scandalous incident referred to as Unigate.

The poor old Ambassador doesn't even get a mention, but then I guess that his low rank compared to the competition combined with his lack of a personality led nobody to notice he was there anyway. I've experienced this before when deployed over the festive period.

I know that once Christmas passes we will become minor-to-no-news and here in KAF we'll be able to settle back into our comfortable routine of talking bollocks while lying in the dirt.

KAF ATLO SITREP
week ending 21/12/2011

▶ Prime Minister's flight diverted to KAF due to dust storm. ATLO detachment will be voting Labour in next election.
▶ Unannounced Royal visit to KAF. Informed by the RAF Warrant Officer Mover at late notice.

110

Royals and crew were well looked after with no complaints. I could go on but I don't want to milk it.
▶ NAAFI have withdrawn their doughnut promotion and now major restructuring in the management is planned.

Thursday 22nd

The shoebox parcels from the UK are now coming thick and fast as it's the run-up to Christmas. Various charities organised the collection and distribution while the general public showed their gratitude by donating the contents, which are a wide-ranging variety of goods such as OXO cubes, pens, knitted hats, keyrings, dice, tea bags, and a massive amount of sweets. We go through each box taking anything that would be useful. The sweets are put into a drawer labelled 'diabetes,' and it is already overflowing with sugary tooth-rotting pleasures.

With each box, there is a letter from the person or persons who packed it thanking us for our service and saying how proud they were of us all. I take the time to reply to a few of the letters to let them know where their box ended up and who we were and what we were doing out here.

A few will later reply, including one from the Sheffield branch of Specsavers. I will hint more than once that it would be nice to get some free quality sunglasses. I will never hear from them again.

On a previous tour in Iraq, we were donated some similar boxes that were destined for the Yanks but, possibly because of the sheer amount, they couldn't cope with them and they found their way to us.

These also had letters in them and I remember one of them from a young boy in a school in Richmond, Virginia, thanking the soldiers for their service. He went on to add that if it weren't for the soldiers in Iraq then he would probably be getting tortured somewhere in Europe. He had spelt tortured incorrectly and someone, whom I presumed to be his teacher, had crossed it out and written it correctly for him.

Saturday 24th: Christmas Eve
Christmas Eve finally arrives and for all of us at KAF and in Afghanistan it's business as usual. There is no excitement of an impending holiday, last day at work, or even a drunken office party. It's just another day that we can tick off the calendar and another day closer to getting out of KAF. I return late from the office and as I walk to the accommodation I can hear people singing. As I get nearer I can make out the tune of Silent Night. I turn around the corner to the central part of the British compound and I see that there are about 30 people standing in a semi-circle all holding a candle in front of them. It almost looks like the scene had been taken from a Christmas card except everyone is in military uniform with green hats, scarves, and gloves to keep out the cold. I am slightly mesmerised by the comforting tune and the soft light of the candles. I stop to watch for a while. As they sing about sleeping in heavenly peace and how all was calm, with their guns slung over their backs. I await for my epiphany moment and when it doesn't come I mutter to myself, "It's all a load of old bollocks," and head off to bed.

Sunday 25th: Christmas Day
I get to stay in bed as the RAF have deemed flying on Christmas Day is too dodgy and have elected to have the day off.

I wake about eight, but stay put as it's a tadge cold. I read a newspaper that is so out-of-date that I almost feel nostalgic. By 10 I am getting bored and decide that I'd better show my support for the ongoing operations and get up.

I meet Ned for coffee in the NAAFI and we have a shouting conversation, which mainly revolves around his impending departure, in competition with the world's noisiest milk steamer, a device that can easily drown out a jet engine running at full power. We get bored of their prices in the NAAFI so we move down to the Echos Centre, which is marketed as the Dutch version of the NAAFI. This couldn't be further from the truth as the staff, who serve reasonably priced coffee, are Bosnian, their coffee grinders have a quiet mode, and their newspapers are recent.

I try to impress the female member of staff by saying "Mogu li popiti kafu," while holding up two fingers as I don't know the Bosnian for two. She smiles and says something back to me which I don't understand. My reaction to this is a blank look followed by my admission that my grasp of the Bosnian language is now exhausted.

"Milk and sugar?" she says. In English.

I thank her and settle down with our value-for-money coffees while talking at a normal level. I pick up a one-day-old newspaper and saw that the text was in Dutch.

"Who fucking speaks Dutch?" I exclaimed.

"Er, the Dutch," says Ned.

"They speak better English than us," I point out, "I bet they speak English when at home and only speak Dutch when they are slagging you off to their mates while in front of you."

The Echos centre was a temporary wooden structure with a much cosier feel to it. The layout was exactly the same as the one that was located at Divulje Barracks in Croatia when

113

I was there in the mid-90s. I am convinced that it was the same one and it had been flat packed, put into storage for a few years, and then sent out here when it all kicked off. Maybe some of the locals had accidentally been packed up with it, which would explain the higher ratio of Bosnians to Dutch staff conundrum. Out of sheer boredom we agree a drive around the entire camp perimeter to kill some time. On the northern side, it is quite devoid of buildings or life but we do pass a few large vehicle graveyards. They are a mixture of armoured and soft-skinned vehicles dating from what looks like fairly recent times to the Soviet invasion era. Someone has taken the time to line them up in neat rows even with their various states of shabbiness and noticeable damage from munitions. Every bit of equipment is grey and some of them are a noticeably orange rusty colour after they had been completely burnt out. The armoured vehicles are just empty shells, as I can seethrough missing side panels and doors that most of the interiors had been removed and they were filling up with sand. The trucks were missing their windows and as their rubber tyres perished and deflated they leant over at different angles as they were left to rot away into the ground.

We pass another graveyard, but this one is made up of helicopters, bits of planes, and rubble. The helicopters were once white and I can still make out the black UN lettering on their sides. Their off-white paint is peeling off to reveal a light khaki colour underneath, which is also peeling off. They look more like they are in storage or a reduced rot programme as their rotor blades have all been removed and neatly placed next to them, with hessian rags covering the delicate machined joints. Their air intakes are also covered up with what looks like specifically made-to-measure red leather cushions to keep the dust out of their turbine engines. They are of Soviet design and, as a testament to their engineering, I reckon that with a jump-start and a lick of paint they could be flying in a couple of hours.

Among a pile of rubble consisting of smashed breeze blocks is the complete tail section of an Antanov-12 cargo aircraft. I can't tell if the rubble was possibly the building that it may have crashed into. There are also bits of wings, several sets of undercarriage, and a propeller laying nearby. We drive down a long straight stretch where there is only a wire fence between us and the big wide world out there. I can see a line of yellow bollards placed on the outside of the fence a distance out which must denote something. We see some shepherds with their flock of goats and they wave to us as we pass. We wave back and we discuss the finer points of the fact that we don't have a gun between us. If they want to have a pop at us, all we have at our disposal is the gas pedal of the pick-up, which would look a bit like a cowardly running-away motion. They don't have a pop at us, which we guess is either because they have the perception that we are armed to the teeth, or they are simply goat herders.

KAF is, in a word, massive. It takes us an hour to travel around the entire base. As we come back around from the desolate north-side perimeter to what is a civilisation of sorts, we hear the all-clear being announced on the PA system.

While we've been away, the French compound has taken a direct hit from a rocket which peppered a building and Porta-loo with shrapnel-shaped ventilation holes.

There was a traditional Christmas lunch laid on for all the troops in the British DFAC. Ned and I couldn't face it, which was why we went exploring around the camp. We do enjoy hearing how everyone ended up eating it under the tables during the attack with paper hats and crackers.

KAF ATLO SITREP
week ending 28/12/2011

▶ Two IDF attacks this week. No casualties. One Portaloo now has an improved ventilation system but leaks a bit. We are now starting to feel the effects of the Taliban campaign of attrition but at least we don't sweat as much when using the Portaloo.

▶ NAAFI has decided to continue selling goods at inflated prices. They are obviously oblivious that there is an American PX[36] down the road selling the same gear for half the price. Imminent collapse of NAAFI expected.

▶ The milk steamer from the NAAFI is now being used out on the runway at night to deceive the enemy into believing a Tornado jet is taking off.

Saturday 31st

As the last Spam-laden Herc of 2011 disappears over the perimeter fence into the dark sky, I call Bastion on the Nokia phone for the usual evening melée of communications on the cheap. It rings for a while, then I hear a voice.

"Camp Bastion ATLO, Lance Corp," it breaks up, as expected.

"Jonesy, It's Staff Lee at KAF here, can you hear me?"

"Camp," silence, "ATLO," more silence, "Jones," then the high-pitched sound of electronic interference.

"Can you hear me now?" I gesture to Joe to start driving

---

36   American version of the NAAFI but a lot cheaper.

with the phone still to my ear in the minor hope that this might improve the signal.

"Camp," static, "ATLO," more static, "Jones," then the sound of silence.

"Jonesy, it's Staff Lee."

"Can you hear me now?" says Jones on the other end.

"Yes, can you hear me now?"

"Can you," more high-pitched interference, "now?"

"Ramp 65, departed, 47 pax in total, 20 for Kabul," I say, knowing full well he won't hear half of that.

I keep the phone to my ear, concentrating on trying to hear what is coming through the tiny dust-encrusted earpiece.

"ATLO," silence, "Jones," static, then silence, then the high-pitched interference.

"Ramp 65, just departed, 47 pax in total, 20 for Kabul," I say it over and over again until in the end, I hear Camp ATLO Jones repeat all the words back to me in several broken-up sentences and, in between, the silence, static and the high-pitched interference.

I press the red button to terminate the call and the green screen comes on for a second, illuminating the dark pick-up in a spooky glow. It switches off and I slide the phone back into the breast side pocket of my jacket.

I imagine the Taliban listening to our call trying to work out if we have a very crafty code or we are just a bunch of idiots.

I attempt to place my head on the dusty excuse of a head-rest that has been designed for someone with a head the size of a tennis ball. It's more like a neck rest and as I lie back my head hangs over the back of it and I feel a slight twinge of nausea for a second. I immediately sit back up and it takes another second for it to subside.

As soon as we get onto the perimeter road back towards the compound, we come up behind a Humvee with a Bulgarian flag adorning its rear. It is escorting some plant equipment that's moving under its own steam. Moving at the pace of a very unfit snail, the Humvee is driving in the middle of the road, which gives us the unconditional message that we are not getting past. There is an open-topped square turret-like construction on top of the vehicle. This is for the soldier on top cover to give his exposed position a degree of protection. I can just see the back of his helmet poking over the top of the rear metal armoured plate as he is facing forward. He then swings the turret around to face us. The front is made up of two pieces of square armoured glass in a metal frame, giving the soldier full-frontal vision. Between the two plates of glass is a hefty-looking heavy machine gun that is pointing high into the air as it sits back on its pivot. He has his hands tucked in behind the front of his body armour, giving him a relaxed look. I'm sure if he were outside the camp he would have been holding the machine gun and looking more aggressive. His face is covered by a black scarf but I can see his eyes through his goggles that he was wearing to keep the dust out. He waves at us to maybe say "Hi" or to let us know that he considers us not a threat and is not going to shred us to tiny pieces with a few well-aimed bursts from his gun.

The Bulgarian soldier continues to watch us as his Humvee straddles the middle of the road, hardly moving.

Joe suddenly says, "Well, what a year that was," as if to break the awkwardness of being watched by our soundless bored-looking companion in front of us, "especially the last two months."

"Any New Year resolutions, Joe?"

"I suppose not getting killed or injured is number one."

He scratches his head and I can almost hear the cogs in his head working.

"Drinking more beer," he laughs.

"That's actually my number one resolution."

We both laugh.

The Bulgarian looks on, like an expressionless statue.

"I hope he doesn't think we are laughing at him?" Joe says with a hint of apprehension.

I sit forward closer to the windscreen and I take a longer look at him, "He doesn't look too happy, does he?"

"I think he's unhappy because this isn't how he thought he would be spending his New Year's Eve when he applied for the job."

"I bet the job advert said something like, 'Do you like working in the great outdoors?'"

"I guess it also said, 'Do you like the feeling of the wind in your hair while looking at idiots and all the dust you can eat?'"

"That sounds good to me, where do I apply?" I say excitedly.

We are crawling along in first gear. I put the window down and I can hear the unmistakeable clatter and squeak of a tracked vehicle. From the individual clanks, I have a picture in my head of a yellow bulldozer moving about a quarter of a mile an hour, "Why yellow?" I wonder as that is quite specific. As I think about this, the word Caterpillar appears on the side of my imaginary bulldozer. The penny drops as I see the Caterpillar marketing machine has just worked on me.

"Fuck me," says an impatient Joe, "If we go any slower we will be going fucking backwards."

I say, "I reckon we could park the jalopy up, walk past the convoy and come back tomorrow to pick it up."

We stick with it and the 40-minute crawl back to the compound is like watching paint dry.

Ned is waiting with Paul in the office for me when we get back.

"Aye up, saddle sniffer," he says, affectionately, "what took you so long? Paul says you should have been back half an hour ago."

"It's the rush hour and the bridge was down."

"Down with what?"

"Malaria, or it could be just a nasty cold. I'm not too sure yet as I'm still waiting for the diagnosis to come back from the Doc tomorrow."

"Why tomorrow?"

"Because tonight he's playing bridge."

Everyone groans.

"What's your plans for tonight?"

"Not sure yet. Might pop into town to watch the fireworks or I might stay in and celebrate with some bottles of champagne."

"It's a tough life for some, eh?"

Ned reveals to me on the way back to the accommodation that he's managed to get his hands on a couple of cans of beer to celebrate the passage into the New Year.

The Army have a no-alcohol-in-theatre policy. Unless you are up in Kabul as it is freely available on the NATO camp at the airport or in the pixelated face brigade's compound as they have their own bar. It was spelt out quite clearly that there was zero tolerance on the liquor subject and if you are caught with it or pissed up you forfeit your Operational Tour Allowance. This allowance is about £2500 and is to compensate us for having to pay tax while we were serving out here. A few years back some MPs had brought the topic of the unfairness of soldiers having to pay income tax while deployed on operations. I don't think the Spams pay tax when on tour so I suspect word got around and someone wrote to their MP about it. The government, never being over the moon about giving money away, finally agreed to pay it but in the shape of an allowance that was based on what a Private soldier would pay in tax over six months.

With an immense sensation of guilt, we lock ourselves in my room, pull the knackered blinds down as best as we can, and turn off the lights. We listen for a while to ensure that everything is quiet and only when we are sure it is do we pop the cans open and quaff a potential £5,000's worth of beer in under a minute. I try to savour each mouthful, but it's the first beer I've had for two months and it tastes on the bad side of strange. We are both burping as we drink it far too quickly. I'd like to say I am enjoying it but I'm not. We finish them and then have to get rid of the evidence. We crush the cans by standing on them and go looking to find a bin to dispose of the evidence. With any luck it's one belonging to someone in the RAF.

British casualties for the month of December
4 killed & 20 wounded

3
JANUARY 2012

Sunday 1st

THE NEW YEAR starts with a bang, about three of them in quick succession. I'm in bed and carry out the immediate action drill of not doing any immediate actions by staying still. My reasoning for this is that I can see the condensation of my breath which makes my analytical brain decide that it's better to risk death slightly than get out of bed and risk being cold highly.

The radar must have picked up more incoming rockets than there were bangs because, as soon as it's quiet, the camp PA system kicks in and an American voice announces in a thick Southern accent, "All movement in all sectooors is to cease while EOD[37] teams try to locate the unexploded ordnance. Ah say again all movement in all sectooors is to cease while EOD teams try to locate the unexploded ordnance."

The Taliban must have got their hands on a bad batch of rockets as there were to be quite a few duds during January.

The EOD teams now have to search the whole of KAF trying to locate those missing bangs.

For once, I'm more than happy to follow an order from the knuckle-dragging inbred making that announcement as I fall back asleep. I am next awoken by the all-clear being sounded and another announcement from the extra from Deliverance.

"All sectooors are now clear. Restriction on all movements

---

37   Explosive Ordnance Disposal. The bomb squad.

has now been rescinded. Ah say again, all sectoooors are now clear. Restriction on all movements has now been rescinded."

I just know that at this moment 80% of KAF's residents are now looking up the word "rescinded" in a dictionary.

KAF ATLO SITREP
week ending 04/01/2012

▶ Ramp flights have resumed after the holidays.
▶ IDF attacks continue.
▶ Lance Corporal Seckerson has watched 80% of his DVD collection already.

Thursday 5th
I arrive in the office to what I initially assume is an RAF police raid or convention as there are quite a few of them all chatting away. I'm introduced to the two new ones, who are known as 'Hamish', as in Hamish Macbeth, from the BBC Scotland police drama of the same name, and 'Tosh', as in Tosh Lines from ITV's *The Bill*. You can't make this stuff I up, I think. Sergeant Macbeth and Corporal Lines are on their umpteenth tour and have served in KAF many times before.

I put Ned on the Ramp flight to Bastion as it's finally time for him to go home and leave me in peace. He's so convinced that I'm going to do something to his luggage that I don't have to do anything. "There's nothing to fear but fear itself," I say to him on the back ramp of the Herc.

"Oh fuck," he says, rubbing his tired worried eyes.[38]

---

38 When we met up a year later he told me that he was still looking though his now empty luggage for months afterwards certain that I would have not let him depart without doing something to his kit.

125

Monday 9th

Troopy Evans decides to tick her job description requirement of pretending to have an interest in the troops by paying us a visit. She comes in on the midday flight and, not one for hanging around KAF a minute longer than required, she ensures that she is booked on the early afternoon flight out. She comes bearing gifts and pulls out a large salami sausage from her daysack.

"This is for you from Staff Tsui, Staff," she says, slightly confusing me with the overuse of ranks. "He got it from the Estonian detachment for doing favours."

I don't think she realises what she is saying.

I pull a face that probably makes me look like I was in slight pain in an attempt to disguise the fact that I'm about to burst out in fits of laughter.

She then passes me a card. I open it and it reads:

'Staff, right now I am standing in front of you with a very large salami sausage in my hand,'

It is, unsurprisingly, in Nick's handwriting

'So if you don't get me some doughnuts to take back to the boys and girls in Bastion you tight bastard, I'm going to shove this sausage right up your arse, love and hugs from the Troop Commander xxx'

It's too much. I burst out laughing.

"What's so funny, Staff?" she says in her Welsh accent, grinning uncomfortably and still holding the salami in her hand.

Having the honour to keep a friend out of trouble, I hand her the card without any hesitation.

"Here you go, ma'am."

Once I see the horror in her face, I add, "I'll be more than happy to be a key witness at the court-martial."

"The little bas-" she says, stopping mid-word as she suddenly remembers she's a commissioned officer of HM Armed Forces.

Then, immediately forgetting she's a commissioned officer of HM Armed Forces, she says in a very unlike-officer manner but fittingly well for someone with a Welsh accent.

"I'm going to shove it up his arse."

KAF ATLO SITREP
week ending 11/01/2012

► New RAF Police staff are now in place. We are hoping for results otherwise they'll be writing parking tickets at Brize Norton for the next three years.
► Lt Evans's visit was a success. Request more Estonian salami.
► Two more IDF attacks succeeded in damaging a patch of dirt.

After I submit the latest SITREP to the Troop Commander, informing her that her visit was a success and informing her of really mundane stuff, she decides she doesn't need to be informed as much and reduces the SITREP to every two weeks. I think "Thank fuck for that," as I'm struggling to fill it with anything meaningful at all.

Wednesday 11th
It's quiet in the office this morning, apart from the annoying sound of Joe slurping his far too hot cofftea from a Styrofoam cup. "Fucking hell, Joe," I say, "I'm sure you could make some

127

more noise if you tried." He takes this as an order to slurp louder.

The phone rings and drowns his slurping out. It's someone from Bastion tasking us to help out the SF guys.

My stomach drops like I've just gone over a humpback bridge at hearing the term 'SF guys'.

I am immediately transported back to the night when Ned and I stole the TV from them and presume that he's dobbed me in for his self-inflicted conviction of luggage tampering.

Trying not to sound nervous on the phone I listen to the voice on the other end. As the unfolding plan is revealed to me I realise that it's not a wind up. I listen intently and absorb the information.

The SF have their own Hercs that they use for SF things that they need to do and we never ever get involved. On this cold wet day, their Hercs aren't available and they've had to commandeer one of the regular Ramp ones. Because it's one of the Ramp flights we will have do the passenger manifest for whoever is onboard.

I'm told that they are "off to Herat, way over in the West, to do a job."

Someone is going to die today, I think to myself.

"They're waiting by the plane for the crew and you."

Joe and I hot-foot over to Whiskey Ramp at a tyre screeching 20mph. As predicted they are waiting there at the Herc in a couple of big black American 4x4s. The RAF crew have set two new records. They have beaten us to the plane and it is looking likely that it will depart on time.

I approach the front vehicle in trepidation to speak with the SF guys. They are highly trained killers who are off to do an unsavoury job and I am just a jobsworth who'll be asking them to give me their names for some paperwork. As they get out of their pick-ups they look eccentric in their kit which has been chosen for practical reasons. Their weapons are ones I've not seen before and are painted in light green and yellow colours.

"Who's in charge?" I enquire.

"That'll be me," says a fresh-faced young guy.

I explain what I will require from him expecting either a tut or some rolling of eyes.

"No problems, Staff," is his unexpected reply. They turn out to be the nicest and politest group of passengers I have ever had to deal with.

"Do you have any bags?" I ask.

"Just those," he says pointing to one of his team unloading them from the back of the rear vehicle.

"It's not grenades, is it?" I ask, jokingly.

"Yes, they are," he says without flinching.

"Aaaaaah," I say, in a manner that gives away that this is going to a problem.

"Is it going to be a problem," he asks, sensing the gist of my reaction.

I explain that because this is a Ramp flight that normally carries nothing but passengers that they are not authorised to carry grenades.

"Give me two minutes?"

I wander off to find the Loadmaster to present this problem to him. He's in the back of the plane going about his checks.

"We have a problem, they have grenades."

"Aaaaaah," is his expected reply. "Let me go and speak to the Captain." I follow him towards the cockpit and I can just about hear him passing the news to the Captain.

"Aaaaaah," goes the Captain.

He removes his flying helmet, produces a mobile phone

from his inside pocket and makes a call. I can see his head moving about as he passes this information to the person on the other end.

He hangs up, smiles and says, "We're all good to go."

I pass the good news onto the killers, who are undoubtedly relieved that they can take their extra explosive firepower with them.

"You haven't got the dangerous goods form for the grenades?" I ask the killer in charge.

"Aaaaaah," is his expected reply.

"Don't worry, I have one in the pick-up."

I quickly fill out the form and hand it to the Loadmaster along with the completed passenger manifest.

Once all five of them are strapped in and their gear stowed on the immense empty interior of the Herc I wish them all the best.

They all thank me individually for my time.

Tuesday 17th

I'm summoned to Bastion for a meeting about the future conduct of the Ramp flights. I know I'm going to be talked at by excited officers, Army and RAF, all trying to make their mark during this tour to hopefully further their careers. I know that my brain will switch off as soon as the meeting starts and I will just end up pretending to take notes and nodding my head in agreement with anyone who speaks.

I go down on the morning flight and even manage to get a seat up in the cockpit. I feign an interest in aviation, but my real reason is the armoured cockpit. As this is my last tour during the twilight years of my career, I am all too well aware that I will be slightly miffed if anything happens while I have the finishing post in sight. I keep my body armour and helmet on for the flight even after the pilots and loadmaster tell me several times that I can take it off.

Nick meets me off the back ramp of the Herc and we shake hands and laugh.

"Aye up, lad," he says in his northern accent, "you're looking well. Life must be far too good up at KAF."

"Well, you know I run a tight ship up there and have the lads doing PT six times a day."

He laughs out loud and adds, "Yeah, sure you do."

All the normal passengers file off into the tent, to be shouted at by a young Lance Corporal Mover, which would pass for their briefing, and to the baggage reclaim area in the dirt outside. We head off in a different direction as we have a date with a cheap cofftea. I'm not to be disappointed.

He knocks up two cups of the MOD's finest in the standard white Styrofoam cups, we both take a sip, we both pull a face, and we both pour the contents onto the floor.

"How is everyone?" I enquire.

"Dave Davidson is good, he's still smoking his body weight a day in arsenic-filled cancer sticks."

He scratches his head. "Troopy is still Troopy, and the rest are, well, grafting their tits off."

Camp Bastion has evolved from the early days of the initial British deployment from a small collection of tents to a huge complex. It's now the main base for all British troops entering and exiting the country. Therefore it has the bulk of the Movers working here, taking the main entry and exit point away from KAF a couple of years previously.

Massive building projects are going on all around the camp. The biggest is a brand-new air terminal that has risen out of the dust. It truly looks out of place because it looks like a real air terminal and not the tabernacle that I'd become

131

accustomed to. It's a good-sized concrete structure with working air conditioning, proper check-in desks with the scales, a proper departure lounge, and even proper luggage trollies.

In the typical military thinking strategy we had been making do with tents since we first arrived in 2002. It's now early 2012 so there's been a real determination to get it up and running in the next few months.

I guess we just want it ready so that we will get the maximum use from it before our withdrawal in 2014. Maybe it's compensation to the local government for ruining this untouched empty piece of desert. At least the next landlords of Bastion will have a shiny new terminal to ruin. It could have been that maybe the military were thinking long-term. Fifth time lucky?

I spend most of the day following Nick around like a lost dog as he goes about his tasks, which seem to be drinking cofftea at as many geographical locations within the camp as possible. He's using the white Tata pick-up to go from one place to another, and it still sounds like it has one bolt holding the engine in place.

"Does that not annoy you?" I say, as he puts his foot on the accelerator.

Clang. "Does what annoy me?"

He takes his foot off the accelerator.

Clang.

"That," I point towards the engine area.

His foot goes back down on the gas pedal and predictably the pick-up makes the noise again.

Clang. "What?" He turns to look at me with a mixture of confusion and laughter.

"Are you taking the piss?" I say.

Clang. "What are you on about, lad?"

"Can you not hear that fucking noise every time you put your foot down?" He looks ahead and moves his foot on and off the accelerator several times.

Clang, clang, clang, goes the pick-up.

"Oh yeah," he says. "I've not noticed that before, I suppose we had better get it looked at."

With Nick's tasks complete for that day, I find myself hanging around the Tabernacle terminal waiting for my flight. I'm watching the comings and goings of everyone as they rush about, not moving much while looking frantic, as they wait to be called forward for their flights. I am part-daydreaming and part-watching a slightly irate, but mainly flustered, Infantry Sergeant running around a pyramid-shaped pile of weapons that wouldn't have looked out of place in Giza. It reminds me of The Generation Game. All the weapons are wrapped up in thick padded bundles made from an extremely hard-wearing green material and they all look the same. With the assistance of a Mover they are checking them in for a flight. This involves cross-checking the weapon serial numbers on the card that is inside a little plastic window on each bundle which lists its contents. The Mover, who also has a manifest, but only in one hand, looks exceptionally bored as he casually calls out a number and then watches the Sergeant run frantically around looking for a specific bundle.

I'm violently slapped out of my daydream world with a blow to the back in the shape of something big and flat.

"Staaaafff, you bastard," I hear a voice bellow. I turn around to see that the big and flat thing is a hand that is attached by an arm that is attached to the one-and-only walking profanity dictionary and well-weathered prune-faced RE Captain whom I got home for Christmas.

"Fucking hell, Sir," comes out of my mouth with a smile, "what are you doing back here? I thought you'd finished."

"So the twatting fuck did I."

He looks slightly less weathered than when I last saw him a month before. The break in the UK must have given his skin time to recover but didn't dampen his use of swearwords to emphasise his displeasure with being back so soon.

"The bastards wanted me to just do one last shitty job. It should only take a couple of cunting months."

"That's a crap deal," I reply.

"I still owe you a big bastard pint for getting me the fuck out of here last month."

He looks me in the eye, shakes my hand, and says, "It was really appreciated."

With those parting words he was gone and I was never to see him again.

(So, Sir, if you are reading this book, I am still up for that pint.)

The flight that I need to jump on to get back to KAF departed Bastion early but it routed to Kabul first, then back to Bastion, before routing back up to KAF a lot later in the evening. It's got the same flight number for both legs which confuses a young, keen, not-open-to-advice logistical officer who is trying to get to KAF. Even after the guidance of Lance Corporal Jones he is adamant that if he got the earlier flight he would get to KAF sooner, so, with the officer's blessing, Lance Corporal Jones books him on and allows him to board. When the

Herc returns three hours later and it's my turn to board for my trip back to KAF, Jonesy tells me about the officers return to Bastion as we are walking out to the plane with all the other passengers.

"So I go to the back ramp to get the manifest from the loadmaster and predictably the officer is still on the plane all on his lonesome," he says.

"With possibly a bit too much enthusiasm, I smile and say, 'Welcome to Camp Bastion, Sir, good to see you again.' The officer remains silent in his seat staring directly forward so not to make eye contact with me. Even in the dim light I can see that he's so red, I can't work out if its embarrassment or anger."

We stop at the back of the ramp and he says, "Wait here a second." He disappears inside the Herc, making his way to the loadmaster, hands him the paperwork, and then points to me while smiling. The loadmaster laughs back at him and nods in agreement to whatever they have just agreed on.

Jonesy walks back off the plane and says to everyone, "You'll be boarding in one minute, so if you could just remain here a little longer."

He taps my arm, winks and says, "Come with me."

I follow Jonesy into the Herc and all the way to the front.

"Hello again, Sir," says Jonesy to the red-faced officer, who is refusing to make eye contact with him.

"Staff, can you sit here? Have a good trip and I'll see you in whenever you're down our way again."

I bid Jonesy farewell as he darts back off the Herc again to deal with his waiting passengers.

I sit down next to the Officer and as soon as I do up my lap belt I turn to him and say, "I hear Kabul is lovely this time of year, Sir."

He looks like he is going to pop a vein or vent high-pressure steam from his ears.

"Fuck you, Staff," is his reply as he bursts out laughing.

 Nothing happens for a while after we are all in and sitting down. I assume the crew are waiting to ensure we will be typically late. I'm starting to feel the chill seep into me and my T-shirt and jacket feel exceptionally thin in the cold night air. My body armour gives me a degree of warmth, as the padding is fairly thick, but it doesn't sit like a jacket so there are a few gaps between it and my body to let the chilly air in. Finally, one by one, the engines start up and the plane begins to vibrate, shake and shudder, and the familiar smell of oil and jet fuel that you only get in military aircraft is amplified. With the little yellow foam ear plugs squashed into each earhole to protect our delicate drums from the racket that four turbine engines warming up make, we're all relegated to our own little worlds of silence. Cut off from communicating with one another other than by sign language, I nod at the Spam sitting opposite me. He nods back to agree with whatever I was nodding to him about. The back ramp and forward side door are both still open and the spinning propellers are now forcing the cold night air through the fuselage giving it an industrial wind tunnel feel. It's also being forced in between the gaps around my body armour and I start to shiver uncontrollably. My teeth are chattering which make my helmet on my head vibrate. The loadmaster is hanging outside the forward door and I'm thinking to myself, "For fuck's sake, close that bloody door."

Wednesday 18th

We land early in the dark morning back at KAF. The Herc is now quite warm inside since the doors were shut but is again reduced to a freezing temperature as soon as the Loadmaster pops the back ramp open. The sharp cold air rushes in to replace the warm air and within a minute I'm shivering again. On the long taxi to the Herc's parking slot everyone's gaze is drawn down the back of the fuselage to the yellow sodium outside world. It always attracts the attention of the passengers, like a fire or a TV. It's also something new for us to look at, after staring at the passenger opposite for the last hour. The pilot is taxiing fairly quickly. I imagine he wants to get to his bed. As he turns the Herc quickly around in a tight corner, the small view we have outside is blurred for a moment until he straightens up again.

The engines wind down and, with that, the forced air conditioning comes to a halt. It almost feels warm again but I still can't stop shivering. I wait for everyone to disembark the Herc to ensure that I am the last one off. I hop off the back and I see a well wrapped-up Paul guiding the passengers towards the bus with writing on the front proudly boasting that it was from Fahrschule Dr. Cüppers[39] of Aachen. There's also their phone number emblazoned down the side just in case anyone should need some bus driving lessons in Germany.

"Alright, Staff," he says.

"Ayyyyyeee upp, Paaaul," I reply, with my teeth chattering at 50 chats a second, "wheeers theeee piiicck-up?"

"Over there, Staff," he points towards the blast wall.

I head straight for it as it is a sanctuary of warmth. I open the back door and place my weapon on the back seat, followed by my helmet. The removal of the weight from my head is a big relief, but my forehead is now exposed to the cold. I un-Velcro the sides of my body armour and pull it off over my head, catching what would be the collar on my ears. It is not

---

39   Dr. Cüpper's Driving School.

the lightest item of clothing, and as I wrestle out of it to one side, the heavy ceramic plates in the front and back swing forward as I direct it towards the back seat on the pick-up.

I now feel as if I'm almost naked as the icy air flows around my body, penetrating my thin uniform. I make for the passenger door and slide myself in, shutting the door behind me. The relief just to get out of the chill is brief. It's just as cold in the pick-up, so I feel around the steering column for the keys. Predictably they are not in there but in Paul's pocket. When he eventually comes over, jumps in the driver's seat, and starts up, the first thing I do is put the heating up all the way to full.

"How's things down in Bastion?" he inquires.

All I manage is a grunt, as the cold has taken away my ability to communicate.

"Nick and the gang all OK?"

I managed a word, "Mmmm."

In my short time away I had forgotten how warmth feels. As we drive the route back to the compound in second gear, the pick-up slowly warms up and the air coming out of the vents finally thaws me out.

Now that my vocal cords have warmed up I am able to converse with Paul more intelligently. I describe how busy they are down there and how lucky we are away from it all. Even with the rocket attacks.

Thursday 19th

We wave off the mid-morning flight that came with its usual hitches and glitches, normally with the root cause being the Spams and their sense of entitlement. I have a couple of free coffee vouchers burning a hole in my pocket and the sun is out which keeps the chill at bay, so I suggest to Joe that we should go and de-fraud the Green Bean once again. On the way over I have Kandahar FM playing with the sole purpose of driving Joe slowly mad as we bounce in and out of the potholes. "He sounds in pain," says Joe, as he looks at the radio.

I look at Joe, then the radio and then back at him.

"He isn't in there, you know," I say, pulling a face, "but if he was, that's the noise he would be making because of your exceptional driving technique of somehow managing to drive through every fucking pothole in KAF."

"Shall I put BFBS on?" he says, hopefully.

"Do you want the word 'incompetent' on your post-tour report?"

He turns towards a large pothole in protest.

We find some parking down one of the back alleys close to the boardwalk that isn't two feet deep in liquid mud. On the way to the Green Bean, I pop into the cigarette shop to buy Dave Davidson's weekly supply of nicotine sticks.

"One thousand of your finest cancer-inducing replica Benson and Hedges, please," I ask the Afghani behind the counter.

"Of course, sir," he replies with a toothless smile as he reaches up to the shelf and picks up five cartons, each containing 200 tabs. He puts them in a cheap blue plastic bag, which instantly splits at the corners of the blunt cartons. Before he can tell me the price I hand over $10 and say to Joe, "That'll keep Sergeant Davidson happy for two days."

Joe, looking like a fat kid in a sweetshop, gazes hypnotically at the wall of tobacco and doesn't surprise me with his insight as he slowly says, "They must have a billion fags in here."

We venture out onto the veranda. "They sell bicycles too," I say, pointing to half a dozen dusty and slightly rusty mountain bikes chained to a post.

"Maybe," said Joe, "we should take up mountain biking and smoking."

I could see his brain working.

"The exercise would cancel out the damage done by the fags."

"Knowing what crap is in these fags," I say, "you'd have to do 15 laps of KAF for every one smoked, followed by a full blood transfusion."

I order two coffees while Joe waits for me at a dirty wooden table in the open so that we can enjoy the warmth from the sun. I place the two coffees down along with enough sugar and stirring sticks for 20 people. We sit in silence, enjoying our coffees and the warmth of the sunshine while the world of KAF carried on around us.

I am just thinking about breaking the silence with some comment about how nice the sun is when we were rapidly shaken out of our semi-hypnotic state.

There's an explosion. It's louder than usual and so close by that we feel the strength of it as the sound and shock wave arrived together. All the wooden structures of the boardwalk seemed to have jumped, windows flexed, and all the people who were walking stop in their tracks. Everyone looks at one another as if searching for an answer or reassurance.

"Fuck," exclaims Joe, "that's a big one."

We both sit at our table, unsure of what to do right at that moment. Everyone has started to move again, tentatively at first, as if expecting another explosion, possibly close by, which is what we were all accustomed to with the rockets. It doesn't come.

"I don't think that was a rocket," I say to Joe, due to the absence of the rocket alarm.

"Maybe they dug up an old bomb?" he replies, as there is an insane amount of building work going on around KAF and, due to its history, it would surely be inevitable that one day an unfortunate digger driver would detonate something nasty.

"Maybe," I say, "but either way I think we'd better get out of here."

I suddenly feel vulnerable out in the open and in a place where large numbers of troops gather. The boardwalk would undoubtedly be a juicy target if the enemy had breached the perimeter with the intent of creating death to the infidels on a large scale. There is also, nagging in the back of my mind, the small matter that we are both unarmed.

"Let's get back to the office," I say, standing up and chucking my unfinished coffee in a nearby bin. "Never an excuse to litter though."

We are both quiet on the short drive through the narrow alleys in the most populated part of KAF. I am feeling more than nervous at not knowing what's going on and every time we round a corner my dread level intensifies a little.

In the office I find the RAF coppers, and a half-asleep Paul, all with full-body armour on and wearing helmets. Hamish is cocking his pistol while looking into the breach before letting the working parts slide forward. He pulls the trigger with the sound of a click.

"Hello, ladies," he says, looking up, and holstering it with the grace of a cowboy.

"Any idea what's happening?" I enquire of Hamish.

"Not a clue," comes the reply from a well-informed RAF copper.

I say to Tosh, looking at his holstered pistol, "I see you are also tooled up with your piece, Mr Gangsta."

"One is never left wanting in the Westside RAF Sons of Averageness gang," he says, in his poshest voice.

"I'm so glad our weapons are two fucking miles away in the fucking armoury."

"At least you have your rounds," says Hamish, handing out our bullets that are in his safe for safekeeping.

We have 60 rounds between the three of us.

"Even if we did have our weapons," I say sarcastically, "it's hardly going to be the defence of Stalingrad-style battle, denying the enemy the use of the movement's office."

The camp PA springs into life with our redneck broadcaster friend. We immediately slide the window open to hear him better and all crowd around it looking sideways so that we each have one ear facing directly outside.

He announces that there has been an incident at the main entrance, all non-essential movement should now cease, the alert state has been raised, and US forces are to make their weapons ready.

We all take a sharp breath together at this news. Not at the heightened alert state or the movement issue, but the fact that the Spams will now be walking around with loaded weapons made ready with a round up the spout, and just the safety catch keeping us safe from a certain death followed by the word, "Oops."

Nobody wants to leave the office, which is understandable. It would be carnage out there with numerous casualties as thousands of Spams are given the green light to do what they like best.

I give Jamie Savage over at the RAF compound a call to see if the armoury is as we now need to be armed due to the heightened alert state. We discuss the Spam issue, both agreeing that it could be a good idea to stay put for the time being.

The PA springs into life again. Again we all stop to find out what wisdom it will bestow on us this time. Thankfully, it rescinds the order for the Spams to be made ready.

"He loves the word 'rescind', doesn't he?" adds Joe.

They are now just to have their weapons loaded with the magazines on. We hear the collective sigh of relief from 5,000 NATO non-Spam troops across KAF.

I ask Tosh to escort us round to the armoury as the route will take us past the Fledgling Afghani Airforce compound, which always has an armed bored-looking ANA[40] soldier on duty there. We all agreed that, due to the increasing 'Green on Blue' attacks that had happened in the past, we all felt very uneasy driving past their compound. Green on Blue was the name given for attacks on NATO forces by Afghani forces due to Taliban infiltration, cultural misunderstandings, or personal enmity.

"Are you scared of the big bad ANA guard?" he says in a piss-taking voice.

Then his voice changes.

"Of course I will... for a Green Bean coffee voucher."

"How do you sleep at night?" I ask him while looking him directly in the eye.

"Very well, thanks," is his predictable reply.

"I hope your next crap is a pineapple."

"If it is I'll make you a Hawaiian pizza."

As we pass the Afghani compound we all have our eyes glued on the guard at the entrance. He's armed with the usual AK-47 and looks as bored as usual, but also more threatening than usual.

"They probably don't give him any bullets," I say, trying to calm everyone's fears. "He'll probably have a paper chit in his

---

40   Afghan National Army.

magazine with the words 'IOU 30 bullets' written on it signed by the Quartermaster." I manage to get a laugh from everyone, which breaks the tension.

Two hours later we are finally armed and back in the office ready to defend it to the last man if required when the PA announces that the alert state has now been returned to its normal level.

"I'm not driving around to the bloody armoury again," I say to no one in particular.

Later on we find out the details of what happened at the main gate. A suicide attacker in an explosive-laden car had driven towards the main gate detonating himself as he got close. He managed to have zero effect on KAF operations but courageously killed seven civilians, including two children, and injured a further eight.

Friday 20th

It's just after lunch and Joe and I are waiting for the mid-afternoon flight back into KAF. I'm sitting in the chair in my usual pose with my feet on the desk whilst looking at the e-mail inbox, hoping for a message to appear that could liven the day up. Joe is going through the diabetes drawer, trying to find something edible and recognisable. No sooner had the leftover processed turkey started to cool than so did the enthusiasm for sending the shoebox parcels. We hadn't received any since before Christmas and the tooth rot drawer is starting to run low. The only sweets remaining are the crap ones nobody liked or American ones, which nobody knew anything about.

An email suddenly appears in the inbox and I say, "Aye, up."

I scan through the text and it is about having to complete a risk assessment for the workstation in the office ASAP.

144

"For the love of God," I gasp. "Right, Joe," I say taking my feet off the desk, "fancy a trip to the old PHF?"

"What's the PHF when it's at home?" he replies, with his head still in the drawer.

"It's the Passenger Handling Facility."

"You mean CATO?"

"Nah, the old PHF that was in use before they started using Bastion for the flights in and out of theatre."

It's on the same side of the airfield as CATO up by the Afghani Air Force compound and is just off the road that we drive along to get to Whiskey Ramp. It's a series of square metal-framed buildings which were covered in a green plastic-looking material, which I suppose made it a tent. It's probably more like a type that you would hire if you owned a stately home and decided to have a big party for all your posh friends on your massive lawn. Some may call it a marquee, but I'd call it a tent.

It's obscured from the road by a long line of soil that had been pushed there by a bulldozer to form a high berm. I'm not too sure if this was to offer some protection or just because it was the only space available for a large pile of crap. The berm runs all the way up to the wall of the Air Force compound in one direction and a good mile or more in the other direction. There are bits of building material, wires, and glass mixed in with the soil, so I suspect it's the remains of a building from when the Spams arrived and decided to do some heavy-handed refurbishments. We scale our way up the side of it like a pair of old men struggling to walk. Upon reaching the crest we bounce down the other side like young boys, kicking up clouds of dust and stones as we descended. Joe catches a buried strip of metal with his boot and it clatters down with us. We both look at it trying to identify it. It's green, flat, and a

145

sort of triangular shape. The sort of shape that is a fin that would be found on a bomb.

"Should we have just climbed over that?" asks Joe.

"Probably not," I say, with a nervous laugh.

We follow the side of the tent looking for a way in. I had been through this PHF a few times back in 2009 but it had always been late at night and now nothing looked familiar.

Skirting around the outside and looking for the entrance, we come across rips in the material where it has rubbed against the metal frame. They're big enough to put your head through. I encourage Joe to pop his head in to have a look.

"Go on, have a peek."

He hesitantly pulls each side back and peers into the blackness inside.

"I feel like a gynaecologist working in a rough part of Swindon."

As he slowly moves his head forward to the hole, I say, "I'm sure there isn't an executioner on the other side with a massive sword."

He pauses.

"He's just been waiting there for months for someone like you to pop your head through."

Joe, still looking into the black hole, starts to move his head closer.

It's all gone very quiet.

With his hands holding the sides open, Joe continues to move his head towards the dark hole. "Go on," I say in a hushed tone.

His head is just about to go into the hole.

Then it happens.

"BAAM." I shout, simultaneously poking my fingers into his ribs for added effect.

"Arrrgh!" he squeals, jumping back from the imaginary danger.

He lets go of the material, closing the hole and adds, "You're such a fucking knob."

"You're such a fucking knob, Staff," I say, reminding him that we are still professional soldiers of HM Army even when acting like eight-year-olds.

My head goes into overdrive as I imagine a seven-foot bearded warrior in full ceremonial battle dress, wielding a huge cutlass, and who had been waiting for this exact moment for two years. The war council had no faith in his plan but he would show them, he thought. He now has tears in his eyes, as we wander off laughing, leaving him to return to the war council in shame to explain that his plan failed.

The search for an entrance eventually bears fruit but only after we had circumnavigated the entire structure. We are now almost back at the point at where we started our search.

"Bloody typical that," exclaims Joe, "it's a 50/50 choice and we choose the wrong way."

"But think of the fun we had with the executioner of KAF."

The entrance had been secured at some point with industrial-size zips, but over time the wind had battered the material and they had come apart.

We pull the flaps back and peer inside timidly. We are looking at total blackness while our eyes adapt from the bright sunlight of outside. I am again thinking of the executioner and I can guarantee Joe is as well.

"You know it takes up to 30 minutes for the eyes to adjust to darkness?" says Joe.

"Thank you, Professor Parkestein," I say, pulling a torch from my pocket with the words, "and this is why I am a Staff Sergeant whilst you is not."

147

"Voila." comes Joe's reply as he also pulls out a torch with a hint of one-upmanship.

"Very good, Lance Corporal Parkes. You could be destined for great things," I say with encouragement, "but nobody likes a smart arse."

"I like what you did there, Staff. Do they teach you that on your promotion course?"

"Of course," I say, "it's the doughnut and mallet approach, similar to the carrot and stick but more extreme."

We venture inside, shining our torches forward as we go. The floor is a rough concrete and we can hear the dirt crunch underfoot with every step. There are breeze blocks stacked waist height everywhere. These are the blast walls that would offer some rudimentary protection from any shrapnel that might have come that way. They form a corridor down the middle with rooms off to the sides and gaps for doors. It gives it a feel of an archaeological dig that's revealed the layout of the building.

On the floor are sheets of A4 paper covered in a heavy layer of dust. We shine our torches upwards and see, hanging from the ceiling, fluorescent strip lights attached by cables. A few of the cables have snapped and the lights hang down perpendicular to the floor.

"It was quite a tent in its day," I say.

We come across a large notice board with the sentence 'WELCOME TO THE PHF,' that shouts at us with its overzealous use of capital letters. All the spare space on the board is filled up with other notices explaining the alcohol policy for Op Herrick or telling us that we aren't allowed to travel in shorts or a tee-shirt. I quickly glance over the other notices, in the same uninterested way I would have when I came through here a few years ago. Far too much info to read, but somebody somewhere says it's got to be displayed. There is an arrow either side of the board with one directing passengers to the check-in and one pointing the other way for passenger pick-up.

We move around to the check-in desks which, by the look of them, have been made locally and are similar to a fairground stall selling candy floss. They're all a glossy deep red in colour, and somebody with too much time on their hands had painted the colours of the RLC on them at waist height. A strip runs horizontally, with a blue band about six inches in width. On the top and bottom are thin yellow stripes, with two thicker red strips in the middle. It's that good that it looks like it could have been painted by a robot. On one of the desks is a big wagon wheel, bright gold in colour and about two feet across. This is the NATO-recognized symbol for Movement Controllers so that our NATO partners, who may not be familiar with how the British Forces operate, know either who is chinning them off a flight or who is to blame when they are late. On the desks are reams of paper, some blank and some with passenger's names on them. There are broken seats, dusty whiteboards with numbers and graphs still written on them, broken wooden pallets, and the remnants of a coffee stand. A curved promotional board that would have been behind the stall is all that remains. It has a montage of pictures of coffee in porcelain cups, successful business types drinking them, and laughing friends sitting together. It advertises that it is all to do with 'Piacetto Espresso' and implies that if we drink their coffee then we can all be as successful as the people in the pictures, and not sitting in a shitty tent in Kandahar waiting to get on a plane to Destination Shithole.

I know that when the plan changed to start using the CATO facilities and to move down to Bastion that it would

149

have been done with strategy and order. But this place looks as if it had been a hastily chaotic withdrawal after the threat of an imminent zombie apocalypse. I pick up a piece of paper, I stare at it and say in my best sounding agitated voice, "Joe, Joe, we need to go now."

Joe turns towards me, shining his torch in my face, which allows me to show him my scared face.

"We have to go now," I say again, staring at the piece of paper in my hand. "We have to get out of here now," I add, raising my voice a bit more.

"What you on about, you fruit loop?" he says, with a minuscule amount of apprehension in his voice.

"I'm telling you we have to get out of here as quickly as possible right now," trying to play on his developing fear.

I turn slowly towards him, looking into the brightness of his torch whilst keeping a look of fear in my face.

"You've..." I pause, "...a dental appointment in 10 minutes."

I crack a smile then add in my normal voice, "And you don't want to be in the shit for missing that, do you?"

Joe bursts out laughing, which, I suspect is partly relief.

We make our way back and are instantly blinded by the bright sun when we emerge outside. As our eyes adjust to the light we look at the berm and then one another, both remembering the bomb fin.

"Shall we walk around it?" ask Joe

"Well, it is such a nice day for a walk," I agree, "be a shame to waste it."

And so we start our half-mile walk to the pick-up, which is less than 20 feet from us on the other side of the berm.

Monday 23rd
The aircraft parking lot at KAF is a fair old size, and it is

constantly busy with a mixture of helicopters, fighter jets, cargo planes, passenger planes and executive jets. I even spot an old Canberra from the 1950s that I was told was operated by NASA. The RAF Movers work here, offloading mainly Russian and Ukrainian cargo planes chartered by the MOD to bring in essential stores such as out of date FHM magazines, UHT milk, and doughnuts. I fancy having a look around one of these cargo planes so I sort of invite myself over when the RAF are unloading the next one. The plane that comes in that day is an Ilyushin-76. It's a high wing one with four jet engines. It's designed to be fixed with just the bang of a hammer, run on cheap contaminated fuel, and land in muddy fields.

We park the pick-up and walk over to the plane, stopping at a huge Antonov-124 on the way for a few minutes to admire its size. This is a similar aircraft to the Ilyushin-76 in design but just bigger. It's self-loading, two shipping containers side by side with its own crane through its back door. When it comes to making cargo planes the Soviets didn't piss about. We continue over to the smaller Ilyushin-76. It's still of an impressive size to us pongos. I find the lanky RAF Mover in charge, whose name is, unfortunately for him, Corporal 'Sandy' Balls, loitering around the back of the plane. He's deep in supervision mode, watching the TCNs offloading the cargo with their forklift trucks and making sure they don't inadvertently put two fork-sized holes anywhere in the fuselage of the plane.

Sandy quickly introduces Joe and myself to the Russian Captain. He's a short, plump, old guy, with bright red cheeks that I think come from syphoning off the fuel from the tanks into his hip flask. The weight he's gained from years of eating around the world has somehow started to transfer to his head, thus making his nose look tiny and his eyes like piss holes

151

in the snow. He wouldn't look out of place in a Bugs Bunny cartoon.

"Can these guys have a look in the cockpit?" Sandy says slowly to the Russian Captain. "*Da, da, da,*" comes his reply.

Sandy then disappears off to continue supervising the TNC's offloading its cargo.

The Captain smiles, slaps me on the back and says, while pointing at himself, "*Ukrainian, nyet Russki.*"

He gestures for us to climb up the metal ladder with the words "Davai, davai." The ladder is attached to the bottom of the door on the side of the fuselage and is at least twelve feet high with no handles to assist you in getting through the door. Suffering from a slight case of vertigo, I shakily manage to get up and through the door into the plane. The floor is the standard uneven, dirty, silver aluminium that we are used to seeing in the Hercs. There are rollers, for ease of sliding the cargo pallets up and down the fuselage, and tie-down points sticking up several inches dotted all over the floor, which make it a health and safety trip hazard expert's personal hell. Joe enters the aircraft with a display of a lack of confidence similar to my own, and add the words, "Jesus Christ, where are the proper steps?" reinforcing the impression that he's not exactly in his comfort zone either.

"If you're crapping yourself at 12ft then what will you be like when you have to jump out of a door like that one day at 5,000ft?" I say, in reference to Joe still having to complete his P Company parachute training.

"I only get scared at anything below 13ft," he says, "my brain can't acknowledge the fear of being at 5000ft."

With the confidence of having done this a thousand times before, the short, round Captain scurries up the ladder and in, with a speed that doesn't match his frame. Again, he gestures us to another set of ladders that leads up to the flight deck, but this time they were the fixed type and with handrails.

"Davai, davai," he says, smiling so hard this time that his eyes completely disappear. The ladders lead us to a tiny corridor that takes us to the flight deck. I briefly look back to see the Captain's belly rubbing on the wall as he shuffles sidewards down the narrow corridor behind us. Given the amount of flying hours under his tight belt, I envisage that his belly is the culprit for the waist-height line of where the paint has been rubbed off, leaving a shiny polished metal finish that runs along the length of the tiny corridor. For such a large plane the flight deck does not match its dimensions. It's about the size of a small garden shed with four seats crammed in. One is immediately on the right and I presume that it's for the flight engineer as it has a small desk and faces a huge wall decorated with a copious amount of dials and switches. Up ahead and facing forwards are the two seats for the pilots and the fourth seat is on the left and seems to be for someone who's just along for the ride. I'm not the tallest of people but I am having to stoop slightly to keep my head from rubbing the paint off the ceiling. I move over and stand behind the right-hand pilot's seat so Joe can get into the cockpit. He positions himself behind the other pilot's seat, and then the Captain barges his way in-between us

The dashboard has the familiar, if confusing to the non-aviation-trained eye, layout of dials, switches, levers, and lights. The areas of the console that are not covered in instruments are turquoise, with matching coloured curtains on each side of the long but thin window. Even the trim for the seats is turquoise. With his customary phrase, *"Davai, davai,"* he motions for us to sit in the seats. We take turns to squeeze in, climbing over the centre console, being mindful that we don't want to accidentally kick a lever or knob that will render the aircraft useless, or, worse, start us moving. The seat is wide, comfortable and a long way from the controls. Captain Vodka starts explaining something in Russian while pointing at the area in front of the seat and makes a forward movement motion. I pick out the word 'pull' from his incomprehensible enlightenment and realise that to make the seat go forward I need to pull the handle under it. I find it with my fingers, and pull it up. The seat slides effortlessly forward towards the controls. My feet find the rudder pedals, which are each the size of a gigantic square dinner plate. The turquoise joystick sits limply forward and has black plastic handles with buttons on each end of the handle. I can hardly see out of the window to the front, as it's so narrow and cluttered with equipment. Right in the middle is a thing that resembles an old-style green screen oscilloscope from the science lessons of my school days. There are a couple of three-bladed fans on swivel mounts, which I deduce is a rudimentary ventilation system.

Captain Neat Alcohol then moves into piloty in-depth explanation mode and starts pointing at things in front of us. I can tell he is more than happy to sit there educating two British soldiers in broken English and fluent Russian about the technical aspects of how to fly a complex four-engine cargo aircraft. He is probably fed up watching the unloading of pallets of old newspapers and FHM magazines and finds this a nice distraction. Because he knows we don't speak any Russian he says the odd word in English as if to reaffirm that we have grasped what that particular bit does. We're finding it hilarious. He points at the power levers and moves them forwards and backwards. I start making up the translation as if I can understand him.

"These are the throttles for all the engines?"

"*Da da,* fast, slow," he nods in agreement with me.

Next, he points at the control column and signals me to pull it all the way back saying "da, da," when I comply with his order.

"So, if you pull back on the stick the aircraft will climb and the cows will get smaller?" I say.

"*Da, da,* climb."

He then motions me to push it all the way forward.

"If you push it forwards the aircraft will descend and the cows will get bigger?"

"*Da, da,* descend."

He then indicates that I should move the column from side to side. "This will roll the aircraft from left to right making everyone sick," I say, looking at him for confirmation.

"*Da da,* left and right."

The explanation continues with him pointing at various dials directly in front of us. It's a continuous cascade of Russian intermingled with my words, such as "height, arrgh, direction and crash," and his words of "*da, da, da.*"

He looks at us, in turn, to confirm that we have understood him and we nod in agreement as if we are fluent in Russian.

Content in the knowledge that we both now know how to fly this aircraft should we ever find ourselves in the situation that requires it, Captain Booze points down towards the floor muttering something unintelligible.

"OK, now that you two idiots know how to fly the Ilyushin-76, let's go downstairs and look at where the bogs are," I continue with my improvised translation.

Joe is almost crying trying to hold back the laughter.

We retrace our route out of the cockpit and back to the cargo area. There is a small doorway to the right of the bulkhead with a few steps going down towards the nose cone. The Ilyushin-76 possibly had a bomber role in mind when it was designed, as most of the nose cone is made from Perspex which must have been for the bomb aimer. As our merry host makes his way down into the nose I pick up the word "navigator" and I realise that that area is now home to the navigation officer. His seat is raised and positioned sidewards which gives him the view out to the front on his right-hand side. The views from his station must be amazing during take-off and landing but possibly the worst when it all goes wrong. He has a larger than normal desk which I assume is to accommodate large paper charts. There's also the standard wall of dials and lights facing him which again mean nothing to us. It's rather dark down here and the walls and ceiling are festooned with pipes, wires, and bracing struts with foam taped on them to protect any unsuspecting heads. A laptop whirrs away on the desk as its fan struggles to keep its insides cool in the heat. On its screen is an aviation chart with lots of numbers, lines, and Cyrillic script. Captain Ethanol pipes up again and points to the wall of dials, so I add.

"None of this equipment is any good, in fact it's so shit, so we use a second-hand computer."

"*Da da,* shit," he says in agreement.

He then points at the laptop, says "Map," and laughs.

I think my translation may have been right for once.

After each bumping our heads on the foam-covered bracing strut we make our way back out to the main cargo area. We shake the Captain's hand in turn and thank him for showing us around his plane. He continues to babble to us thinking that I am now fluent in Russian.

As we shakily step off the bottom of the metal steps back onto terra firma and walk off in the direction of our pick-up, he shouts after us waving excitedly while hanging out of the door in the fuselage. "I think he's going to miss us," I say to Joe.

"I think he's still pissed," replies Joe.

KAF ATLO SITREP
week ending 25/01/2012

▶ Heightened threat level now means we are permanently armed. We have 20 rounds each so we should be able to defend the office for at least three minutes.

▶ Lance Corporal Seckerson has discovered a thriving black market in DVDs so he's now prepared for the remainder of the tour.

Saturday 28th

I'm sitting in the office with Joe reading the latest article about who were the favourites to win the 2006 World Cup and contemplating putting £10 on Germany to win. We're holding our feet up while the young Afghani cleaner sweeps around our feet. It reminds me when I was little when I would be sitting on the settee with my brothers watching Tiswas on the telly. We would hold our legs up so that our Mum could hoover under our feet. The cleaner and his Indian escort leave the office just as the attack siren starts its merry song. The sound always makes me jump a bit. Joe and I look at each other without smiles and we undoubtedly simultaneously think, 'I'm not getting on the floor unless you are.'

The closer-than-usual bang and shock wave pass through the building override our hesitant posture as we head towards the floor as fast as gravity will allow us.

"Fucking hell," we say together.

"Someone's day has just been ruined," I add.

We stay on the floor waiting for the next one to fall. I'm thinking that if they were launched in a salvo then the next couple of incoming examples of China's finest ordnance are probably going to be landing fairly close to the last one. We wait, with that black dread hanging over us like the Sword of Damocles.

"Get up and put the kettle on, will you, Joe?" I say to break the tension.

"Errr, OK, boss," he replies in a deep, comical, sarcastic tone.

The attack alarm winds down and our Southern American friend comes on the PA system announcing:

"Movement in all sectooors is to cease while EOD teams try to locate the unexploded ordnance, Ah say again, movement in all sectooors is to cease while EOD teams try to locate the unexploded ordnance."

We get up from the floor and dust ourselves down.

"He's just swept the bastard floor, why am I so bloody filthy?" whines Joe.

The dust in the office is a white colour and we look like we have been very busy working in a bakery making bread.

"He's not a cleaner, he's a dirtier," I reply to Joe's remark. "He's employed to make sure we are continually covered in dust, it's not an easy task you know. Takes years of training in the ASS."

"In the what?" he says, initially surprised. "Go on, then."

"The Afghanistan School of Sand," I say triumphantly

"Oh, dear God, why couldn't that rocket have landed on us?"

Tosh enters the office and he too is covered in dust, all over his front. It's outside dust and has a more a yellow colour to it.

"Fuck me, did you hear that?" he asks, like an idiot.

"Hear what?" I exclaim. I look to Joe and say, "Did you hear anything?"

"Nope, not a thing. You must have imagined it Tosh."

"You're a pair of bellends," says Tosh.

He then notices that we are covered in white dust, laughs, and says, "Busy day at the bakery, I see? While I'm here, can I have a white bloomer, a baguette and a couple of baps?"

"Knuckle sandwiches are on offer today," I say to him.

"Buy one get 50 free," adds Joe, showing him his fist.

We then both jump on him and proceeded to shower down a rain of punches as he adopts a standing foetal-like position. I chuck in a haymaker while Joe tries to give him a dead leg with his knee.

"Fuck off, you pair of twats," laughs Tosh as we continue the assault and force him into one of the comfy chairs side-wards.

"Can you believe we are being paid to beat up an RAF copper?" proudly exclaims Joe as he carries on in his attempt to inflict a dead leg. "I love my job."

With Tosh firmly squashed into the chair and Joe and me sitting on top of him still trying to get in one last punch to an exposed shoulder or leg, we all start laughing as our energy dwindles. The all-clear sounds so we start to punch him in time with it.

"All."

"Ow."

"Clear."

"Argh."

"All."

"Oomph."

"Clear."

"Fuck off, you pair of lunatics."

The door opens and a Spam officer enters the office, and what he witnesses is not what he was expecting to see when he thought he would ask the Brits about getting on a flight later in the day.

"Am I interrupting something?" he asks in a deadpan tone.

"Oh, hello," I say, as I look over my shoulder and then add, "sir," as I realise he's an officer.

"You just caught us beating up the Air Force, sir,"

I push myself up from the mass of limbs and dust and turn towards him.

I notice that he too must have recently been taking cover as he is also covered in the yellow dust from outside.

"Did you hear that incoming rocket?" he says, with a face like thunder, as if to try and inject some guilt for finding us laughing.

As he is an American officer, I decide against any sarcasm as it would be wasted on him and I take the route of least resistance by just saying, "Yes, we did."

"I didn't hear any ambulance sirens, which is always a good sign," I say, trying to defend our actions and starting to feel slightly remorseful that we were arsing about while there could have been people dead and dying not far from us. I then identify in ourselves that we have started to become desensitised to the attacks as they were now just a part of our daily life. I suddenly start to feel a hostility towards this guy for trying to make us feel uncomfortable for becoming used to situations that aren't normally normal.

"What can I do for you today, sir?" I say, in a now-expressionless tone.

"I was wondering what the chances are of getting on this evening's flight to Camp Leatherneck?"[41]

"It's full up, I'm afraid, sir," I lie to him.

"Ah, that's too bad," he thinks for a second, then turns around and leaves the office.

Afterwards I feel bad about lying to him and for taking his reaction a bit personally. I see him hanging around the terminal that afternoon so I approach him and tell him that a seat has become available later on that day. I explain that if he still needs to go I can get him to Camp Leatherneck. Surprisingly, he apologises for his earlier behaviour saying that we are all under stress one way or another and have our own coping mechanisms. We shake hands as if we were good friends and I do what I would do to all of my good friends.

I ensure he will be placed next to the urinal on that evening's flight.

We find out later that our near-miss had landed on a patch of open ground about 200 metres from us. This small area of unclaimed land is between the compounds belonging to a few different nations, therefore, it's surrounded by thick high-blast walls. It's used mainly as a shortcut for pedestrians moving around the area. Nobody was about when the rocket impacted and all the shrapnel was contained by the blast walls. I wonder if our luck will hold out until May.

The EOD do a good job of locating all the duds apart from one. Rumour has it that it had landed in the Poo Pond and they declared it safe without even attempting to look at it.

British casualties for the month of January
3 killed & 17 wounded

---

41   The Spam camp next to Camp Bastion.

4

FEBRUARY 2012

Wednesday 1st

I ALWAYS THOUGHT February was a dreary month back home, but it's nothing compared with out here. The deep blue skies, sunshine and cold dry air had left us late in January to be replaced with silver nitrate coloured clouds and a slight rise in temperature. This change in weather has also brought with it rain, dampness and dullness. The water-filled clouds that cover the sky block out the usual yellow light that we became accustomed to when it was overcast but dry. There isn't normally a wide spectrum of colour to be found in KAF and this is now magnified by this dreariness.

The weak, beige-coloured dust has turned to a brown mud with the addition of the rain and we are now constantly covered in this sludge from the knees down. This limited range of colour that we are treated to is now restricted even further to just two shades of brown. Big, dark brown clumps of mud that stick to our boots like goat shit and the watery splatter of light brown mud that decorates the bottom part of our trousers. The mud on our boots is brought into the office even after some rigorous stamping of feet on the wafer-thin mat as we come into the main building. These clumps fall off, dry and return to dust. Our Afghani cleaner brushes it up, puts it in a bin bag and throws it into a skip where it will be sent to landfill. This could be a long-term strategy by the enemy to relocate the whole of KAF to the local tip. Everything is damp, really damp. My uniform feels damp. In the office or the pick-up it feels damp. Even when I pick up a pen it feels damp. Everyone I see around KAF seems to walk about with a hunch which gives the impression that they have the weight of the world on their shoulders while looking damp at the same time. The rain that falls is mixed in with dust and I can see this on the white paintwork of the pick-up as the coffee-tinted water splashes on the bonnet. The wipers manage to keep the windscreen clear, but there is always a dirty smear left.

I'm in the office this morning with my jacket on as there is no heating. We did have one of those cheap heaters that cost £100 a minute to run but it has been borrowed indefinitely by persons unknown. I have sent Joe off on an errand and take this time to fire up the computer, hoping that the little heat that it produces will warm me up a little.

I've received a damp email that has been forwarded several times telling me that back at the Sergeants' Mess in South Cerney there has been a proposal to get every mess member his or her own personalised pewter beer mug. It's no doubt the idea of a newly-promoted Sergeant, who is so keen to impress that he will have volunteered for the Mess Committee and is now spouting ideas like a runaway volcano. After a quick search on the internet, I find an article on pewter poisoning. I print off all twenty pages and add the usual Post-it note.

'SSM, we need to be careful on this one as it could come back to haunt us. Have a read of the attached paying particular attention to para 1.1.23. It would be good to know your thoughts on this one?' I sign it off with the familiar scribble and stick it in the post to Lee Mulligan. It will be on its way back to the UK tonight, and by Monday morning Kiwi will be spending hours worrying about it, scratching his head, and pulling a face.

Friday 3rd

It's still raining and we are informed that 'Operation Noah' has been called.

"Any idea what Operation Noah is?" I ask Joe.

"I presume it's a water-themed operation?" is his reply. "Maybe the next operation is an assault on Afghanistan from the sea because the Navy are feeling left out?"

"Thinking outside the box, I see," raising my eyebrows as high as they can go. "Maybe we are expected to build an ark due to the rain?"

"It'll be a quicker way of getting home than waiting for the RAF."

"Walking backwards would be quicker. Are you any good at woodwork?"

"I made a bookend in school once," he says with pride. "It was really just a lump of wood with a flat bit nailed to it."

The pride then drains from his face, as he obviously re-members that is was probably crap.

"Right," I say, "you're on Ark building duties and I'll go and round up the cockroaches, ants and flies."

We eventually find out, after asking the Base Warrant Officer, that it is less exciting than building an ark and that we are to start placing sandbags around the entrances to the buildings to stem the rising water levels. By the time I find out where we are supposed to get some sandbags from, someone has already done the job for us.

The stench from the poo seems to be getting stronger and I suspect that the poo pond had had a little accident and burst its banks. This now means that KAF is the world's biggest effluent lake.

Saturday 4th

I get into the office after some watery wallpaper paste that could have been masquerading as a crap porridge and send Joe off to do the laundry run. I open the inbox on the computer and see that it is going to be a busy day as three emails are requiring my attention. Suddenly a Spam bursts into the office, bringing a load of mud with him. He comes in so fast that his knock is two seconds behind him. Standing there in his greyish-greenish-looking uniform, which is full of massive badges on both upper arms, he starts saying something wholly unintelligible, which is not uncommon for our American allies.

"Sorry, I didn't catch what you said there?" I say "How can I help you?" just managing to stop myself from adding 'old chap' at the end of the sentence in case he realises I'm taking the piss.

He says something again and then I realise that he's speaking with a southern English-sounding accent. My ears then tune into the dialect and I start to understand what's coming out of his mouth.

"Alwight, mate, are you the guys I need to speak to about the RAF flights?"

"What you wearing that shite for? Problems at the laundry?" was all I can come up with.

"Nah, me Mum is from Dartford and me Dad is from the US, but I grew up in Essex," he says with a well-practised script, as I know this anomaly must be an recurring question.

"Listen, listen," he says, getting all excited. "I was on the fucking Ramp flight last night and I lost me fucking daysack. I fink I've left it on the plane."

"Should you have really been using your daysack during the night?" I point out.

"Eh?" comes the reply with an added look of confusion. As soon as that look disappears, he starts again,

"It's got all me kit in it. Can you ask the pilot he found it?"

I ask him to describe it to me, and as soon as my mouth closes I realise the futility of the question I have just posed.

"Er, it's like light brown, with a US flag on it and, err, well, like a US forces issued daysack I suppose."

That narrows it down to about five million bags that are in KAF.

I give the RAF a call over at Whiskey Ramp and while I'm waiting for someone to pick up he starts again all excitedly.

"If you can't find it do you fink you can give me a statement or somfink so I can claim on me insurance?"

Somebody answers, so I raise my hand to indicate that I cannot listen to him and talk on the phone at the same time, no matter how good I am at multi-tasking.

"Hi, it's the ATLO here over the other side. Did you know if anyone found a daysack from the Ramp flight last night?"

"Dunno, mate, I just fix the things."

There's a considerable length of silence as we both wait and presume one of us is going to speak next.

"Is there anyone there who would know?"

"Dunno, mate, they're all out working on the planes."

"Can you ask about for me?"

"I'm just about to go off shift, mate."

"Can you leave a note for someone to call me back?"

"We haven't any Post-it notes, mate."

"Can you leave a message on the whiteboard?"

"The marker pen has run out of ink, mate."

That conversation pretty much sums up the RAFs relationship with the Army.

I hang up entirely unsurprised about what I have not managed to achieve on the phone. "They'll have a look for you and get back to me," I say, lying through my teeth, "and if you can leave me your details on how to get hold of you I can give you a bell as soon as I hear something."

"I can claim it on my insurance if you can give me somefink in writing, as I had my iPad, my Kindle, my Bose earphones...", he says, rattling off his list that was akin to a Christmas list of must-haves for that year. I know exactly where this is going and it's in the direction of a massive fraudulent claim stating that he had had a number of expensive items squeezed into his daysack that would have clearly filled a shipping container to the roof.

"I'll email later," I lie.

Not wanting to be complicit in his scam, or talk to him for any longer than required, I say, "I have to go and deal with some passengers and planes and stuff."

Lying for a third time that morning, and all before 10am, I get up and start putting on my jacket, just as Joe walks through the door.

"About turn," I say immediately, giving him the look that would best convey the situation that I was stuck in a room with an idiot and I was trying to get out quickly.

"We've got some Movery-type things to do."

Thankfully, he reads the signals correctly and plays along. As we usher him out of the office, locking the door behind us, Dodgy Derek of Dartford continues to list the items in his bag.

". . . My laptop, my iPhone, my telescope, my Harley."

Once outside we open the doors of the pick-up and start to get into it to keep up the sham of having to rush off. As soon as he disappears out of sight we get back out, shut the doors and promptly go straight around to the NAAFI for a brew. I don't feel too bad about it as he was technically a Yank, but I do feel an ounce of repentance when I realise we are standing behind him in the queue.

Later that day, when I am over at Whiskey Ramp, I ask one of the RAF Movers what they do with all the carry-on luggage that they find left behind on the Hercs. He shows me to a room with over fifty bags piled up in the corner. One stands out as it's adorned with the US flag. On the way back to the office I sneak a peek in his bag. Predictably, he was lying like a cheap NAAFI watch.

Monday 6th

It's my turn to collect the dhobi this morning, so I head off in the pick-up through the sea of Kandahar as it's another rainy day. I manage to find some parking fairly close next to some muddy ground that's above water. I hop from one muddy island to another muddy island eventually making it to the front door with dry feet. The high wooden steps that rise out of the quagmire are a welcome relief from constantly having to look where I am putting my wacker plates[42]. It's more welcome relief as I go through the main door getting out of the rain but unfortunately, I have to join a queue of Spams all talking bollocks. With my hands in my pockets and reading the posters with the dos and don'ts of handing in your laundry to pass the time I patiently await my turn to hand in the numbered tags. Efficiently as ever the TCN disappears out the back with the tags and returns seconds later whereupon he slides across the counter four full off white net bags. All the bags have just come out of the industrial dryer as they are really quite warm to the touch which is comforting in the cold of the morning. I retrace my steps back to the pick-up without managing to

---

42   Wacker plates - Military slang for feet, normally reserved for someone who has clown sized boots.

drop any in the brown goo. I throw the cooling bags on the back seat and set sail back to the office. Upon my return Joe, Tosh and Hamish are busy reading the latest magazines from five years ago. I hand out the bags as if it's a mail call.

"Lance Corporal Parkes."

Joe looks up and I throw his bag directly in his direction forcing him to drop his magazine.

"Sergeant Hamish."

"Aye," he says, holding one hand up in the air, ready to catch the bag that is sent his way.

"Corporal Lines, one bag of women's clothes, you filthy little deviant."

I swing his bag by the string that keeps the end closed so that it lands on his head.

"You fucking knob," is the unimaginative reply.

Something metallic flies from his bag, bounces off the wall and back on to the middle of the floor in-between us all. It's spinning round very fast and, as it slows, we see that it's a 5.56mm round.

I bend down to pick it up. It's red hot and straight away I am juggling it from one hand to the other like I was try to hold a red hot potato.

"Oh dear Toshy boy," I say, laughing, "you're gonna be doing bird for this."

I place the round on the desk mindful that the heat might set it off. "I know us pongos are a bit mad when it comes to cleaning stuff but washing your bullets is going a bit far."

"It's not mine," he says straight away in his defence. "You know I only have a pistol."

I turn to Hamish. "I'll happily give a statement Sergeant Macbeth indicting Corporal Lines in bullet laundering."

"Me too," adds Joe.

171

"I'm going to keep this bullet, Corporal Lines," I say, pointing to it in an accusing manner, "but do I file it under B for Blackmail, I for Insurance or F for Favour?"

"B for Bore off," he says, as he carries on reading his magazine.

It will sit on my desk for the remainder of the tour as the one and only table decoration.

Tuesday 7th

It's the afternoon and we are on our way to meet the inbound flight from Bastion. The ring road that skirts around the airfield is undergoing some maintenance as the Spanish engineer battalion attempt to lay some tarmac down on a section that was slowly turning into a realistic reconstruction of the Somme. They've put some temporary traffic lights up to control the traffic while they try to solve the problem. These have now caused some biblical sized tailbacks that are alien to KAF traffic. We decide to drive over to Whiskey Ramp via the active airfield which is allowed. We don't normally bother going this way due to the 10 mph speed limit for us and that we have to give way to all taxing aircraft. It can sometimes take forever but today it's the quickest route. We enter onto the airside part of KAF near the CATO building past a sleepy Spam guard sat on a polyprop chair. He just waves at us with a sense of hopelessness.

We return his wave as we pass him without stopping. For some reason, these guys do 12 hour shifts on their own, sat out in the open with no protection from the elements alone with only their polyprop chair for company. They normally have a crate of energy drinks stashed under their chair to keep them going through this painfully long shift. Just past the entrance is a metal grate that has been laid down on the tarmac that we have to drive over. Its sole purpose in life is to shake any loose mud from the vehicle whilst waking up the sleepy Spam. It's been designed to violently shake vehicles quite hard to ensure that the mud falls off at the grate and not on the taxiways as that could be dangerous for the planes. They are so bone snakingly brutal they also manages to shake off parts of the vehicle and the passenger's fillings. After our mind-scrambling vibration we stop the pick-up as we try to refocus our eyes. Now under the scrutiny of the guard we are expected to get out and walk around the vehicle looking for potential lumps of mud, wet or dry, that may still be stuck to the underside. He is under strict instructions to dob us in if we don't.

We wait off to the side of the taxiway as a 60 tonne Antonov-12 cargo plane passes by at such a speed that it rocks the pick-up violently. The high wing tip goes over the top of us and the noise from its four engines drowns out Kandahar FM even with the windows closed.

With his fingers in his ears, Joe shouts, "10 mph, my arse."

We continue down the taxiway pulling over every time a cargo plane screams by.

"Are you sure we aren't on the runway," I say to Joe as we are rocked about inside the pick-up.

We see a helicopter coming our way flying low down the taxiway. It's a Mil Mi-8 which is a Russian design that's used by every country who were ever in the Warsaw Pact or an old Soviet ally. After three months here my aircraft recognition skills are becoming quite good. We pull over again to let it pass and as it floats past, this time very slowly, we are again deafened by the engine that's on full power. The blades pass over us and we can feel them chopping brutally into the dense air. The downwash from the spinning knives rock our pick-up more viciously than any of the cargo planes previously. It gives a sensation that it's trying to prize us up and away from the gravity of Planet Earth but our brute industrial weight just manages to hold all our four wheels on the ground.

As it heads off into the distance we move back onto the taxiway both breathing a sigh of relief.

"I don't mind the odd traffic jam," I say to Joe realising that trying to save a few minutes driving was a probably bad decision.

"Yeah," he agrees "they're sort of a novelty around here."

We are approaching a junction and we see an unmanned US Reaper Drone now coming our way.

"Oh for fucks sake," exclaims Joe, "at least the planes have a pilot in them." His remark is directed at the fact that they are piloted remotely from somewhere in the US. I did hear that it was somewhere near Las Vegas. We pull onto the side of the taxiway in anticipation to having to let it past.

This thing is the size of a small plane with a propeller at the back and a V-shaped tail that gives it a futuristic look. Under each of its spindly wings are a cluster of small unassuming rockets that don't match their precise destructiveness. At the front where the cockpit would have been located is a bulge that gives it look that invokes a primeval fear in me because I think it looks like the Xenomorph's head from the film Alien. That film terrified me when my parents let me watch it at the age of 10. Underneath the head and about the size of a football is the camera that moves back and forth like the eye of Sauron looking for its next target to vaporise. Not knowing which way it will be turning at the junction we decide to hold back. It also stops and we can see its camera swivelling left and right either looking for traffic or trying to decide which way to go.

"You know that right now there's a pilot in Las Vegas at the control of this multi-million dollar killing machine claiming to be lost," I say to Joe.

The camera that was moving suddenly stops with its gaze fixed on us.

"Oh fuck," says Joe.

For a moment the unease of being in this things sights scares me deep down inside. It's ridiculous as I know that it's not going to unleash its ordnance on us but it's like looking over the edge of a high cliff knowing you are close to death.

From behind the drone and out of nowhere a brown pick-up races towards it. "He's not doing 10 mph," says Joe.

The driver jumps heavily on the brakes and as his pick-up squats forward it squirms about as the tyres fight for grip on the tarmac. A pair of legs appear out of the passenger door and as it comes to a stop in a little cloud of burning rubber the legs are already on the ground. Out pops a man in the beige uniform of a civilian contractor. He runs around the side of the drone wildly waving his arms to try to attract its attention.

This seems to work as the camera picks him up and now follows him as he continues to move around to the front of it. It's all very reminiscent of a film where someone is trying to gain the attention of the monster thus distracting it away from eating the children. This works and once he sees that he has its attention he puts his arms above his head making an X shape. Now he starts to walk backwards away from the beast still showing it the X sign. As he backs towards the edge of the taxiway he moves both his arms to his right indicating for it to turn left. After a short pause, its engine increases in power and it slowly rolls forwards before turning to its left.

As soon as the man sees it turning he gives it the thumbs up. Once it's past and safely moving in the right direction he walks slowly to his pick-up. He briefly turns to us and gives us the double thumbs up.

"Was it just about to obliterate us?" says Joe.

"Maybe there's a monkey at the controls," I reply. "He's currently in Las Vegas Zoo and he was just about to press the fire button, but thankfully his trainer turned up."

Joe sighs a sigh that is actually him saying "Fucking hell," and adds, "I thought I saw that bloke waving some bananas at it,"

We pull back onto the taxiway to continue our 10 mph journey towards Whiskey Ramp.

"You know what?" I ask Joe.

"What's that then?"

"Every day something abnormal happens but because it happens every day it doesn't seem abnormal at all."

Wednesday 8th

It's still raining and it seems that all colour has finally been washed away from KAF. The rain has eventually cleared the sky of the dust and is now a clear liquid as it falls but it doesn't give that cleansing feeling as the mud is still present. The heater still hasn't turned up and the office is now on the side of fucking uncomfortably cold. Joe, being a potential Paratrooper, occasionally gets up and either starts jogging on the spot or drops down onto the floor and does hundreds of press-ups. As soon as I think he's about to finish I say, "One more for the Queen."

"One more," comes his eager reply.

"One more for the Colonel in Chief," I spur him on.

"Colonel in Chief."

"One more for the Royal Family."

I'm now sat on the edge of my chair leaning over him looking like his trainer.

"The Royal Family," he says through clenched teeth.

I can see that he's starting to struggle.

"One more for the German *Bundeskanzler.*"

"Eh," he says surprised, stops and cocks his head to one side to look at me while still in the press-up position with his arms extended.

"Don't give up now Lance Corporal Parkes, pain is just failure leaving the body," I start with the cliché sayings of an Army Physical Training Instructor.

"You'll never succeed in life if you give up now," I say with a raised voice, "one more for the Ukrainian Minister of Agriculture."

He manages to push one more out with a groan.

"One more for me."

He collapses on the floor trying to catch his breath.

"You piece of crap, so you want to be on your deathbed in Swindon with your family around you all tutting and shaking their heads at what a total failure you were in life?"

He stands up panting and attempting to wipe the dust off his uniform which results in him just spreading it to parts of his uniform that were dust-free.

"Now that you have finished fucking about let's do warming up Staff Sergeant Lee style."

I chuck him the keys to the pick-up.

As soon as I get into the pick-up I put the heater and Kandahar FM on.

Joe gives out a groan. He has beads of sweat across his forehead. "Where to, Staff?" he says as he backs out of our parking space.

"I'll let you know when we get there."

We drive around the inhabited area of KAF in 2nd gear bouncing in and out of potholes the size of large ponds. On one of the back roads by the hospital, there are some trees

177

poking over a high concrete blast wall. I have noticed them before but their leaves were always covered in the yellow dust so that they blended in with the background. The clear rain had finally washed the dust off the leaves revealing a deep lush green in the ocean of dullness. It was the most colourful thing we had seen for a long and our eyes are fixated on this treat.

"Would you look at that?" I say to Joe.

Without telling him he pulls over onto the side of the road and switches off the engine while we are still moving. The radio and heater fall quiet which is an instant relief.

As the pick-up rolls to a halt, we sit in silence staring at this simple but immensely satisfying luxury with just the sound of the rain falling on the roof of the cab for an age.

KAF ATLO SITREP
week ending 08/02/2012

▶ Due to rising water levels Operation Noah has been called. The HMS ATLO office is prepared for sea and Lance Corporal Parkes is now running sea survival lessons.

▶ The NAAFI have started selling out-of-date doughnuts as life rings but are still charging a premium for them.

▶ A rocket landed on the waste ground near the office. We are thinking of making a pond out of the crater. I'm looking into funding for some plants, fish, a water feature, and a bench.

Thursday 9th

The phone rings and it's Jamie Savage, the RAF Warrant Officer Mover.

"Hey Staff, how's it going?" he enquires in his strong Glaswegian accent. I'm half-expecting a threat of violence towards me at any moment.

"All good, sir."

"Ave ye heard what the thick spams have din noo?"

"Surprise me," I reply.

"They've apparently burnt a Qur'an up at Bagram by accident."

"Oh," I say, understanding of the seriousness of the situation.

"The shit will hit the fan now, just ye watch," he predicts. "I've noo gotta now give ye all a briefing on why burnin the Qur'an is bad and why ye shouldnae burn one."

"Yeah, we are free this morning after the flight," I say.

We head over to the RAF compound on the other side of the airfield. The ANA guard at the Afghan Airforce compound with his AK47 looks even more menacing today. I'm sure I detect a scowl as we drive past him and I keep my eyes fixed on him for any signs of vengeance.

We all meet in the large RAF crew room, which is well stocked with appliances, brew-making kit, snacks, just out-of-date magazines, and newspapers.

"Flippin' 'eck, they've got a good set up here," exclaims Joe, as he makes us both a rich Italian roast coffee with fresh milk in a pair of Royal Doulton porcelain cups.

"Budgets," I reply. "The RAF has always had a bigger budget than us. They were the first to be issued Gore-Tex kit back in the late eighties so that they didn't get wet going to and from the cookhouse. Meanwhile, the Army's playing silly buggers

179

out on the training areas in the pouring rain in 1960s plastic bloody waterproofs,"

"Must have been good for weight loss, wearing a plastic bag?" he says.

"I fell asleep on exercise while wearing a full set once. I woke up wetter than I would have if I'd slept in the rain. On the plus side I'd lost two stone."

"Gore-Tex eventually found its way into the Army inventory but it was as rare as rocking horse shit," I say, continuing to enlighten Joe on the logic of the Military.

"On my first tour of Northern Ireland, we were finally issued a Gore-Tex jacket."

"All good things come to those who wait," he says, before taking a sip from his coffee.

"Yeah, one between fucking four of us."

"Fucking hell," he says with a mix of laugh and coffee followed by a snort and then some coughing.

"It was like one of those game shows when the host says to the losing contestant, 'Here's what you could have won' and they look utterly dejected.

"We'd take turns wearing it, but you always knew you'd have to take it off,"

"The cruel bastards," says Joe, while wiping his mouth with a pure Egyptian cotton napkin.

The crew room fills up with an assortment of personnel in different uniforms. There's more Army in desert combats than the RAF in their ground crew coveralls and piloty-looking flying suits.

Jamie Savage arrives, thanks everyone for taking the time to attend and passes on a brief that has obviously been written hastily by a Staff officer somewhere in a dark office thousands of miles away.

The crux of the message is that the Spams are stupid bastards and burning the Qur'an or throwing it in the bin upsets the locals, even if it is an accident, therefore we shouldn't do it, and, if we do it, intentionally or accidentally, then we are all in for a world of pain. He can now report back up the chain of command that he has ticked that box saying we have all been briefed and will all be good boys in future. I imagine later that day one of the pilots, whilst dropping a 1,000lb bomb on some armed locals, is glad he didn't get rid of the Qur'an he found.

On the way back as we again pass by the scowling ANA guard, I eyeball him and say, "Come on, then, if you think you're hard enough."

"He can't hear you," says Joe.

"Well, I don't want to upset the poor guy."

Friday 10th

During the tour, we get to go back home for a couple of weeks on R&R, and today it's my turn. It's several days to and from the UK which makes it feel more of a chore than a rest without recuperation.

My time in the UK is spent with my wife and two children, counting down the days until my return in just under two weeks' time.

Sod's law sees me suffering from a very severe case of tonsillitis which I spend four uncomfortable days in bed and trying to get registered with a doctor to get some antibiotics.

Thursday 23rd

Far too quickly the precious time together has passed and my family have to drop me off at Brize Norton. My wife has a German passport so she is told by a grumpy-looking MOD policeman that she's not allowed onto the base. My daughter and son are too young to comprehend why I have to go away again. There are tears all round as we do the pain of separation again in front of a now-embarrassed policeman.

Friday 24th

Another dust storm arrives in Bastion and after several aborted attempts to land in the poor visibility the TriStar pilot is finally defeated. He reluctantly announces that we will have to divert to Muscat in Oman where we have to sit out the storm for a few days. The in-county resident RAF transfer us from the airport to their camp, which is in the middle of the desert and a three-hour coach ride away. One of our fellow passengers is a pretty female reporter who becomes ill. On our arrival in the desert camp, she is taken away to the medical centre not to be seen again during the remainder of that day.

Saturday 25th

Apparently there is a possibility of getting out today so we endure another three hours on the coach back to Muscat airport. Our reporter friend isn't with us so I presume she must be quite ill and I feel sorry for her. After hanging around the airport until late evening an RAF Flight Lieutenant turns up to tell us that the visibility is still too bad and we will have to return to the desert camp. Back on the coaches we go for another three hours. We arrive just before midnight to see a dissipating party in the RAF bar. I clock the pretty reporter, now healthy, drinking and laughing with some of the RAF camp staff. I can't but help think that the trip to Muscat with the non-existent promise of the departing flight was just a ploy to get us off the camp so that us walking freight didn't gate-crash their party.

Sunday 26th

I arrive back at KAF just before midnight in the pouring rain and it's utterly miserable. I jump off the back ramp of the Herc and feel that I need more than ever some extra R&R to recover from the emotionally charged rollercoaster of my R&R.

Monday 27th

My first morning back and the email traffic has increased twofold. I see that we have been receiving up to four a day during my absence. I'm down as an action address so have to read them all. These emails are written by high ranking officers with brains the size of planets and some are longer than Tolstoy's War & Peace. I spend the best part of most morning poring over them, trying to work out what is happening and where we are to be in the grand plan. What I can gather is that there's a proposal to start using the Hercs to ferry injured Afghani soldiers and civilians into KAF from Helmand Province. Their main hospital is located in downtown Kandahar and I presume, previous to this, that they were moved by road. That couldn't have been enjoyable for anyone, let alone someone with injuries, as it's a long hazardous drive on rough roads. It's hazardous due to the Taliban threat, yes, but even more hazardous because of the local population, who would be driving on the road at the same time. The Afghan DVLA and road safety campaigns were a long, long way off and not even a spark of an idea in some minister's head. The quality of driving is just awful, and we're always hearing of fuel trucks crashing into crammed buses with reports of massive casualties.

Today the first Herc will arrive with its cargo of poor souls. The plan is for the wounded to be moved from the Herc by UK and US medics to the back gate of KAF. The back gate is a bit more discreet and closer to the hospital, and, going by the enemy's persistence towards killing civilians, they wouldn't think twice about having a crack at this convoy. On arrival at the gate, they will be handed over to local medical services for onward movement to the hospital with a heavily armed escort. I've arranged for the Herc to park next to the CATO terminal so at least it's a shorter route from here to the back gate. With all the medics informed of the plan, they turn up at the right time at the right location. Everything is in place now, so we wait patiently for the arrival of the Herc at 1400hrs.

Joe and I are sitting in the pick-up at the end of a line of several ambulances. The rain has stopped, so the crews are all out of their vehicles, some sat on the bonnets and some gathered in groups talking amongst themselves. Like a taxi ignoring a drunken fare on a Friday night, 1400hrs promptly comes and 1400hrs promptly sails by.

A bored-looking lanky female medic with her hands in her pockets wanders slowly up to my side of the pick-up. Expecting something about the tardiness of the RAF, I am ready to point out that I am not personally responsible for the Herc that we are waiting on.

"Ere, why you gotta Jammy Dodger on your arm, Staff?" she says in a South West accent, referring to the big red Movements badge that is stuck to my upper arm with Velcro.

"It's the NATO symbol for who is in charge of making the brews," I say with a straight face. "It's so everyone who is a member of NATO, no matter what their nationality, knows who to speak to about getting a brew."

"Well, fuck me sideways, I didn't know that," she replies

also with a straight face. I can't tell if she is playing along with me or being serious. "Funny how it looks like a big red Jammy Dodger and you're in charge of the brews, eh, Staff."

"I'm sure they thought about it long and hard before they decided to go with it," is my reply.

"I love Jammy Dodgers, me," she says, looking to the sky. "I once stole a pack from my local shop in Frome when I was a kid."

"Did you get away with it?" I enquire.

"I would've, but Katie Matterson," she says, as if I know who this other girl is, "grassed on me to the police and I had to apologise to the shop owners and pay them back for the Jammy Dodgers." She pauses, then adds, "Fucking bitch."

Every couple of minutes a plane departs and another one lands. Some of them are Hercs so Joe says, "Here we go," followed by, "Aww, bollocks," as it turns off the runway and heads off in another direction.

We often mistake planes and more than a few times we have called Bastion to say the plane had just departed, as we had both seen one disappear down the runway into the night sky, only for ours to come taxiing around the corner, heading back to its parking stand with some problem or other.

Finally, one of the Hercs turns off the runway in our direction. It begins to follow the maze of taxiways zig-zagging left and right across the open area. At each turn that favours it coming to us, Joe makes an "Oooh" sound.

When it turns on to the big open apron that we are waiting on, he shouts "Bingo."

It drives straight at us, with its four menacing engines still turning at what sounds like full speed. The plane continues to head directly our way, and then, when it's almost upon us, it turns sharply to the right. The wingtip accelerates with the

185

turn of the plane and speeds over our heads. It straightens up, and the front end of the fuselage dips down slightly as the nose gear suspension soaks up the force of the pilot applying the brakes. The engines continue to run for a while as the crew do their shutdown procedures. Not wanting to suffer from premature deafness or death, Joe and I decide to stay in the pick-up and wind up the windows to give our ears some protection from the deafening noise and our skulls from the spinning blades. As the engines are cut, this makes the plane shudder slightly as the propellers seem to release their grip on the air. I see the back ramp start to open, and I hop out of the pick-up, doing the usual routine of placing myself in view of the loadmaster, who is moving about on the ramp. He is checking the area around the ramp, while still attached to the plane with his communication cable. I wait for him to spot me and, once he sees me, he beckons me forward to the back of the plane. Instead of the grey and green sea of military uniforms, there's a different sight that catches me out for a second. Stretchers are strapped to the floor all down one side of the plane, with unmoving human-shaped lumps covered in thick dark blankets. On the other side sitting along the seats are 20 or so Afghans in a mixture of civilian and dark green military clothing all looking slightly distressed. I presume this is from the flight, as flying is alien to most Afghanis.

The loadmaster takes off his leather glove, shakes my hand, and announces how many souls he has on board. As I'm concentrating to hear what he is saying, I look down to the end seat and see a mother holding on to her young daughter. She must be about three, and both her arms are wrapped in white bandages from top to bottom. The daughter is crying frantically while the mother sobs. A British female medic is trying to comfort them both as she attempts to give the child oxygen. She's trying desperately to keep the plastic facemask on the child, who keeps pushing it away. The loadmaster gives me the go-ahead to bring the ambulances over. With a pre-arranged signal to Joe, which is me just frantically waving my arms while looking in his direction until I get his attention, we start things moving. The walking wounded are taken off first. Assisted by more medics than the injured, they are led to a waiting bus. The fleet of ambulances then moves in and, one at a time, they are reversed up to the back of the plane with their back doors open and ready. The stretchers are picked up carefully by teams in both British and American uniforms with the softly spoken words "3,2,1 and go." Delicately, and with a feeling of compassion, they move down the plane keeping the stretchers horizontal as they negotiate the drop off the ramp on to the ground. The delicate cargo of human life is slowly passed into the back of the ambulance and, once they're safely in, they re-enter the plane for the next one. A medic in the back of the ambulance looks down at each of the patients. In turn, he puts his hand on their shoulder, and smiles at them. The doors are swung shut and, with a flat-palmed double bang of the hand, it drives away to be replaced by the next one ready for its load. Slowly the line of loaded ambulances that is on the edge of the apron, patiently waiting as, one by one they drive, over to the plane, reduces. Once loaded, they move over to join the back of the waiting convoy. At the front of it, the expressionless Bulgarian escorts are grouped around the front of their Humvees, with helmets and body armour on, ready to go. They are talking amongst themselves without any emotion and could be discussing their lottery win.

The last of the patients is taken off the plane and the final ambulance moves away. There is lots of shouting over by the convoy and the Bulgarians climb into their vehicles. I see a head appear out of the top of the turret on one of the Humvees. The machine gun moves up and down, then the turret rotates left to right a few times. It moves off and the ambulances trail behind it one at a time in a cloud of dust and fumes.

As they disappear into the sunset we turn and walk into the back of the plane. Some remaining medics are cleaning up the inside of the plane with the crew. I go to find the loadmaster to let him know that we are going. He hands me a big black bin bag as a reward for our efforts with the words.

"Can you do me a favour and get rid of this?"

Instinctively, I grab it and reply, "Yeah, no problem."

Noticing it's on the heavy side, I instinctively pass it to Joe and repeat the Loadmaster's words, "Can you do him a favour and get rid of this?"

Joe grabs it and also notices that it's a bit on the heavy side.

"Jesus, what's in it, body parts?" he says, as he takes the strain of its weight. The loadmaster laughs nervously and scurries off back into the dark depths of the plane.

"I'm tempted to look in it now," says Joe.

"I'm not."

We say bye to the medics and wander back towards the pick-up. "Well, that was different," says Joe, as he opens the back door of the pick-up and starts to swing the bag into the back seat.

"No!" I shout. "Put it in the back, you cockwomble."

"I am putting it in the back."

"No, the back back," I say, frantically pointing at the open back part of the pick-up. He swings it into the back back and it lands with a dull damp thud. We look at each other and pull faces of repugnance, distress, and uneasiness. That's not bad considering we have only two faces between us.

We find a big industrial bin in a discreet area and get rid of the bag. I don't know why but we look around nervously, drop it in, then walk away with a look of guilt. It's the type of guilt you get when you arrive in a country and have to hand your passport over to the customs official. You know you haven't done anything wrong, but, as they look at you to compare you with your passport picture, you're trying to look relaxed but your guilty conscious goes into overdrive and you feel the need to confess to something. "What do you reckon was in the bag?" says Joe.

"Severed head, couple of arms maybe, some cocaine, who knows," I say, "I wasn't prepared to look in there, were you?"

Tuesday 28th
It hasn't stopped raining for most of the month. The flood defences, four sodden sandbags, are holding up but struggling. Not from the height of the water but from constantly being walked over by everyone entering the building. Most of the floors inside all of the building are starting to look like the ground outside. The cleaners are doing a sterling job, but the mud isn't drying so their brushing efforts are just spreading it about. However, they are paid to brush, so that is what they are doing. It must be good for the environment, as the amount of dust going to landfill has been reduced.

I am waiting for 'Operation Man The Life Rafts, Women and Children First' to be called any moment now. Some of the back roads are now so deep in mud that even the big off-road armoured vehicles with high ground clearance are getting stuck. We quite often come across a recovery in progress with several other of the same vehicles, all connected by thick wire ropes trying to pull their stuck comrade out of the thick brown liquid.

Someone has put wooden duckboards down between

some of the most visited places. Initially they work, but, as the water continues to rise, they disappear into depths of the brown murk. Our boots aren't waterproof, so damp feet are the order of the day, depending on where you needed to go. I did have a pair of waterproof boots, but they were in a box 3,000 miles away back in South Cerney. The words of one of my wise old Sergeants from way back when I had just joined the Army rang around my head. "Any dickhead can be uncomfortable."[43]

Wednesday 29th

It's a boring Wednesday afternoon, it's still raining, and nothing particularly interesting has happened for a while now. We haven't even had the excitement of a rocket attack, which is a surrogate for any form of excitement, apart from the thrill of getting out of here for good. "We haven't had a rocket attack for ages now," I broadcast, as the thought rattles about in my head.

"The wet weather must keep putting the fuses out after they light them," says Joe.

"I hear the Taliban health & safety rep is a bit of a Nazi for the rules about returning to a 120mm Chinese rocket once lit," I say. "He insists that they wait a few weeks to confirm it's properly out."

Joe has a rummage round the diabetes drawer, through the remnants of the tooth-rotting shite that nobody will touch, and pulls out a small box. "Why don't we play this?" he announces, holding up a small oblong box.

---

43   I eventually ended up with a bad case of athlete's foot. I tried using talc for the next few months to take care of it but it just wouldn't go away. One of the first things I did on my return to the UK was to visit a pharmacy to get some strong medication to tackle it. "That'll teach you not to dry your feet properly," whined the old lady behind the counter as she passed me the medication. I snapped back at this telling off with, "I've just spent six months in Kandahar." She was befittingly embarrassed.

"I can't stand Trivial Pursuit, unless it's the thicko version?" I reply. He holds it up to the light to read what's written on it. "It's not Trivial Pursuit," says Joe "it's..." he pauses as he struggles to read it. I grab it from him and start emptying the contents on the desk. It's full of cards and a bit of paper with the rules on. I pass the rules to Joe.

"Read and learn them in the next two minutes, Lance Corporal Parkes, I shall expect an in-depth back brief on how we should tackle this cheap game with a Powerpoint presentation on a blue background with yellow text in Times New Roman."

Joe says, "Well, there's a word on the cards and you have to explain what it is without saying what it is and the other person has to guess what it is I guess."

We are so bored that we decide to play it. I order Joe to go first. "Sinking ship that's not broken?"

"Submarine."

"Correct."

"Chavvy dove?"

"Pigeon."

"Well done."

"Car with a missing wheel?"

"Reliant Robin."

Joe throws the entire game in the bin, stands up, and says, "What a shit game, shall we go for a coffee?"

There's no movement from me.

"My treat," he announces.

I spring out of my seat like the Taliban are coming to town.

KAF ATLO SITREP (Delayed)
week ending 29/02/2012
▶ Water levels remain but we are managing to keep

our heads above the effluent.
- ▶ Roads on KAF are deteriorating from relatively bad to exceedingly bad.
- ▶ No proposals of marriage from any women on the 29th February.

That evening I get word that one of the RAF blokes in the block is leaving soon and has a sofa that requires a new home. I track him down and, with some empty promises of preferential treatment on the plane departing KAF to Bastion, I secure a sofa, yes, a sofa. I wonder how it came to be here in KAF. Was it purchased locally, or was it flown in? It's a dirty mustard in colour and I'm doubtful that the dirty look is intentional. I soon learn that it's designed more for looks than comfort, which makes me suspect that it's a locally produced. The cushions, which are fixed in place, are about as thick as a couple of folded newspapers but with less give than compressed steel, which ensures a numb arse within five minutes of sitting down on it. Underneath the cloth exterior is a wooden frame with all its wooden hardness and wooden angles.

"It's really a bench covered in leftover material made by someone with no experience or skill in making sofas", declares Hamish, looking at it in revulsion.

With my massive acquired TV and comfy looking sofa, I will soon become the centre of attention for film nights. This won't last long as cases of lower back and spinal problems in KAF will increase. With a bit of training and self-discipline, I can lay down on it as if I were lounging at home, and, because I'm not at home, I don't even have to take my boots off.

It turns out I will spend many hours on that sofa letting my mind wander, taking me to past chapters of my life, and trying to imagine what the future held after this tour and after the Army. This was not how I expected my tour to be and I accept that this is not how normal people visualise a soldier's time in Afghanistan. It was just bizarre. I'd feel a sense of guilt, as not everyone is having such an easy time out here. The guilt would then melt away as I think about the circumstances that led to me laying on that sofa and how they were due to choices from way back in the past that I could never have predicted. These are choices like the day I wandered into the Army recruiting office in 1989 and saw they needed drivers for the Royal Corps of Transport and not the infantry, or the posting in 1999 to 2 Close Support Regiment in Gutersloh, Germany, that put me in a freezing Tent somewhere in Poland with Nick and George's turd which led to a career change and eventually to me being here in KAF. It would be on that sofa that I'd decide to write this book.

British casualties for the month of February
1 killed & 4 wounded

5

MARCH 2012

Thursday 1st

IT'S EARLY IN the morning, pouring down with rain, and I'm outside the compound next to the road waiting for Joe to arrive in the pick-up. I have my rifle slung over my right shoulder and in my left-hand several laundry bags with their drawstrings tied tightly around my clenched fingers to keep them off the ground and out of the mud. I have my waterproof jacket on, but I can feel the cold of the raindrops as they land on my shoulders, giving me the illusion that my jacket is not waterproof. The sky is dark, with low clouds that emit such a greyness that makes me feel as if I'm watching the passing traffic in black and white.

There's a drainage ditch, which runs parallel to the road, that is full of brown water that doesn't look as if it's flowing away anywhere. Hundreds of empty plastic water bottles float about in it on their sides with the look of a large navy. The brim of my hat starts to sag under the weight of the water and starts to drip as the material becomes saturated. The raindrops splash in the mud and send the brown liquid to stain my trousers up to just below my knees. I look about for a bit of drier ground and move over to a small pile of gravel that is a little island poking out of the sea of mud. The drawstrings are now cutting into my hand and making my fingers go tingly as the blood supply is reduced. I see the white pick-up coming down the road, and, as it pulls up just in front of me I walk over to it, open the back door, throw the laundry bags in and slam it shut. My hand reaches for the familiar handle of the passenger door pulling it open. Taking my rifle off my shoulder I slide into the passenger seat which it's an enjoyable reprieve from the cold rain. I rest my gun on my lap and reach around to grab the seat belt to strap myself in, while saying, "You took your time, you fucking cocknugget."

I click the seatbelt in and then look to where Joe should be sitting.

But he's not there. In his place is someone I've never seen before in my life. This bearded guy staring back at me looks as confused as I feel. He has both of his hands on the steering wheel and is leaning forward with his mouth open in what can only be described as a state of paralysis. I immediately undo my seat belt, climb back out into the pouring rain, retrieve the laundry bags from the back seat and say, "Sorry, mate, wrong pick-up."

I notice another pick-up behind the one I'm just exiting, but this one has Joe's ugly mug staring at me through a rain-splattered windscreen. I note that he's not in a state of paralysis and leaning forward with both of his hands on the steering wheel because I can see him laughing. I amble over to the correct pick-up and repeat the same process. I sling the laundry bags into the back of the correct pick-up then I reach for the familiar door handle on the correct pick-up. Sliding into the correct vehicle this time I again relive the enjoyment of getting out of the rain but have to put up with Joe's howls of laughter.

"Weeeeeell," I drag the word out, "they all look the fucking same, these pick-ups."

197

"I bet the poor bloke was shitting himself thinking he was getting car-jacked," says Joe, managing to gain his composure.

"I called him a cocknugget, hardly the chosen dialogue of a desperate criminal."

The pick-up is still stationary in front of us so Joe pulls around him as we head off to the laundry. I smile and wave at him as we drive past. He glares back at me like I've just slept with his mother.

"I think he was a Navy officer," I say.

"What gave you that impression?" replies Joe. "Did he say, 'Permission to come aboard?' and then blow your whistle?"

"Nah, the scruffy creature had a beard."

We both laugh as we bounce our way down the road through the mud.

Friday 2nd

Tosh departs on his R&R today so I think about what I can do to make his journey a little bit more unbearable. He turns up at the terminal and presents himself at the desk, takes one look at me, and groans.

"ID card, and if you're going onto R&R from Bastion today I'll also need to see your passport please, sir," I say, acting all official, but with a slight grin on my face.

He hands them both over to me. I pass his ID card to the Indian TNC, who looks for his name on the manifest. I check his passport very slowly like a border official who loves his job. I have it open on the photo page and hold it up to compare the likeness. I look at the passport, I look at Tosh, look back to the passport then back to Tosh and say, "How can you be so ugly with only one fucking head?"

He laughs, grabs the passport from my hand and replies, "You're such a tit."

"Just the one bag today, sir?" I enquire.

"Stop calling me 'sir'," he says.

"Would sir like one to stop calling him 'sir', sir," I drag out the last sir.

I continue to annoy him. "Would sir like to drop one's bag over there, please, sir?" I'm now putting the emphasis on the word 'sir'.

"I know what to do, you gimp."

He uses his foot to slide his bag across the dusty floor over to the hole in the wall that doubles as the bag drop. Due to the distance and weight of his bag, it takes him a couple of attempts, all of which makes him look like a crap footballer playing football in very sticky mud.

"Would sir like help to place sir's bag on the..." I'm cut short as I attempt to lift his bag onto the conveyor, and my body strains to lift the weight. "Jesus, I haven't even put anything in here yet!" I say, through gritted teeth, thinking that he's suddenly nailed it to the floor.

"If I find anything in there that shouldn't be," he says, pointing a finger at me, "I'll be sorting you out."

"You can now proceed to the departure lounge, sir, and help yourself to the many refreshments that we have on offer in there today."

As he wanders off, he looks back over his shoulder and says, "I'm fucking warning you."

I smile, wave him farewell, and leave him with one last thought to go on his way.

"I won't crap in your bag."

I realise what I've just said out loud in the busy terminal, and I am suddenly aware that I'm being now looked at by several surprised people. I carry on smiling and waving. It's all very melodramatic, but I'll be seeing him in an hour as I count him onto the plane. Once he is out of sight, I go through to the back and intercept his bag. It's just about to be loaded onto the pallet by one of the Romanian baggage handlers. I grab it and say to him, "Just give me five minutes?"

I spend a good ten minutes wrapping it up in several rolls of Black Nasty, while the confused Romanian baggage handler looks on. It eventually looks like a big plastic shiny black lozenge and I pass it to him adding "OK, it's good to go."

It should take him a good hour to get back into his bag.

Saturday 3rd
It's Saturday so it's Bazaar day. The venue is the large uninhabited area of mud that took the direct hit back in January. There's no sign of where the rocket impacted. They come in on such a low trajectory that, when they detonate, just a patch of the top soil is removed. Sometimes they bounce and detonate somewhere else, or they just fail to go off. One had landed on the apron before I had arrived in theatre but the damage was still evident. It had come in from the North over the runway, bounced off the concrete, and continued its course towards the TLS at quite a lot of hundreds of miles per hour. It punctured a neat hole in the wire fence that was the waiting area for passengers from incoming flights at waist height. It then hit the thick wall of the TLS, leaving an indentation about a foot deep, then ricocheted straight up and finally came to rest several hundred metres away in the middle of a road. Thankfully, it didn't explode, and, doubly thankfully, there was nobody in the waiting area.

There's a pond in the middle of the area that I think is just a large hole as it is far too large to be a normal rocket crater. The Spams could have possibly created it when they were removing the last tenants and had felt the need to target their vegetable garden with an even larger rocket. It's now full of stagnant rainwater, empty plastic bottles that have been blown into it by the wind, and the odd dead rotting bird that maybe couldn't stomach the manky water.

The Bazaar is a hearts-and-minds venture to allow a select gang of local traders onto KAF to rip off the NATO troops by selling us a variety of counterfeit goods. They set up their wooden stalls, and by that I mean they bring their own wood and nails and build them from scratch. Each stall has its own extended awning that offers their potential customers some relief from the sun and or rain.

The stalls are set up around the manky watering hole and they neatly lay out their wares. The merchandise on offer is just extraordinary - history books on Afghanistan, decorative wooden boxes, cheap jewellery, huge Persian rugs, DVDs, brass instruments, antique muskets and watches. Lots and lots of watches. More watches I have ever seen in one place and predominantly Rolex and TAG Heuer. There must be a factory somewhere churning out thousands of these things. I'm not an expert on fake watches but they look very convincing until you turn them over. The flat piece of metal that covers the back of the watch has been attacked by an angle grinder leaving a very rough finish that could possibly lead to lacerations of the upper wrist.

We all decide to visit that Saturday morning and browse the merchandise that's on offer. Hamish, Joe, Paul, and I walk along in a group, four abreast like cowboy outlaws entering a town. We do a slow lap of the bazaar first to check out what is on offer today. On the second lap we have all seen something that catches our eye and home in on that stall. I have a look at a TAG Heuer watch, and as soon as I pick it up the seller is in my face. "You like, sir?" he says with a toothless smile.

"How much?" I say, expecting to start a haggling war.

"Today's special price just for you, sir, $20."

My haggling skills are stopped dead by the cheap price he has just told me.

"Is it an original?" I ask.

"Of course, sir," he reaches around the back of his stall and produces its display box and a card that says it's an original. "Here is the warranty card that you can send to TAG Heuer."

"Really," comes my reply, with an expression of surprise that's even more fake than his watch.

I have a look at the back and the angle grinder worker must have been in a rush as it has more than its fair share of sharp metallic burrs.

"I'm not too sure about this, my good friend," I say rubbing the back of the watch with my thumb and shaking my head in disappointment.

Quicker than the time you have to wait for a Spam to start talking shit, he produces a bit of wet and dry and starts rubbing the offending burrs out of existence.

"How's that now, sir?" he says passing me the watch for my inspection.

I nod with satisfaction at the now smooth surface and ask him, "Will the warranty not be void now that you have carried out an unauthorised repair?"

He looks at me blankly and I realise that I've probably just exhausted his knowledge of English.

"You like, sir?" he repeats.

"How much?" I say playing along with him.

"Today's special price just for you, sir, $25."

I laugh at his cheekiness and say, "I'll give you $10."

"Today's special price, just for you, sir, is $25," comes his well thought-out counter offer.

"$15," I say, playing hard.

"Today's special price just for you, sir, $20."

I feel that I'm grinding him down and go for the deal.

"$17. And that's my final offer."

"Yes, sir, that'll do nicely."

I hand over a $20 bill, he puts the watch in its display box, and hands it to me. He then moves around to behind his stall while I wait for my change. He just stands there not moving and smiles at me.

"Err, my change," I ask him.

"No, sir, $20, thank you, sir, good day, sir," he says, nodding at me from behind the relative safety of his stall.

"You cheeky twat," I say to him, partly amused by, and partly disbelieving of, his blatant brazenness.

"Yes sir, good day, sir."

We all get back to the office with our thin blue plastic bags of stuff from the bazaar and start checking them out in detail. I've also bought my children some Afghanistan football kits, which should go down well during PE at their primary school. I take my new watch out of the box and inspect it a bit closer. I give it a shake and I can hear something rattling inside.[44]

Paul had bought a massive bag of DVDs for $1, which have turned out to be of such low quality that they are unwatchable.

"Fucking hell," he moans, "the bastard ripped me off."

---

44   The watch worked for a few days then started slowing down and eventually stopped. I did write to TAG Heuer in Switzerland to claim a repair under the warranty, but I never received a reply. One can only hope that by the time that they did reply I must have departed KAF. A few weeks later, when the bazaar was back in town, I did manage to find the seller and asked him for a refund, but he denied ever selling me the watch. I waved the warranty card at him, but he just tried selling me a Rolex.

"Did you not get a receipt?" I reply, sarcastically.

"Of course I did."

I was initially surprised until he showed me. It was a small piece of paper with some unintelligible scribbles on it.

"It probably says 'Fuck You' in Pashto." I point out.

"$1 is $1," he says in a voice that has a broken spirit.

Joe has bought a decorated box that is already starting to come apart.

"At least we'll have some firewood," he says optimistically, as he tries to put the loose joints back into place.

Hamish is the only one who got a good deal today because he bought fuck all.

Tuesday 6th

I am woken by my cheap alarm clock with its miniature buttons that make switching it off or putting into snooze mode such a faff that, by the time you work out how to do it, you're wide awake. It's cold, so I pull the clock into the warmth of my bed as I fumble with it to try and find the snooze button for nine minutes of respite. I fall back asleep and dream that I am riding a motorbike that makes a high-pitched sound every time I open the throttle. I close the throttle and the sound decreases in pitch. I pull the clutch in and drop it down a gear and now it starts beeping. The sound increases as I once again open the throttle. I see a tree stump disappear under the front wheel and I brace for the impact which comes with me jolting violently back into the land of reality. In my dreamy state I quickly realise that the engine sound is the rocket alarm and my alarm clock is enlightening me to the fact that my nine minutes are up. I decide to stay put as I would like to die warm and not shivering on the floor. I hear the thumps, three in quick succession, that make the windows vibrate.

"And on that bombshell, it's time to get up," I say aloud to myself. I swing my legs out from the warmth, put my bare feet onto the rug I bought back in December, which offers me protection from the cold floor, and, for the hundredth time, think that it was $10 well-invested.

Like a monkey, I use my feet to search out my flip-flops and align them both so that I can slide my wacker plates in. They slot seamlessly into place, and I feel the cold of the plastic Y-shaped strap in-between my toes.

I reach for my softy jacket and pull it over my shoulders without putting my arms in the sleeves. It's cold, but I pull it around me knowing that it will quickly warm up. Looking like one of Napoleon's soldiers during the retreat from Moscow I shuffle over to the window. I put my finger on one of the dusty and damaged blinds and pull it down slightly to peer outside. It's initially too bright that I cannot see anything. As my eyes adjust I can see that it has stopped raining and the skies are blue. I feel a mild sense of euphoria that Spring has arrived and realise that I will be going home in just over two months. I keep peering out of the window and see some small birds hopping about on the gravel floor looking for scraps of food. The all-clear sounds with its single continuous note. It's not quite the scene that you associate with the arrival of Spring.

Saturday 10th
One of the DFACs has been advertising a Mexican night, so, with nothing else in the diary that evening, we decide to pop down to it to try it out. We don't normally go down that way, due to it being a ten-minute drive away and in the rough part of KAF that houses all the TCN workers. It's a suburb of KAF that's made up of prefabricated modular accommodation that's stacked up to four-high in places. The planners, or

non-planners, have crammed these accommodation blocks in more tightly than they would with the military. Each dwelling has a balcony with a safety rail that is festooned with an assortment of clothing and towels placed there to dry. There are extremely narrow mud-filled passages in between them, leading deeper into the claustrophobic metropolis. All of this gives the entire area a ghetto feel in that you wouldn't want to find yourself down here on your own at night without a gun. It's night, but we are armed and travelling in force. We park the pick-up next to a very tall blast wall which has the words "Keep Out" spray-painted on it haphazardly. I don't normally lock the pick-up, as car theft doesn't seem to be rampant on KAF, but I do tonight. As I walk away from it, I give one more backward glance half-expecting never to see it again.

We go looking for the end of the queue by following it from where it enters the DFAC. We follow it around the outside of the building, and every time we turn a corner we can see it disappearing off around the next corner. After several more corners of frustration we find the end and take our place. We slowly shuffle back along towards the entrance, retracing our route around the outside of the building as more and more TCN's join behind us. "There must be nationalities from all around the world here," I say.

"Funny, isn't it?" says Joe.

"What is, your social life?" replies Paul, quickly.

"The baddies, and I mean terrorists in general. They are trying to divide nations but here we all are, working together," says Joe, trying to sound all intelligent.

"I think you'll find that most of the people around us are just in it for the money and probably hate us just as much," says Paul.

"It's like a rogues' gallery," I say. "Just look around us."

We look behind us, at a group of skinny young black guys wearing woollen hats and orange hi-vis vests. One of them is wearing his vest as a hat. They are laughing and chatting amongst themselves in an unknown foreign language.

"They're out-of-work Somali pirates. If they weren't earning $5 a day here they'd be taking us hostage faster than you can say 'arrrrrrrrr'".

"They're probably laughing at how shit of a ransom they'd get for you, Paul," says Joe.

"Look behind them," I say, nodding in that direction.

There's another group, but this time it's some white guys who are quite well-built, all wearing beige fatigues.

"They're ex-Uzbekistan government contract killers who've fallen on hard times after the financial crash of 2008," I say. "If they weren't getting paid for mopping out the bogs they'd happily cut your throat in your sleep for an affordable fee."

"I'm glad we are armed," says Joe.

"You think that'll protect you?" replies Paul. "They could kill you with a toothpick."

"I bet the FBI have never thought of looking here for Bin Laden," says Joe.

"I heard that he works at the Spam DFAC emptying the bins," I add.

"Here we go again," says Paul, drawing a deep breath, rubbing his eyes with one hand, he lowers his head and mutters quietly, "For the love of God."

"He saw an advert in the Tora Bora Times for kitchen hands in KAF."

"Fucking hell," groans Paul.

"Anyway he thought he'd have a bit of that as it would be the last place the Spams would be looking for him, so he puts on his best bib and tucker..."

"I could just imagine Bin Laden in a dark grey suit with a waistcoat and gold pocket watch on a chain," interrupts Paul.

"...He gets his arse down to the KAF front gate, presents himself and somehow gets in for an interview."

"Did no one notice that it was the world's most wanted man?" asks Joe curiously.

"No," says Paul, loudly, "because it didn't fucking happen."

"He's not daft is our Bin Laden," I say to Paul, as he rolls his eyes. "He'd shaved his beard and hair off by this point."

"The Spam doing the interviewing wasn't too bright, sees his name on the application form and..." I pause to let Paul interrupt me again.

"Let me guess, he saw the word 'Bin' on his application form and thought bins were his speciality?" he says, predictably in a groaning manner.

"You know the story?" I ask Paul in a tone of mock-astonishment.

"No, but it's blatantly obvious where this yarn was going."

"Yeah, but I bet you didn't know what happened next, though?"

"Go on, then," Paul says, reluctantly.

"He won employee of the month. Not just once," I pause, "but three months on the run," I throw my arms up to add to the incredulity.

"Yaay, that's not bad going," says Joe with a smile.

"He's now been worryingly promoted to a position of authority," I say, changing my tone to one of concern.

"IC[45] slop jockeys?" enquires Joe.

"Not quite that high," I say, shaking my head. "He's 2IC[46] menus."

---

45   In Command

46   Second In Command

"Aha, it's all making sense now," says Joe.

"Only two bastard months and I'm out of here," cries Paul. "Let me guess, he's using his position of influence to come up with disappointing menus?"

"And that's why you should be a copper, PC Seckerson," I pat him on the back. "Your analytical pea-sized brain knows no bounds."

In a monotone voice, Paul continues, "Thus he's able to continue his War of Terror by wearing down the morale of his enemy one meal sitting at a time."

"Fucking hell, Paul," I say, surprised. "You're wasted in the RLC, you should be in military intelligence or even a spook."

"I wish," Paul says. A pause. "I wish I wasn't here."

As we continue to queue, we eventually get around the corner into the bright glare of an industrial-sized lighting tower that has been positioned to blind anyone who is entering the DFAC. With a continuous slow shuffle, whilst shielding our eyes from the bright light, we move closer to the entrance with its swinging doors.

"It's like being at a shit funfair on the slowest ghost train," says Joe.

"I hope you've paid," adds Paul, "otherwise I'll have to eject you."

As we pass through the doors, we are in almost complete darkness, which isn't helped by the retina destroying light outside.

I'm half-expecting a shit-looking skeleton to fall unconvincingly from the ceiling.

I poke Paul in the ribs and say, "Whoooa," trying to make him jump, but all I get is a "Fuck off, you knob" in reaction.

There's another set of swinging doors that opens up into a dimly lit corridor with rows of sinks on either side. We wash our hands and, after the tapping of the meal cards on the electronic reader, we are finally in through the last set of doors into the super bright fluorescent-lit dining hall. Everyone coming in is in varying states of blindness, as they all hold their hands up to offer some protection to their eyes.

As my own eyes adjust, I see that there are Mexican flags everywhere. Big ones on the walls, medium ones hanging from the ceiling, and miniature bunting ones hanging from the rows of serving counters. All the staff are wearing over-sized sombreros with big black moustaches painted on their faces. I do notice that some of the more outlandish ones are real.

There are several serving stations that are offering different types of food, so we split up to go to check out what delights await us. Somehow, in the madness that is 1,000 people eating their dinner, we manage to find a free table and all home in on it.

"So did anyone find any Mexican food?" I ask.

"I've got a Mexican pork chop with Mexican roast potatoes and a selection of Mexican vegetables covered in Mexican gravy," says Joe.

"Oh nice," says Paul "I went for the authentic Mexican chow mein, with an authentic Mexican spring roll starter. I wish I could have completed the experience by being able to eat it with some authentic Mexican chopsticks."

"I was going to go for the Mexican soggy sausage roll with a side of Mexican chips and Mexican baked beans, but in the end I was swayed by the soggy Mexican Cornish pasty."

We all giggle at the ridiculousness of the situation.

"I did get some tortilla chips," announces Hamish, holding them up in a small white plastic bowl.

We start to howl with laughter that's a bit too loud. The

Uzbekistan killers stop eating and stare at us.

Paul notices that there are some postcards on the table. He picks one up and reads it while shovelling some Mexican noodles into his gob.

"They're after customer feedback and are offering a fantastic free prize for one lucky customer," he says, with a few noodles still hanging from his mouth.

"A week of severe dysentery?" I enquire.

"A week of pan bashing?" says Joe.

"Actually it's free food for a year," he announces.

"That's handy on a six-month tour," replies Joe.

As we shovel the scoff down our throats ,we each pull out a pen as we start to think of what feedback to add.

"Dear sire," I say in my best posh voice "whilst visiting your culinary eating establishment during my Spring vacation I found your pepper to be of inferior quality. I suspect that you may have watered it down with the addition of grit."

I sign it off as Mr Bin Laden. "You know some poor sap will have to go through all of these to try and find one that's real," I add.

"Mongo like food," starts Joe, imitating the man child from *Blazing Saddles*. "Mongo like chicken. Mongo like chickens still alive. Lots of love. Mongo."

"I've been sensible," says Paul, holding up his card to read it.

"Dear Egg Technician, one can simply not put Mexican before the name of the fodder on offer and then call it Mexican. A turd is a turd even when covered in hundreds and thousands. I also find the wearing of oversized sombreros and painted on porn-style moustaches highly offensive. Yours truly, Felipe Calderón."[47]

---

[47] The then-current President of Mexico. How he knew this I have no idea.

"Mexican pudding, anyone?" says Joe, optimistically.

"Fuck that," says Paul, which is followed by a loud scraping of metal chair legs on the painted concrete floor as we all stand up at the same time.

"It sounds like a form of torture," I say.

"Hey, gringo," says Joe in a crap Mexican accent. "We're gonna give you a Mexican pudding and you'll be screaming for your mama."

We make our way towards the exit, passing the unemployed Somali pirates, who eye us up to see which one of us would raise the most cash. We head back outside into the darkness, and the hundreds of TCNs are all mooching about. Being the only ones in uniform, we feels like we are no longer on a military camp, and we hurriedly head towards where we left the pick-up. I'm slightly relieved to see it still there. I wasn't worried about the actual theft but rather the paperwork that would have to be done explaining the specifics of the theft.

"I feel like someone in a film who's trying to get into their car in a hurry whilst they are being pursued," I say.

I start to give a running commentary.

"I'm so nervous that I'm shaking too much I can't get the key in the door. The Somali pirates and Uzbekistani killers are now moving in for a hostage and a paid kill."

I turn the key, the central locking pops all the doors open, and everyone piles in.

"I'm so panicky, I'm now struggling to get the key in the starter," I put the key in and start to twist it. "Oh my God, it won't start, we're gonna dieeeeee."

All I hear from the back seat are groans and sighs.

The pick-up starts and we drive off, bumping through the potholes into the dark back to our compound in the quiet atmosphere of disappointment that was the Mexican night.

Friday 16th

Tosh returns from his R&R. He left some of his kit in the laundry with instructions for Hamish to collect it. I volunteer to collect it, with a plan in mind. Once it's in my hands, I go through his laundry bag, looking for trousers of which I find two pairs. I take them to one of the posties, who just happens to be an amateur tailor, and he takes the waist in just an inch. Deed done, I pass the bag back to Hamish with only me aware of my dastardly plot.

Saturday 17th

I'm in the office glued to the computer when I hear Tosh muttering to Hamish that he overdid it on leave and will have to start hitting the gym a bit harder. I keep my head hidden behind the screen, pretending to be engrossed in my work, so that he can't see me struggling to contain my laughter as the tears run down my face.

Wednesday 21st

I can't keep it to myself anymore and I have to confess to Joe and Hamish what I have done. Tosh is struggling with his new gym routine as he has overdone it. Every time he mentions a pain or stiffness, we are creasing up and can't contain our secret.

"You fucking bastards!" he exclaims. "I've nearly put my back out on the rowing machine thinking I'm a fat bastard."

"It was nothing to do with us," say Joe and Hamish.

He glares at me through his pain-filled eyes.

"You better sleep with one eye open from now on," he tries to say in a threatening manner, but, with his West Country accent, it just sounds comical, and I burst out laughing.

Thursday 22nd

I can't find my hat. I have looked in all the usual places, such as on my head and in the big map pocket on my trousers. I struggle to think where I last had it and start contemplating getting a replacement. I feel naked walking around without a hat so I dig out my beret from somewhere deep in one of my bags. It's covered in dust and misshaped after months of neglect.

I hold it by the rim and bang in on my thigh a few times, which creates a dull thump and small clouds of dust. I place it on my head and use the roundness of my bonce to reshape it. I get the usual alien feeling after not wearing it for months and the leather band feels sticky. Now that grey clouds have given way to sunny skies and the temperature is rising I can't think of anything better than wearing a big dark heat-absorbing thing on my bonce.

Friday 23rd

I find my hat. It's in the office encased in a block of ice the size of a portable TV on the floor, with a smiling Tosh sitting in the chair, pretending to be all innocent.

"I'm going to use your fucking head as an ice pick," I say in a threatening manner. The North West accent makes him swallow nervously. He pretends not to have heard me and picks up a two-year-old newspaper to bury his head in.

"You hide your head in shame," I add.

It takes me 20 minutes to free the hat from its ice prison using just a penknife. After all the hacking, during which I miraculously manage not to stab myself in the finger, wrist, or artery, there's a substantial pile of smashed ice left on the floor.

"It's a pity we haven't got any rum, fresh mint, and soda," I say, standing over it, out of breath, after the physical exertion of hacking at a 10kg block of ice, "as I do like a good mojito."

The ice now has a brown tint as it's collected the dirt and dust off the floor.

"It even looks like it's already got the brown sugar in."

"We could market it as the Kandahar Mojito," says Tosh.

I bend down and scoop up a large amount with both my hands. I start to move towards Tosh and his survival instinct kicks in. He puts his paper down rapidly as he knows what's coming.

In the ensuing scuffle the majority of the ice is back on the floor but some small bits succeed in finding their way down the back of his top.

"You fucking knob," he says, arcing his back as the chilly ice makes contact with his skin.

"There you go, sunshine. Can't be having you overheating now, can we?" I say patting his back to make sure it's in contact properly. "We don't want to lose you to heat exhaustion now, do we?"

Saturday 24th

My mind goes into overdrive planning a retribution for Tosh. I wonder if the SF guys would be up for a minor-roughing up with a drop-off outside the wire. Could I bribe the Somali pirates to kidnap him or get the ex-Uzbekistan government contract killers to give him a dead leg? Before things get out of hand, a truce is mediated by Hamish and agreed by both of us. The war of the clothing comes to an end.

Sunday 25th

I read an email from someone pretending to be in charge of things happening on KAF.

"Can we get phishing emails on the military computer net internet thingy?" I ask nobody in particular.

Nobody replies, so I chuck my biro at Tosh, who is reading a paper. It hits his paper square on, making him jump and automatically spout the words "Fuck off."

"Well?" I say.

"Well, what?"

"Can we get spam emails on this system?"

"I dunno?"

"Didn't you tell me you were some sort of cyber expert?"

"Yeah, I am."

"Well why don't you know the answer to my question?"

"Because that's an IT issue. I deal with the content and who it's from."

"Well, this is from someone who says they are in charge of

running things here in KAF."

"Someone's running things here?" he says, raising his eyebrows. "That sounds decidedly suspicious."

I start to read out the email, "Apparently, due to increased attacks on convoys travelling along the ground resupply routes, KAF is starting to run low on fuel reserves. We are reminded that only vehicles essential for base operations are to be used and rationing will be implemented from today."

"I don't think many people are driving around here for fun," replies Tosh, "but we may have to cancel our trips to downtown Kandahar for the bingo evenings."

"I'm parched," I announce. "Anyone for coffee?"

We drive the 30 seconds to the Green Bean coffee shop as we consider it a journey essential for base operations.

KAF ATLO SITREP
week ending 28/03/2012

▶ Due to shortage of fuel reserves, rationing has been instigated. Boot wear will increase and we may need to request replacement boots.

▶ My hat has disappeared, can all personnel in theatre please check their workspaces and accommodation? Description – It's a desert camouflaged hat.

▶ My hat has been found. Please stand down the Quick Reaction Force, CSI Afghanistan, and Cobra.

▶ Rocket attacks continue like they have done before and will do long after we have departed.

Thursday 29th

Joe departs on his R&R in the morning, so Bastion agrees to send up a replacement so that I won't have to do all the work on my own. Lance Corporal Emma Norton, known as Norts, turns up on that morning's flight.

Joe then spends the day with her ,showing her the ropes, specifically where to put the dhobi in, and how to blag free coffees from the Green Bean café. She is very keen militarily and I get the feeling that she would be happier in the infantry than as a boring Mover.

Friday 30th

I wave goodbye to Joe, as it his turn to commence the task of trying to get to the UK and back in two weeks. He knows that I will have done something to his bag and I can see the dread on his face knowing that when he opens it up in Bastion it will be full of something unsavoury. I haven't done anything to his bag, but I still say to him, "Enjoy your holiday, Joe," in an Oscar-winning style that keeps him convinced that I have.

He wanders into the back of the plane with his head down in defeat muttering, "Oh, for fuck's sake."

Norts and I drive back to the office and I put Kandahar FM on, expecting a moan, but, to my surprise, she says, "I love this song." In shock, I nearly swerve off the road and into a ditch. "Really?!" I reply, once I've regained control of the pick-up.

She laughs and says, "Do I fuck?! Joe told me you play that shit all the time."

"I only do it because it drives him banonkers."

"What the fuck is banonkers?"

"It's a little bit bananas and a little bit bonkers."

"How about bonkanas?" she adds.

218

"Sounds like Dutch for an orgy," I say, pulling a face. "Speaking of the Dutch, I've arranged to meet up with the coppers for a posh brew in the Echos so that you can meet them."

"The what?"

"The Echos, it's like a Dutch NAAFI but staffed by Bosnians."

"Who are the Bosnians?" she asks. "Whose side are they on? Are they the Taliban's allies or ours?"

"Bosnians, you know?! From Bosnia!"

"Is that over by Herat or is it in Pakistan?"

"Are you winding me up again?"

"I've never heard of them, honestly, I swear."

"Bosnia is in Europe," I start fishing for the lightbulb to go on in her head. "Used to be part of Yugoslavia."

"Yugowhatia?"

"Down in the Balkans,"

"I think I've been to a Balkan restaurant, food was minging."

"Oh, for fuck's sake," I say, while breathing in.

"The civil war that they had when Yugoslavia broke up?" I say, still trying for that flicker in Norts's head. "Croatia and Slovenia?" I add.

"Oooh, I think I've been to one of them places, but it was called Slovakia," "Different country," I say quickly. "It all kicked off in the early nineties."

"I was only born in 1988." She says in her defence.

That stops me dead. I turn to look at her and say, "Really?"

"Oh thanks, do I look that old?"

"No!" I say trying to backtrack. "I can't believe that it was that long ago," realising that she's the physical manifestation of twenty-plus years. "So you'd have only been eight when I

219

was serving there?"

"Well done, Johnny Ball."[48] she says laughing. *"Think Of A Number?"*

"Eh, he's way before your time, how come you know him?"

We arrive at the Echos and see Hamish and Tosh already sitting on one of the other sofas that has found its way into theatre. This one is slightly different from mine as it's comfortable for more than ten minutes at a time and clean.

Tosh has his back to me so I ask, "Busy, ladies?" whilst slapping him on his shaved bald head.

"You're such a fucking knob," he says, while rubbing the red hand mark I've left behind on his bonce.

"You been up all night thinking of that one, Toshy boy?"

I jump on the sofa next to Tosh and say, "White one, please."

"It's your round," he replies, a clear octave higher.

"Tosh, this is Norts," I start the introductions. "Norts, this is Tosh, who's just about to go and get the brews."

"Nice to meet you, Tosh," she shakes his hand. "I'm Julie Andrews."

"Eh," says a confused Tosh.

"White nun?" replies Norts, referring to how she takes her coffee.

"Eh," says Tosh again, then, "Oh yeah," as the penny drops.

"It's not my fucking turn," he adds, while getting up and managing to go another octave higher.

"You'll drive all the dogs mad if you go any higher," says Hamish.

"How come you know who Julie Andrews is, young'un?" I ask Norts, "She's waaay before your time."

"I've no idea who she is, I just heard it mentioned once and

---

48   TV presenter and father of Radio 2 DJ Zoe Ball. He presented a hugely-popular children's programme about how brilliant maths is. Things were very different in the 1980s.

know it's how I take my coffee."

I point to one of the ladies walking around collecting dirty crockery and say "Norts, she is a Bosnian, she's on our side, she is not the enemy, so don't kill her. I say she's not the enemy, but that's apart from when they give you food poisoning."

The rocket alarm starts to wail. "I think we'd better get down," announces Hamish, while leaning forwards, trying several times to overcome gravity to extract himself from the low sofa. We all find a slot in-between the table to lie down with our hands on our heads. The first boom is so far away that I only just hear it. The second one is much nearer.

I feel the shockwave through my stomach as it arrives. The plastic windows rattle in their frames and some crockery breaks in the kitchen as it's dislodged from its perch on to the floor. One of the Bosnian ladies gives out a little scream.

"You'd think she'd be used to it, coming from Bosnia," says a muffled Hamish, keeping his arms over his head.

"It's such a relief being up here away from Bastion," says Norts, in a muffled voice

Saturday 31st

It's mid-afternoon, Norts and I are waiting for the returning flight in the office as usual. Typically we have our feet on desks while slumped in the chairs with the customary air of incredible boredom. I'm looking at the KAF website, clicking from page to page, when I suddenly grasp that it's the end of March. The monotony of a fixed routine seems to make time move so slowly but quickly at the same time, or is it time moving quickly while slowly at the same time. Before I have a minor mental meltdown trying to figure out this conundrum in my head, I realise that I can change the weather reports before we print them out. If I had only known about this back in November, I probably wouldn't have had the material for this book due to an early forced departure from KAF for being an arse.

The web pages are run by the US military, who are possibly not aware that it's open to abuse from bored soldiers with too much time on their hands. Maybe they are and they have done it intentionally so that we may amuse ourselves or maybe they aren't aware but amused that they are aware and that we are not aware. I feel another tediousness mental meltdown coming on so I do a bit of editing and produce the weather according to me. I print it off and put it in its place on the wall, hoping to bring a bit of joy to someone. Nobody takes any notice of the weather report and it's the beginning of May before someone does notice it and laughs.

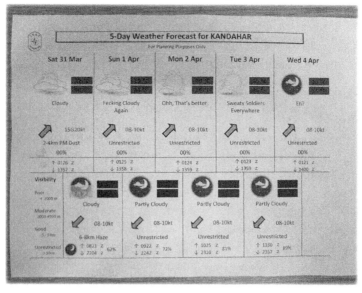

British casualties for the month of March
9 killed & 10 wounded

6

APRIL 2012

Sunday 1st

ON OPERATIONAL TOURS everyone, from the top soldier in charge of everything down to the bottom soldier in charge of nothing, is handed a report, which is called an 'insert slip'. The insert slip goes towards your yearly Confidential Report, which is like the end of term report that you used to get when you were at school. A board then uses it to grade your performance and suitability against all the other soldiers of your rank and the outcome is promotion or no promotion. A couple of well-placed words such as 'outstanding' or 'mediocre' could make or break careers. They are normally written by your boss, or someone just up the chain of command from where you sit.

I have to write Paul's and Joe's, and over the last few weeks I've been making notes and slowly putting them together. Mine is to be written by Troopy Evans, but this morning I get an email from her with the subject heading 'Tour Report Staff Sergeant Lee'. She goes on to explain that, as she is on another camp miles away and has only been to see us once, she wonders if I could I be a star and write my own insert slip? I interpret this as meaning that she can't be arsed.

At this point the rules are that you can't be promoted within the last two years of your service and this is where I currently find myself, with just under 18 months left to serve.

I reply that I would be honoured to write my own report,

trying to convey a feeling of blatant sarcasm, so that she would instantly regret asking me. With the use of a thesaurus I start penning it, imparting the general theme that I am the best soldier ever to have served in HM Forces.

The scent of the MBE is again in my nostrils, which makes a pleasant change from the normal aroma of shit. I declare that I will be sorely missed and that this will have an impact on smooth logistical operations, which, in turn, will degrade our ability to take the fight to the Taliban. I decide to mention brazenly that I should be put forward for an MBE for diligence in running the detachment that would win us a commercial award if we were a civilian company.[49]

Thursday 5th

An email catches my eye, as it has the words 'Replacement' and 'ATLO' in the heading. It's the official notification of who will be replacing us next month. I quickly scroll down looking for a name to jump out at me from all the usual pointless blurb that is used to pad the email out. I see a name and let out a laugh.

"Have you just had your end of tour report?" says Norts from behind a newspaper with headlines informing us that David Cameron has won the 2010 election.

"Better than that, it's our replacements."

The paper collapses as Norts's interest in the election outcome suddenly withers.

"Go on, who's it going to be?" she says, with the paper on her lap.

"Geordie fucking-whey-aye Tucker," I say in my best North East accent.

"I don't know him."

---

49   I'm still waiting for the MBE.

"Lucky old you," I say, still grinning, "he's a right wheeler dealer."

"A what?"

"A wide boy?" I attempt.

"Is he fat?"

"Yeah, but a fat wide boy."

"That makes no sense."

"You know, like a spiv."

"I've no idea what you're on about now," she says, looking confused.

"Bloody kids," I say, shaking my head at her. "How come you don't know what that means? It's only from the 1940s."

"Duuuuh me."

"He would sell his own mother if he thought he could make a few quid out of it."

"Ah, I get you now,"

"He will have sold everything in this office within a day of arriving here."

Geordie was a bit on the short and podgy side and had been blessed with a small pair of arms and legs to match. His dumpy stature made his arms stick out at an odd angle which gave the impression that he was carrying a pair of invisible rolled-up carpets under each arm. He was another one who had an ongoing medical condition and, due to the Army being short-staffed, they wouldn't kick him out. Whatever the condition was, it excused him from doing any type of PT or a fitness test. He was fit... to drop. I had the unfortunate experience of being in the back of a car driven by him a few years before. The first thing I noticed was that his arms were too short to reach the seatbelt, and, even if they had somehow, I doubt whether the seatbelt would have reached across his belly. We were in Germany at the time, and he had taken a wrong turn down a dead end. It was a typical cobbled German street and not particularly wide. He decided to do a ten-point turn to get the car pointing back up the street. Even though it was an automatic, the exertion of spinning the steering wheel from lock to lock and selecting the stick from D to R to D to R was enough to get him out of breath and sweating like he was on a five-mile run.

I remember seeing a message a few days earlier from the KBR maintenance department telling me that the pick-up was due for a service and its annual MOT equivalent check. An idea starts to formulate in my head. With minimal planning, I reckon I can have it in place for his arrival to make the chubby sod sweat a bit and earn his money.

Friday 6th

Norts enters the office, looking all sweaty and flustered. "Can you still not find the dhobi gaff?" I ask her. "It's only 200 metres away".

I remember it took me at least a couple of weeks to find my way round KAF, as everything looks the same.

"I've just had an accident in the pick-up," she declares.

"For fuck's sake," is my natural reaction, before I realise that she could be injured.

I make a note that there's no blood and all her limbs seem to be present and fully attached.

"I presume you're OK?" I guess, after my quick assessment.

"Yeah, yeah, I'm all good," she says, "but the pick-up has a dent in it."

"Big?" is all I can say.

"About that big," she describes the size of a saucer with her hand.

She goes on to explain what happened, and, unsurprisingly, it involved a Spam in a large articulated truck. While he was trying to get around a tight bend, Norts and the pick-up found themselves looking at the trailer coming towards them at an angle. She couldn't reverse due to the traffic behind her so all she could do was sound the horn. This got the driver's attention and he stopped just as the underside of his high trailer came into contact with the top of the pick-up's wing.

We go outside to look at the damage.

"Is that it?" is my reaction when she points it out, as the dent is no more than a few centimetres across.

"You've added to the value of the pick-up," I add.

"Eh, how's that," she says scratching her head.

"Look at the paint off the Spam's truck," I point to the green that is now etched on top of the white of the pick-up, "there must be at least a few dollars worth of his paint on there now."

Norts is worried sick about disciplinary action being taken against her for the damage, as the military has a knack of making you feel that your career is over should you damage any equipment.

"I had a go at the Spam driver but he just shrugged his shoulders, said it wasn't his fault, and fucked off."

"Don't worry about it," I say, "there must be trillions of pounds in damaged equipment every day in Afghanistan. No one cares."

Months later, I would receive an email from Geordie asking me if I could shed any light on a dent in the pick-up that I handed over to him, as he was looking at a bill from KBR.

Wednesday 11th
Joe was due back today but the creaking RAF airbridge, that was struggling under the weight of the job that it was tasked to do, gave way again. As the broken vintage plane was pushed

into the hangar and the engineers headed off to Duxford museum to see if they could source some spare parts, someone was frantically calling around the airlines to see if that had a spare plane sitting about doing nothing. Until they could get their hands on this last-minute replacement charter aircraft he would be stuck at Brize Norton.

KAF ATLO SITREP
week ending 11/04/2012

▶ Preparations are in place for the handover to Staff Sergeant Tucker and his team.
▶ Lance Corporal Norton has settled in well and can now find her way to the laundry unaided.
▶ Latest NAAFI promotion is a free iPad once you've spent $4,000 in store.

Friday 13th

I'm sitting in the office along with Norts. It's quiet as we all have our heads buried in the very latest newspapers from the previous year. I'm trying to wear down the heels of my boots on the table while reading The Times and the key points from the 2011 budget.

"Good news, peeps," I announce "the personal tax allowance is rising by £630 to £8,105 in April 2012."

"What does that mean for me," she says.

"That's a real increase of £48 a year or £126 in cash terms," I read verbatim from the paper.

"Great," she says, not looking up from her copy of The Sun.

"I'll save that towards a deposit to get on the property ladder."

"You should have enough for a two-bed rabbit hutch by, errr, about 2050, I reckon," I add also not looking up from my newspaper. We hear the outer door slam, which sends a shudder through our office, as the damping mechanism thing fell off a few weeks ago. I can hear muffled voices outside our door now and we both stop reading, look over the tops of our papers, and make eye contact at the expectant inbound persons though the door any minute now.

There's a weak half-hearted knock at our door, we all place the papers down, and I swing my feet off the table to look a bit more professional.

"Hello," I say.

There's another knock, this time with a bit more effort.

"Come in," I now shout.

The door slowly opens and a chubby head appears tentatively from behind it as if expecting to stumble on something dangerous or something they shouldn't or wouldn't want to see. When the face sees us, it smiles and the face's owner opens up the door fully to reveal two fat blokes in American uniforms that are straining to keep their bulk in check. The first one into the office has a jolly John Candy look about him, the second one is still wearing his sunglasses and looks like a miserable twat, as his face shows no emotion.

"Hello, sir," says the jolly one with a smile, "are you the guys we need to talk to?"

"Depends on what you want to talk about," I reply. "We can't offer financial advice concerning your personal tax allowance, but we can get you on a flight to Kabul."

The jolly one looks confused while the serious one's face doesn't flinch.

"If it's regarding incoming or outgoing Ramp flights or trying to just blag a free seat then we are your guys."

The look of confusion stays with Mr Jolly.

He introduces himself and explains that they are both civilians working for the USO.[50] This enlightens us to their lack of military appearance, but the acronym means it's our turn to look at them with confusion. He continues to explain that they are running the tour of a certain famous person around Afghanistan on a morale-boosting visit to the troops.

"Who is it? Anyone we know," says Norts, excitedly.

"Sorry, ma'am," replies Mr Straight Face, without any emotion. "Their identity needs to remain a secret I'm afraid,"

It's like good fatty/bad fatty, I think to myself.

Mr Jolly continues, "Our client will be arriving on one of your planes this afternoon and we would like permission to collect our party and their luggage direct from the aircraft."

"I see," I reply. "It's not going to be really practicable for you to collect them."

I go on to describe the process of incoming aircraft, which means that the aircraft will park miles away from the terminal, and that their baggage will be delivered to the terminal still strapped down on a pallet with all the other passengers' baggage for collection. I point out to them that, as they are civilians and visitors to KAF, they won't be allowed airside anyway, and we can arrange for their team to be brought to the terminal by a bus. I put my Bad Mover face on and reiterate that their only option is for them to collect their secret person, team, and baggage from the TLS.

They both turn to one another and begin talking in a lowered voice to one another. I'm expecting them not to be happy with this arrangement and am prepping myself for standing my ground.

---

50   United Service Organisation. They entertain the Spams.

"OK, sir, we are happy to go with this," says Mr Bad Fatty.

They leave us their number and ask us to call them when the aircraft touches down.

We head down to the terminal after lunch with a bit of excitement buzzing between us.

"Who do you think it is?" Says Norts.

"Barack Obama, maybe?"

"Really?" is her surprised reply.

"Somehow I can't see Mr Obama travelling on a manky RAF plane when he has a big shiny jumbo jet," I point out.

"It'll probably be an actor," she exclaims. "I'd love to meet George Clooney."

"Maybe it'll be someone more noteworthy, like Chuck Yeager or Peter Charles Conrad."[51]

"Who the bloody hell are they?" she says looking at me.

"Chuck Yeager was the first man to swim the Atlantic in a pair of welly boots and Mr Conrad invented the paperclip,"

There's a pause as Norts takes a minute to realise that I'm taking the piss, then she laughs.

"One of these days you're going to say something, I'm going to believe you and it gonna get me into a world of trouble," she says.

"That's what I'm hoping for," I grin at her.

We park the pick-up and wander into the terminal which is the usual hive of activity of dossing soldiers busy waiting for their flights. We go straight to the office to be met by the sight of Bogdan, who is in his usual position with his feet on the desk watching something on the computer.

"Bonjour, Herr Bogdan," I say to him.

"Hiya," he says, raising his hand in a half-hearted greeting but not removing his eyes from whatever is so interesting on

---

51   Who? The 3rd man to walk on the moon, that's who. I didn't know it then but he had passed away ten years earlier.

his computer. "Flat out, I see," I say, as I come around to see what is so interesting on his computer. He is watching a car crash compilation on YouTube. "Getting some revision in before your driving test I see," I say.

He chuckles and keeps his gaze fixed on the screen.

"Has the bus gone to Whiskey Ramp yet?" I enquire.

"Not yet, Jamillah is driving it today and I think he's still in the back,"

The door opens and a small Asian-looking man walks in. Bogdan says, without moving a muscle or looking up, "Hi, Jamillah."

"Your eyes will go square one day," I say to Bogdan.

"Why's that, then?" he says, finally looking at me inquisitively.

I can't be bothered to explain.

Jamillah announces very quietly that he's now going to go over to Whiskey Ramp. Norts goes with him on the Number 040 bus to Munchen Flughafen that will take her over to Whiskey Ramp and, unfortunately, not Munich Airport.

I bid farewell to Bogdan as I warn him not to work too hard. I exit the office and head outside making my way around and over dusty sleeping soldiers. It's a five-minute walk to the TLS down what could be classed as the main road in KAF. There are no pavements as such, but someone has had the foresight to put up concrete barriers to keep any pedestrians safe from the endless stream of armoured vehicles that are passing by. The crews of these armoured vehicles are encased inside a protective steel box with only small thick bulletproof windows to see through. The vehicles are all designed for off-roading, with big wheels which place the cab quite high up. These factors mean that the driver and crew have limited visibility and could easily drive over someone without even realising it. As

233

they drive by, they kick up dust and belch out fumes, and I can taste all of this in my mouth, along with the smell of the poo pond. I momentarily wonder what the state of my lungs will be when I leave here, and if the pathologist who does my autopsy will tut, shake his head, and say, "Bloody smokers."

I enter the dark cool interior of the TLS through its big arched door. It always surprises me as to how thick its walls are. I keep walking straight through, and come out airside into the fenced-off waiting area for people collecting their passengers. I take a seat on one of the benches to take in the sunshine and enjoy the relative quiet now that I'm away from the main road. I slouch on the bench, put my head back and take a deep breath. I get a taste of an ashtray. I look down to my left and there's an old industrial-sized tin of beans that's full of black liquid, with cigarette butts floating in it. I move to the other end of the bench to get away from the stench. My relief is short-lived, as an aircraft turns up and parks no more than 20 metres away and keeps its engines running for the next 10 minutes. So now there's the stench of jet fuel too.

Eventually, the pilots switch off the engines and peace returns as and the turbines wind down. Sitting there in the sun is very pleasant and time moves by slowly as I watch the endless stream of aircraft arriving and departing. I'm just thinking that I should be hearing from Norts soon, when the duty phone vibrates in my pocket. I pull it out and see that I have a text message from Norts.

"Ramp flt arrived late :(, Bge & pax inbound to you :). No idea who the famous pax is"

The bus turns up with a smiling Jamillah at the wheel. Norts is first off and points the passengers to the waiting area. I jump up and make my way over to the gate and take the security bolt out of the latch so that I can get airside. They all move over to wait by that wall in front of the big "Welcome to Kandahar Airfield" sign as Norts had instructed them to do. While we wait for their baggage to turn up, I look for someone famous in the mix of passengers. I see the usual military, both Brits and Spams, and civilians in their beige uniforms but nobody stands out. I then notice a couple of Spams, who are in the fenced-off waiting area, start to become excited and point in my direction. One of them goes back inside the TLS and a minute later emerges with even more Spams in tow, and they are all just as excited. I'm standing next to a civilian guy who has the sort of moustache that wouldn't be out of place in the RAF. His greying hair is combed back and he's wearing a pair of coloured sunglasses. As we wait, I turn to him and say, "I hear there's someone famous on this flight."

"Yeah, I heard too," he replies.

"Any idea who it is?"

By now there are even more Spams crowding into the waiting area. Again I notice that they are excitedly pointing in my direction.

I turn to the guy standing next to me.

"Oh!" I say, and I smile. He smiles back and laughs.

"Don't take this the wrong way, but I've no idea who you are," I say to him.

"It's nice to be anonymous once in a while," he says, laughing.

"Can I get a photo?" I ask him "I promise I'll Google you later."

"Sure thing," he replies laughing as I fish around in my pocket for my camera. I hold it up at arm's length and we squeeze together to get into the shot and I take a few snaps.

The bags turn up on the slow-moving forklift that's carrying the pallet. I say to him, "I've got to do some work

235

now I'm afraid, but it was nice to meet you whoever you are."

We shake hands and he says, "No worries, man. Take care and stay safe, buddy."

I walk over to Norts and stand next to her as she waits for the forklift to place the pallet on the ground.

"Any idea who our famous passenger is yet?" she asks.

"Yeah, I've just been talking to him," I say.

"Eh, where?"

"Over there," I say I pointing in his direction.

She squints trying to work out which one he is in the gaggle of waiting passengers.

"He's right there," I say again, jabbing my arm in his direction. He waves over to us as he can see that I'm struggling to point him out to Norts.

"Oh, him? I was sitting next to him on the bus over here," she says, pauses, then adds, "Who the fuck is he?"

"I've no idea," I reply, as I shrug my shoulders, laughing.

Our attention to our famous passenger is interrupted as the forklift drops the pallet on the ground with a loud clang. We both turn around and start taking the straps from the baggage mountain.

I had no idea who to Google later so I had to ask some of the spams at the TLS who he was. It was Geraldo Rivera, who is an investigative journalist and talk show host who's very famous in the US and virtually unknown in the UK.[52]

Saturday 14th

There's a pub-style quiz in the NAAFI that evening and, as we all have massive sliding patio-style windows in our diaries, we wander down *en-masse*. Our team of four is made up of Norts, Tosh, Hamish and myself, and we are confident that

---

52   Geraldo Rivera is one of the 51 people on Twitter that Donald Trump follows, at the time of going to press...

we should do well as we have a fair old level of IQ between us. As we claim a table, we can see the other teams from all the different departments of the supporting staff on KAF. "Oh, for fuck's sake," says Tosh, "we haven't a hope in hell of winning."

"Why's that?" I ask.

"The FCO[53] boys are in town," he says.

"Are they that brainy?" says Norts, "Like privately educated and, err, you know, all that university stuff too?" not sounding as if she ever experienced either of them.

"You know those bastards have smartphones on them all the time," says Tosh, enlightening us all. "They are FCO department ones and they aren't restricted from communicating with the outside world like us."

"The sneaky bastards," I say.

"They'll be looking up the questions on their phones," says Hamish. "Watch them all suddenly have a bladder problem as they keep disappearing off to the bogs."

The quiz starts and we all close in around our table, with our heads down, as if trying to keep any prying eyes away from our answers. After lots of head-scratching, pulling of faces, and whispers of "George Lazenby, it's George Lazenby" or "Geneva, I swear Geneva is the capital of Switzerland," the quiz finishes.

Predictably the FCO take the prize of $50 with a nearly perfect score while the runners-up are nowhere near them.

"I bet they had to answer at least one wrong to detract any suspicion," says Tosh.

"Can't you arrest them for fraud or something?" I ask him.

"Probably, but I can't be arsed with the paperwork," he replies.

---

53   Foreign & Commonwealth Office

"Crime," I say to him, "it won't crack itself you know."

"We have our own smartphones," says Norts.

"What, our crappy Nokias?" I say.

"We can turn them into smartphones," she says, holding up a finger like she has just discovered faster-than-light travel.

"Go on," says Tosh, looking doubtful.

"One of us can stay in the office while the others text the questions through to them," she says, without an ounce of sarcasm. "All we need is an encyclopaedia or something similar and whoever's back in the office can look it up,"

We all look at one another, pulling faces of disbelief.

"Please let the rocket alarm go off right now," says Tosh, while I say, "It could work, you know."

"We'd give those cheating FCO gits a run for their morally bankrupt ways," she says.

"You'd have to be able to text at 500 words per minute to get the question sent," says Tosh.

"I can text fast," says Norts.

"How long have you been in KAF now, Norts?" enquires Hamish.

"Couple of weeks," she replies. "Why's that?"

"I'm surprised that it took that long,"

"What took so long?" she says, with a look of curiosity.

"For this place to turn you into an idiot." We all laugh. "Look at these two," Hamish says, pointing at Tosh and me in turn. "Both fucking idiots."

Our laughing stops abruptly, as we look at him in disgust.

"Aww, Hamish," I say, "you'd be bored if we were all fine upstanding members of Her Majesty's forces."

"If we pull this scam off think of what you could do with twelve and a half of your English dollars," adds Tosh.

"I'm in," says Norts. "Anyone else?"

"We're in," says Tosh, while speaking for me by slapping me on the shoulder.

We all look at Hamish, waiting for his reply. "I'm..." he says, slowly, pausing to keep us in a state of suspense.

"I'm..." he says again, looking at us in turn as we eagerly look back at him.

"I'm..."

We all look at him eagerly for his words of wisdom.

"I'm off to fucking bed."

Sunday 15th

Joe finally arrived back late last night.

"Where the fuck have you been," I say to him, as he sheepishly shuffles into the office like the Prodigal Son, with the hair of someone who was dragged through a hedge backwards. He's scratching his head, while his eyes are barely open.

"Bloody Crab Air," he replies. "I now know that four days in Brize Norton is like four months here."

"Abit like Professor Enstone's theory of brevity?" I say, trying to confuse him, with success, as his reply is an "Eh?"

"Like time passing slower or faster when you're next to a black hole,"

"Yeah, something like that."

Norts doesn't want to go back to the Army ironed uniform discipline hell that is Camp Bastion after experiencing my superior style of management. Using my aforementioned skills, I manage to arrange that she will see out the rest of the tour with us here in KAF without an iron.

Wednesday 18th

It's the afternoon, and all is quiet in KAF, apart from what sounds like a man somewhere repeatedly banging a metal pipe with a hammer. I'm putting the final touches to my confidential tour report, while Hamish is slowly writing an email, and Tosh is cleaning his pistol. The quiet is disturbed, as Joe comes in the office excitedly announcing that there's a five-a-side football tournament taking place next week. "Let's enter a team," he says.

"Good idea, but there's only the three of us," I say.

"Four," he says confidentially to correct me.

"Three, Count Paul Dracula goes on his R&R this Friday."

"Oh, bollocks, I forgot," he says, with disappointment.

"The coppers will be up for it, though," he says, as if they aren't in the office.

"Like shite, am I," announces Hamish, while Tosh says, "Count me in."

"I'll speak to the RAF Movers to make up the numbers," says Joe. "I'll be able to get a couple as they don't get out often."

"Sounds good," I say. "Looks like football's coming home. You can be the manager, Joe"

"Make it so, Geoff Hurst," says Tosh.

"First we need a name," says Joe.

"Movers FC or ATLO United," I suggest.

"Oi!" squeals Tosh. "It's not just Movers in your team,"

"Coovers FC?" I spurt out. "It's like coppers and Movers mixed together."

"How about BIFF?" says Tosh.

"Sounds about right," I reply.

"British Individuals For Football," he declares.

We spend hours debating the name and nothing else – no lineup or tactics. We eventually come up with Team B Football Club, hoping this will deceive our opponents into thinking we are an inferior team.

Friday 20th

The fixtures are announced for the tournament and we have our first game on Sunday evening against the Romanian MP detachment. "I haven't seen any of them since last December, when you caught that Romanian guy for drug smuggling," I say to Tosh. "That was the biggest bust ever in the history of the Romanian Military Police," he says. "They probably got a bonus and a few months back at home off the back of that."

"You never see them anywhere on camp. Maybe they have a secret compound somewhere?"

"Dunno," says Tosh.

"Where do you think they hang out?" I ask him.

"Bucharest?" he suggests, shrugging his soldiers.

"What about Joe?" he adds. "He's on nights now, isn't he?"

"He's not a DVD addict, so he's available for manager and playing duties."

"Game on," says Tosh, rubbing his hands together.

Sunday 22nd

The team line up is Tosh, Joe, Norts, a lanky RAF Mover whose name I've already forgotten, and myself. We have another RAF Mover, whose name I've also forgotten, as a reserve, and Hamish as the water boy. We wander down to the square patch of dust that will masquerade as a football pitch like the characters of Reservoir Dogs.

The pitch is in the middle of the boardwalk, and it has been marked out with white paint that's been painted onto the dust covering the hardened mud underneath.

"It'll blow away if we get some strong winds," says Tosh, kicking some white painted dust onto the pitch.

A couple of small wooden benches have been placed on the sideline for each of the teams, and, somehow, somebody has managed to find or make some proper small five-a-side goals from metal tubing. They have used yellow camouflage netting for the nets. To be honest, we were expecting jumpers for goalposts.

"Looks like they are trying to hide the goal," says Joe.

The opposition is already there, warming up in their matching professional-looking kit with a sponsor adorning the front of their tops. "They're fucking ringers," announces Tosh. "They've flown in the Romanian national team by the looks of it."

If this is a tactic to intimidate us then it's worked. We suddenly feel like a ragtag team of biffs dressed in our attire of whatever it is we had to hand. Our team strip is green. That's a mixture of green in different shades but with an overall green theme. One of the RAF Movers has his boots on, as he forgot his trainers when he deployed.

The Spanish referee also has better kit than us, explains the rules, which turn out to be one rule - simply that it's ten minutes each way. This makes it sound like anything else is on the table and it's going to be a game of injuries.

Joe and the Romanian Captain shake hands, the referee blows his whistle, and five of the best British military footballers in this small patch of foreign dust thousands of miles from home take the game to their opponents.

Ten minutes later we are 4-0 down.

We walk back to the bench in various states of exhaustiveness as Hamish hands us each a bottle of water. In his capacity as water boy, he gives us his assessment on our performance.

"You lot couldn't score in a fucking knocking shop with wads of cash hanging out of your pockets."

"Thanks for that, Bobby Robson," says a puffing Tosh. "I'm going to google Romanian professional footballers."

"They're pretty good," says Joe. "But we can turn this around."

He goes on to give us the sort of pep talk that could be used in a military academy as an example of excellent leadership.

With those words of encouragement, we head back on to the pitch. The final score is 9-0.

Tuesday 24th

It's late in the evening and I'm in my room with Joe and Tosh watching a film. The rocket alarm starts its wailing, and, as usual, we all look at one another, pausing to see how the others are going to react. It's almost as if you don't want to embarrass yourself by being the first on to get on the floor.

Tosh says, "Well, I don't know about you, but, with only weeks to do, I'm not chancing it," as he starts to get down. We agree and follow him. There's not a lot of room for us all and I end up with my head in my trainers, which are slightly damp from my last run in the wet and very stinky. Tosh's leg is underneath mine and Joe's feet are in my ribs.

As the wailing recedes, the computer voice starts announcing, "Rocket attack, rocket attack, rocket attack."

We hear three impacts in the distance and continue to wait, face down on the floor.

The all-clear sounds, and, as soon as I get back up it changes back to "Rocket attack, rocket attack, rocket attack." We look at one another, slightly confused.

"You think the operators just put his coffee on the wrong button?" I say.

The next impact tells us this isn't the case and we are indeed under attack again. It's another salvo, as another couple of impacts come just seconds behind the first one. We all continue to wait on the floor, me with my face back in my smelly trainers. A few minutes later, the all-clear sounds again. We pause this time instinctively as what just happened was unusual and may happen again. Our instinct is correct.

"Rocket attack, rocket attack, rocket attack," sounds the alarm again, as the radar picks up another incoming salvo.

"Fuck," mutters Tosh.

This time it's only a single impact, but it's so close we feel the shockwave, which makes the building shake as it passes through. "Fuuuuuuck," says Tosh again, but this time considerably louder.

Under the unusual circumstances, we decide we should all stay on the floor. The tannoy announces the all-clear again, and further announcements regarding the movement in various sectors tell us that there are now unexploded ones somewhere on the base. "It must be the end of their fiscal year," I say. "They have to get rid of excess rockets so that they don't get any budget cuts for next year."

Just as we place our arses on my hard sofa, the alarm sounds again. This time we all get down with the quick reaction that we should always have. Another salvo of impacts interrupts the rocket attack announcement.

Number one is close, number two is closer. "Here we.." is all I manage to say just as number three detonates. It's the closest one yet. The violence of its shockwave is more pronounced, and I feel as if I am momentarily lifted off the floor. Or maybe the floor drops by an inch while I remain hanging in space. Either way, we hear the building flex around us as the shockwave passes through, and I am tremendously relieved that it doesn't collapse on top of us. Somehow it remains standing as it strains with the passing wave. I'm hoping this might have fixed some of the squeaking doors.

"Jesus Christ," says Joe. "They're hammering us tonight."

"You think we've done something to annoy them?" I reply.

"Maybe they're annoyed at the referee's decision during the match between the ANA and the Polish engineers," says a muffled Tosh.

The all-clear sounds again, but we all remain where we are, expecting another round. After a good ten minutes it seems that the barrage is over and we slowly get up. As I brush the dust off the front of me, I declare that I need to do more sweeping up. We wander out into the corridor and are met by the others of the block, who are all looking as dazed as I'm sure we look to them.

There's another round of attacks just after midnight. I think the guy cutting the fuse on that batch of rockets must have got his imperial and metric measurements a bit mixed up.

KAF ATLO SITREP
week ending 25/04/2012

▶ The enemy continue playing their peculiar game of darts, using us as the dartboard. They must have a new player on the team as they are consistently scoring 180.

▶ At the recent KAF cup football tournament, our joint Army and RAF team were runners-up in a respectable 12th place. Out of 12 teams.

Monday 30th

The evenings since the big attack have been quiet, which is welcome as I wake as normal after a good nights' sleep. I say "quiet" as there is nothing especially quiet about waking up in a massive airbase in Afghanistan. I walk zombie-like for the morning's ritual of washing in the ablutions with their off-white plastic fittings, which were now taking on a mouldy shade of green with hints of more green. They look like our five-a-side team.

As soon as I sit down in the office, I am suddenly overcome by a feeling of not-feeling-quite-right. I am scrolling through the emails that had come through in the night, and I become conscious that I am struggling to keep up my concentration, as I now keep focusing on how "this not feeling quite right" is not quite a right feeling. Joe is lounging in the fire risk chair, busy reading the Daily Mail from eight months ago, and must have noticed my aura of not feeling right. "You alright, Staff?" he says, while not looking up from the paper as he reads an article about how immigrants give you cancer.

"I've felt better," I say, while arching my back in a stretch and simultaneously scratching my head and rubbing my fairly unkempt mop of hair. I only had a shower twenty minutes ago, and already my hair has the same composition as wire wool due to the dust. "Fuck this," I announce. "I'm going back to bed for a few hours. If the Taliban or the Queen turns up, just hold them off with your gun until I come back."

"The perks of being the boss, eh, Staff."

"Well, young Joe, maybe just maybe, one day, if - and it's a big if - you climb up through the ranks of the British Army and you find yourself in charge of a bunch of idiots while serving in a shithole, you'll cast your mind back to this day and think that that Staff Lee was an outstanding leader, led by example, and was more switched on than the national grid."

"Like as soon as you felt a bit rough, you fucked right off leaving the Lance Corporal in charge of the entire movement's hub for KAF, overloading him, bringing the internal flights to a crashing halt, thus undoing years of counter-insurgency operations and putting ISAF on the back foot, which meant their mission in Afghanistan failed and the world was plunged into a dark age."

"You'll go a long way," I say, as I vanish through the door.

I've been back in KAF since November and I put this 'under the weather' feeling down to the dust, dirt, water, filth, Yanks, flies, smells, endless barrage of stupid questions, etc. As I lie on my bed, I doze on-and-off for a few hours, sometimes waking to find myself sweating. The late April midday sun means we are now at about the same temperature of an unusually hot British summer. I listen to the constant noises that sound different from the evening's constant noises for some strange reason - the man with his hammer still hitting the pipe, the aircraft taking off with full power, the drone of hundreds of generators dotted around the camp, the growl of the endless procession of armoured vehicles passing by on the near road. I have this image in my head that they are the same twenty vehicles driving around the airbase all day long, with drivers working shifts. It could be a decision from high up for the benefit of the locals who were employed on the camp who no doubt pass on what they see to the Taliban. Is it to give the impression that we have thousands of these vehicles with a view to making them change their minds and not go back to growing drugs?

The general feeling of being unwell is slowly getting worse, and lying down, trying to sleep, is just making me focus on it more and more. Not being very well medically trained, apart from putting large field dressings on unwilling volunteers pretending to have gunshot wounds, I decide to have a poke around my belly. I don't know what I am looking for, but as soon as I feel a sharp pain as I prod my fingers in the area of my appendix, and I think, "Oh, bollocks."

I was led to believe that appendicitis is normally something that happens in your younger years. I remember when I was young a few school friends having theirs removed. My brother had had his removed in a Russian hospital at the age of 43 and, due to complications, mainly their inability to identify the symptoms, he had nearly died. The surgeon felt so bad about it afterwards that he gave back the bribe my brother had paid for preferential treatment. I am 41 and in a strange country, so I accept that my time has come too for a spot of appendix removal. By now, the pain is becoming more severe and getting dressed is a bit more of a struggle now. I have to stop after every dressing movement to rest from the pain. One leg in the trousers and rest, then the other and rest again, with a bit of panting and sweat now forming on my brow. I try to do up my trousers but my lower abdomen has become quite sensitive so I have to leave the button undone. At least I can leave my shirt over the top, so as not to look a sex pest, or fat, or a fat sex pest. Putting my shirt on is akin to doing some minor upper-body exercises after a long period of inactivity. All the time, I'm thinking that this will be the end of my tour. I will probably be medically evacuated back to the UK, and Joe will have to sort all my gear out. Another SNCO will have to be found from somewhere to come and cover my post. I am facing the possibility of some minor surgery, hopefully, without complications, that is going to put me out of action for a while and my thoughts are solely focused on what an inconvenience this will be to everyone else. Bloody Army indoctrination.

I shuffle down to the Medical Centre to see if I can find a medic to get some sympathy from. In the DFAC during feeding time, there are normally more medics than Yanks. But today in the place where they should congregate it's more like the Mary Celeste. I plonk my backside on a plastic chair in the waiting room facing the reception desk, waiting for some help to appear. The most comfortable position for me by now is to lean forward with my elbows supported on my thighs, which I hope gives the illusion of being really ill and not just a normal malingering soldier. After about ten minutes, help arrives, in the shape of a young medic with a shaven head coming in through the back door. He's holding a cup of tea in one hand, and is finishing off a conversation with someone out of view with the words, "It just popped open and that was that." Before the door closes behind him, he flicks a cigarette butt back outside the door with his free hand. As soon as he sees me he goes, "Ooh, I'll be with you in a minute." He goes looking through some filing cabinets and flicks through the thick files one at a time. Now and again he'll stop and pull a file out, turn his head to one side to read the name, pause for a second, and say, "You're fucked," before dropping the file back in its place.

"So what's the matter with you then, Staff?" he says, sounding like I've interrupted his afternoon plans.

I want to reply, "I'm feeling brilliant. In fact, I was hoping you'd have something that will make me feel like shit?"

Instead, I just whimper, "I think I have appendicitis."

Before I know it, I'm sitting in the doctor's office, and while he is taking my temp and blood pressure my head starts spinning, my hearing becomes dull, and cold sweat dribbles off my head down over my temples and into my eyebrows.

I manage to say, "I think I'm going to pass..." and then it all goes black.

I surface from the blackness sluggishly. As my brain restarts, after its unplanned shutdown, my thoughts start to reorganise themselves as I have a conversation with myself in my head.

"Where am I?" I think, with my eyes still shut.

"Oh yeah, I'm on tour in Afghanistan. Am I up in Kabul with the Yanks? Nah, that was the last tour." I give a mental sigh of relief.

"I'm in Kandahar, I've been here for a while, which means the tour is nearly over." I treated myself to a little smile.

"Are you still in pain?" says the doc, in a muffled tone, mis-interpreting my smile as a painful wince.

"Doc?" I think, in surprise, while raising my eyebrows, and immediately I presume the worst.

"Oh, bollocks," says my brain as I realise I am lying down with a doctor attending to me.

I'm now desperately trying to think about what has happened to me. Was I run over by one of the awful drivers of the Belgian Army.[54] Did I walk into a spinning Herc propeller? Was I blown up by a goat herder's lucky hit with a rocket?

I try to open my eyes, but it's far too bright so I raise my hand to cover them. I roll my head to the right and look out of one half-open eye. I comprehend that I am in the medical centre, and I can see the chair that I was sitting in. Suddenly, all the memories from before passing out drop into place, and I treat myself to another smile as I am now mildly overcome that I am not horrendously mangled up, but just possibly having a bout of appendicitis.

"Are you still feeling pain, Staff?" His voice is still muffled

54 Belgium somehow produces some of the worst drivers in Western Europe. Every time I have driven in Belgium I have had a near-death vehicular experience and their military are just as bad at driving, if not better at being bad.

and again misdiagnosing my smile for discomfort.

I'm now conscious that I am lying down on his examination table with my shirt undone. My arm, still with the thing for taking blood pressure attached around it, hangs off the edge of his table. As I become a little bit more awake I realise he is asking me something again.

"Can you hear me, Staff?" he says quite clearly now, sounding as if I've just taken out some earplugs. I manage to give him the thumbs-up sign.

He starts poking around my stomach, and when he presses on my tender swollen appendix, I make the actions associated with "Ouch, that really fucking hurts," and he asks, "Does that hurt?"

I do think, "What do you fucking think?" but I can only manage an "Urrrrghhh."

Doc drives me down personally in his own battered white pick-up to the American hospital on base where I'm to be admitted. You wouldn't get that service on the NHS. Driving sick soldiers isn't his forte, as he manages to find all the big potholes between the medical centre and the hospital. In his defence, there were so many potholes that KAF was one big hole, and it made you wonder if the engineers used high explosives to grade the roads. I'm sitting in the passenger seat, holding on to the little God-knows-why-it's-there handle above the door with both hands, hoping it will help me steady myself and lessen the pain. As he bounces the pick-up out of one pothole and into the next one, I say, "Argh," and he says immediately, "sorry."

"Argh!" I cry.

"Sorry," he says in an apologetic tone, while pulling a face as if he's the one in pain.

"Argh!"

"Sorry."

"Argh!"

"Sorry."

"Sorry."

"Eh?" I say, as we drop into another large pothole.

"I just thought I'd pre-empt that one," he says.

"Argh!"

We are now out of sync.

I'm handed into the care of the Yanks and as I'm taken away down the corridor I glance back to see the doc who reminded me of a parent waving his child goodbye on their first day of school. I'm guided into a room where the nurse tells me in a Deep South deadpan accent to strip off and put one of those ludicrous gowns on with my arse hanging out. She attaches a band around my wrist with my details on and asks.

"Is your date of birth 9/2/70?"

"Nope it's 2/9/70." I correct her.

"Strange, it says the second of September 1970 here," she adds as she looks at her clipboard.

"Yeah, that's correct."

"That's what I said first, soldier," she says, with a look of mild fury, as if she were at the end of a very long shift and I was doing this on purpose to annoy her. I just try my best to look sick.

I'm then escorted by two extremely tall and well-built medics who look more like henchmen. I'm in no shape to run away if that's what they're worried about. It's all a bit mysterious, like a film, as I'm shown to a door which opens to the outside. Silently they beckon me to follow them across a concrete courtyard. As I do, I feel the sand and dust stick to my bare feet. The concrete is pretty hot, and I start to go "Oooh," and "ahh," as I do that monkey walk that you do when walking barefoot on uncomfortable surfaces. The afternoon wind isn't helping my attire preserve any semblance of my modesty, as it repeatedly tries to lift up my gown over my head. My reactions are still pretty sharp in keeping the front of the gown down, they're not as effective with the back bit, thus giving anyone within sight a fine view of my milky white buttocks. Still not too sure where we're going, and with me being politely British, I keep completely silent, playing along with their game. We approach a green shipping container that looks brand new, as it is devoid of any scratches, dents or rust. It's got lots of cables protruding from it, and air conditioning units bolted to the side that are whirring away. Unlike a normal shipping container, there is a door in the side of it. Henchman number one opens it and silently gestures with his hand for me to enter, while henchman number two stands just behind me giving the impression that he's ready to violently shove me through the door in case I get cold feet. There's no danger of that with this hot concrete underfoot. As I cross the threshold I have a TARDIS moment, as it's huge inside. I also have a "Thank God I'm not going to be violently interrogated by their psychopathic criminal boss" moment, as I realise it's a just a type of MRI scanner.

A short unmilitary-looking man with dark thick bushy hair and a "Noo Joisey" accent, who could be the love child of Groucho Marx and Tattoo from Fantasy Island steers me towards the scanner. He's the first remotely medical-looking person that I have seen since entering the hospital, as he's wearing a blue scrub uniform. He's also the first person to explain what they are going to do. "We are going to inject you

253

with a contrast fluid containing iodine which will give a metallic taste in you mouth and an urge to pee. Please don't pee."

He continues to explain that I am going to be inserted into the high contrast scanner. This will enable them to see the blood and stuff flowing around my body and will hopefully show up any anomalies. As I lie there, the medical orderly hooks me up with various cables and leads. He finishes off by tapping my arm looking for a vein and, without hesitation, inserts a massive needle into my arm. Immediately I feel a cold sensation travel up my arm and the metallic taste in my gob materialises, followed by the sudden impulse to get up, go out the door and around the back of the building for a quick leak. They push me into the scanner and then retire to their computers while telling me to remain completely still.

After 20 minutes, we are all done and I'm starting to shiver in the cold air-conditioned container. I've now got a stiff back and, with the potential appendicitis, I have to grunt and groan on the stretcher until someone takes the hint that I need help in getting up. With henchman number one's assistance I manage to flash my arse to Groucho Marx jr as I roll off the stretcher. I'm glad to get back outside into the warm dusty air with my pair of personal henchmen. I haven't had a haircut for a while now and, as I haven't uttered a word, I wonder if they think I'm an Afghani and, therefore, a potential enemy.

I'm taken back to where we had come from earlier, shown to the ward and put in a bed. I thank the hired muscle for keeping me safe and not letting me run off into the desert.

"You're welcome, sir, have a nice day now," says henchman number two, without cracking a smile or showing any emotion. As they depart I guess that they're now off to rough up the local, who I buy fags from for Dave Davidson, for not paying their protection money.

The RAF doc appears. It's good to see a familiar face, I think, and he stands in the corner listening to somebody, who I presume is his American counterpart. He looks at the floor, scratching his chin with one hand, and is nodding his head frequently as he listens patiently to what he is saying. They are out of earshot, so I can't hear what they are saying, but when two doctors are together and one is talking I accept it to be bad news.

My doc eventually comes over to me and smiles nervously.

"Well, your tour is over, Staff."

"Riiiight," I acknowledge slowly, "I was due to finish in two weeks anyway."

"Oh, goodo," he replies suddenly, perking up as if I was going to take the news of a short tour badly.

"Well they aren't sure it is appendicitis, and they haven't the ability here to test your appendix to see if that is what it is, but they are going to remove it anyway."

While this conversation is going on, a medic on the other side of the bed is trying unsuccessfully to insert the needle for the drip into the back of my left hand.

"They are going to operate on you this evening," he adds

I look to my left and see blood coming from my hand, running down my fingers and dripping on the floor. "You'll be in overnight at least," says the doc, as if trying to distract me from the carnage that is going on the other side of the bed. "I'll be back in the morning to see how you are."

He departs and I look at the butcher of Kandahar Hospital who has finally got the cannula well and truly buried in my hand and is now mopping up my blood.

Everyone disappears and I'm left in the room looking up at the bright buzzing white fluorescent lights. Now that the noise of the staff is removed, and with just the lights to concentrate on, I notice the buzz starting to reverberate. There are no windows, and I guess it must be about 7pm. I can hear inaudible voices a way down one of the corridors and the clip-clop of someone in hard shoes walking on the pristine polished vinyl floor. I'm left like this for about an hour and feel myself start to cool down in the chilly ward. Although I didn't notice at the time I am now glad that someone has placed a blanket over my feet and legs. I pull it up and my feet pop out the bottom and are exposed to the cold air. My toes are starting to feel cold already. The blanket is folded in half so now have to decide which part of me is going to remain warm and which part I'm going to sacrifice to the cold. I then have a minor brainwave, if I choose to unfold it, thus reducing the overall thermal protection by 50%, at least my tootsies gain 50% of something to keep them warm. I realise that I am quite bored.

Finally the time comes for me to go into theatre. A few medics in their blue uniforms arrive and wheel me off down the corridor. I see more staff on my horizontal journey in their immaculate blue outfits and I suddenly find it rather strange and a little bit comforting after months of only seeing everyone in only shades of green, brown, and dusty uniforms. It's like a small journey back to a little pocket of normality for a while, even if I am on my back hooked up to a drip about to undergo surgery.

I'm placed next to the operating table, and, before I can say, "Would you lick a Taliban's flip-flop for $10?" hands are grabbing my ankles and more slide under me supporting my shoulders and the small of my back. I hear someone say, "Ready? OK and one, two, three, move." I'm speedily transferred over to the operating table in a swift well-choreographed moment. I feel that I am now just a passenger along for the ride. They are all busying around me and I feel a plastic click through the cannula that is still in the back of my hand. A face with a surgical mask and a soothing voice appears upside down above me and says, "We are going to put you under now. You'll feel a cold sensation moving up your arm, so if can you count to ten for me that would be just super?"

I nod in agreement and start counting.

"One, two, three..." and nothing.

What feels like a few seconds later, I start to hear sounds but it's still quite black as my eyes will just not open. I'm aware that I have now been moved to another room and I am no longer lying completely horizontal but I'm slightly propped up in a bed. It feels like a hangover on steroids, my mouth is drier than the desert outside, and I start to shiver. Somebody puts an already-warmed soft blanket on me and almost lovingly ensures that I'm covered from my toes right up to my neck. The atmosphere in this room has a calm and sedated feel to it. There are people talking quietly and even the buzz of the lights sounds as if they have mufflers fitted on them. The medic obviously notices I'm awake and says.

"How you feeling, man?"

I can only manage a pathetic murmur, because my vocal cords don't work after having what feels like my mouth was swilled out with extremely absorbent sand.

"OK, so you're in the recovery room right now, and I'll be monitoring you for the next hour and if you need anything then you just holler and let me know," he says.

I make my best hollering grunt to let him know I could do with a sip of water. "OK, buddy, you just lay there and relax," he replies to my pitiful holler.

My brain is fully awake but my body isn't as the anaesthetic is still coursing around my veins. All I can do right now is roll my head a bit from left to right. I try to open my eyelids but it feels like that they have a ten-ton weight attached to them and I don't have the strength to overcome the gravity that's keeping them firmly shut. I assent to my condition and decide to just carry on lying still in my darkness. The blanket is lovely, soft and warm. Another one is added and I immediately feel the heat on my body, which is soothing. I again attempt to open my eyes, and it is still not happening. I wonder why I'm bothering as I doubt there will be much worth looking at. A minute later I'm bored and try again. Several attempts later, I manage to crack an eyelid open and immediately shut it in reaction to the super-bright florescent light that I have been placed under.

I am moved in my bed from the recovery room to a new ward by an orderly. By now I have the strength to keep one eye half-open so I can observe my journey through the hospital corridors. All I can see is the ceiling whizzing by, which reminds me of films when the main character is rushed into the hospital and pushed at speed down the corridor to the operating theatre. The ward doesn't have windows, but it does have eight empty beds with four against each wall. They place me in the corner and push the existing empty bed out of the way. It makes a clang as it bumps into the other one. The orderly makes some small talk with a nurse about the Denver Broncos getting their asses whooped and then departs. Now I'm in the nurse's charge and she takes my temperature and pulse, checks my drip, and says, "Do you need to pee?"

I shake my head, and, before I can try to ask for some water, she wheels a table in front of me with a plastic water jug and cup and says, "Would you like a sip of water?"

"FUUUUCCCCKK YYYEEEESSSS," I scream in my head.

She holds the cup to my lips and finally I relive my parched mouth. The relief as moisture is reintroduced back into my gob is just exceptional. I take a few more sips and finally manage a comprehensible "Thank you," to which she smiles and says, "You're most welcome, sir."

Later on, I am able to hold the cup to my mouth as I sip some more. Of all the times to go down the wrong hole it chooses now. I cough, and my sides explode into a ball of pain. I feel like someone is cutting me open with a serrated knife and I can feel every cut as each individual tooth rips my flesh, thus prompting me to say, "Fucking hell!"

The nurse looks over, smiles, and says, "I just love your accent." Undisturbed by my profanity, she offers me some painkillers. I work out that it must be late evening as the operation couldn't have taken too long, but, with no windows and only bright lights, I am not entirely sure what time of day it is. I'm left in the corner with the ceiling lights on in my face and I start to doze. I am vaguely aware of the nurse coming to check on me infrequently as I float in and out of a disturbed sleep.

Sometime during the night, if it is indeed night, someone else is wheeled in. All I can see is them laying on their side with their back to me covered in a blanket. The new casualty has someone with him and he is dressed all in white. Through my groggy eyes I presume he is a doctor, but then realise he is a local wearing the long gown with grey waistcoat and Pakol hat perched on his head that is the attire of the locals. The nurse talks quietly to the man in white who nods as the information is passed to him. Once the nurse is finished he puts his hand on his friend's shoulder, bends down, and talks gently in his ear relaying the information. The guy in the bed gives out a soft moan in response.

I lie there looking up at the annoying buzzing bright lights shining in my face and I feel like I'm about to be interrogated East German-style. Are they are doing some sort of physiological conditioning that will make me pause to think next time I'm not well and considering going to a doctor, or are they punishing me to break the boredom. The poor guy two beds down has been moaning consistently for the last few hours while his friend, still sat in the chair, ignores him, sleeping soundly, and snoring loudly. All that is missing is some death metal cranked up to 11 on the volume.

> *A bar in downtown Milwaukee during the Kandahar Role 3 end of tour party a few months later:*
> "So we have this idiot Brit come in after an emergency appendectomy operation and I bet Gerry $10 that if I leave the lights on all night, put the local guy with chronic toothache a few beds down, and get Snoring Sammy the Duty Doctor to sleep in one of the chairs, he'll not complain once. I wanted to put the death metal on the hospital PA system but Chief Surgeon said no."

I'm starting to get really uncomfortable after lying in the same position for hours now. I try to move myself into a more bearable position, but the searing pain comes back with such a vengeance that it makes me think the painkillers are just placebos. I'm starting to feel abandoned and quite miserable.

British casualties for the month of April
3 killed & 10 wounded

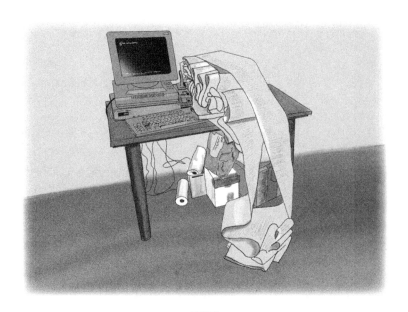

7
MAY 2012

Tuesday 1st

I LOOK UP through the window at what I thought was a part of the upper blast wall painted black and realise that I have been looking at the night sky all this time. I can now make out the first faint red and orange colours appearing in the clear sky as the sun starts to make its entrance. I don't feel so miserable at the prospect of a new day. The nurse also notices that the sun is coming up and switches the lights off on one of her infrequent visits to see if we are still here. The relief of having the bright lights finally turned off is overwhelming and I manage to get some more sleep in the dim morning light. I am soon disturbed again by the mounting noises in the corridor as the hospital wakes up and the normal day-to-day work starts.

I am served breakfast and it's a greasy piece of flat round meat, NOS, with some cold toast. It's good to see that the culinary disappointment is kept up for the sick and injured. I pick at it, even though I haven't eaten since yesterday's breakfast, as my appetite is like the Afghan department for the environment: non-existent. Nothing like a bit of appendicitis to shift a bit of weight I think, cheaper than Weight Watchers too.

A doctor in his blue outfit appears at the bottom of my bed, and I presume he has come to see how I am doing. I presume correctly.

"So I hope you're being looked after by my staff, err, Staff."

He says that last bit slowly and with a slight look of confusion on his face as he reads my rank on the clipboard. "The operation went well, but, as I mentioned last night, we have no way of testing the appendix to see if it was the problem, so we will presume that is what it was."

I nod in agreement, as in this situation I'm not going to ask for a second opinion.

He comes around to my side and removes the sheet and says, "Can I take a quick look?"

I oblige by lifting my gown up to reveal a small rectangular dressing with a couple of dots of blood that have soaked through. It's the first time I've seen it.

He sits on the side of the bed and peels the dressing back. Thankfully the adhesive is weak and I have been shaved so I'm not screaming in agony as my belly hairs are pulled out of my skin one by one.

"Looking good," he says. "We glued you up, as stitches are so last year, and you'll have a neater-looking scar."

I strain my neck and new wound to have a look. The cut is about five inches long, and I can see it's covered all around in a shiny film, which I deduce is the superglue.

"You'll be in a bit of pain for a few days but we'll give you some painkillers to take away with you."

"That's too bad. I was hoping to go to the gym this afternoon," I say.

"Eh, er, no." He looks at me puzzled, then the penny drops and a smile appears. "Ahh, you and your crazy British sense of humour."

I smile back at him.

"I would try to take it easy for a few days, and definitely no heavy lifting for at least three weeks." He goes back into serious mode, "Did I hear right that you are at the end of your tour anyway?" I gladly announce, "Just a couple of weeks away then I'm out of here. Last tour ever as I retire next year, yippee."

"Well, thank you for your service, sir, and I wish you all the best for the future and hope you stay safe for the rest of your time here."

He pats me on my shoulder, gets up, and adds, "You'll be discharged this morning as we need the beds later this morning." He pulls a face which tells me there has been another load of soldiers or civilians mangled up in the conflict. "I'll ask the nurse to get your clothes."

The day shift nurse turns up with my uniform in a back bin bag and announces, "OK Mr English Soldier, you're all done here." She drops it on the bed and buggers off. I'm still attached to the drip and I wonder if I can take it with me. Before I decide how much I'm going to sell a genuine drip and its stand from a war zone, she returns and unhooks me from it. As the cannula's oversized needle is pulled from under the skin in the back of my hand, it feels good to have a foreign object removed from my body, and I get a sense that I am returning to a semblance of normality.

I swing my legs off the bed and wince in pain. I get dressed at the speed of a snail, taking breaks in-between to catch my breath and prepare for the next bout of pain. Finally, I have on my trousers and my shirt, which are both unbuttoned. The bed is far too high for me to be able to bend down to put my boots on, so I have to transfer to a chair on the other side of the ward. I start to shuffle across the room with my boots in one hand and my other hand holding my trousers up. I have to let go of something to reach for the end of a bed to steady myself. I choose unwisely and, as I let go of my trousers, they instantly succumb to gravity and fall down around my ankles.

Of course, the nurse walks in at this point, because that's how things happen to me when I'm in a vulnerable position.

She tuts and says, "What yer doin', mister?" as she comes over to me and starts pulling my trousers up for me. "Why don't you just sit in that there chair and put your boots on." and she guides me backwards into the chair. Leaning down to put my boots on is the most painful thing I've experienced so far until I lean down to tie my laces and realise it's now the second most painful thing.

Finally, I'm dressed in as good a state as can be expected for someone who underwent surgery 12 hours ago. I manage to button up my shirt, but all I can do with my trousers is to pull the zip up in the hope that it'll keep them around my waist. I leave my shirt out so that it will hide my unbuttoned trousers and prevent funny looks from anyone I should meet. I'm sweating buckets and feeling quite nauseous by now, so I have a little rest in the chair. I then venture out into the corridor, walking like a zombie with two bad knees and an overdue hip replacement. I turn right and hear the nurse say, "Other way, soldier."

I make it to the reception and I have no idea how I am going to get back to the British compound. I know where I am but it's over a mile away and I don't feel like a nice relaxing walk right now. I ask the guy behind the counter, who is chewing gum, "Could you call the British medical centre for me, I need a lift back to our compound?"

"Sure can, sir," he replies reassuringly. "What's the number?"

I give him the extension number that I think is for the medical centre. He picks up the phone ready to dial and says, "OK, sir, but what system is that on and what's the code?"

"Bollocks," I mutter. "I don't know it."

I'm now pulling a face while thinking that I'm not looking forward to this impending walk.

"Can you call Roshan phones from here?" Roshan is the Afghani phone network that serves our duty mobile.

"Sure can, sir, but I have to go via the operator in the US."

I write the duty number down for him, explain my predicament, and add that if I pass out on my walk back I'll end up back here and we will be having the same conversation tomorrow.

He pushes a quick succession of numbers on the phone and is dead still. After a minute he says. "Good day to you ma'am, it's Sergeant Hutchinson from the Role Three medical facility here at Kandahar airbase. I'd like to place a call to a Roshan number, please."

He says, "Yes, ma'am," several times, followed by, "Yes, ma'am, it's official business, ma'am." He throws in a few 'uhs' and a short 'mmmm' then passes the phone to me.

I can hear it ringing faintly through the earpiece. It keeps ringing and I'm thinking, "For fuck's sake, pick it up."

The ringing stops and I think that we have been cut off. then I hear Norts's voice. It's quite faint, giving the illusion that she is a million miles away and not down the road.

"ATLO Kandahar, Lance Corporal Norton speaking, sir."

"Norts, you lazy twat, it's me," speaking louder than normal to take into account the poor line quality that comes from the electric signal having to go to the other side of the world and back again.

"Aha, Staff, we thought you were dead," she says, laughing out loud. "I've sold all your gear for $2 and I told David Cameron that you had given your gun to the Taliban in protest against changes to your pension."

"Well you better un-sell it because unfortunately for you

I'm alive, I have risen from the grave and decided that you're a massive bellend. Now come and pick me up from the hospital before I place my boot up your arse and put that you're the shittest Mover ever in the history of the RLC on your tour report."

"I'll be down as soon as I've finished my latest book. It's War & Peace," comes the still-laughing reply. I hand the phone back to Sergeant Hutchinson, thank him, and shuffle over to a seat. The poor guy looks in mild shock and highly confused by what he has just heard. As he puts the phone down slowly whilst gawking at me, his chewing gum falls from his motionless open mouth. I suspect there's a female operator somewhere in the US in the same condition.

After thirty minutes Norts finally walks through the door of the hospital, sees me slouching in a plastic chair, and, with the expected sympathy for a fellow soldier in pain and discomfort, immediately bursts out laughing.

"Oh, God, this is hilarious," she adds, "you were taken out by your dodgy appendix?"

I pull a face and ask her, "What took you so long?"

"I had a call from David Cameron asking how you are."

I prepare myself for the searing pain as I get ready to stand up. I pull a face full of pain and I slowly rise to my feet.

"You alright there, Staff?" says Norts, still giggling.

"Just dandy, considering I've had a doctor's scalpel make a medium-sized cut in my lower abdomen no more than twelve hours ago."

I follow her out to the where the pick-up is parked.

"I'll drive if you want today, Staff?"

"Fuck off," I say, through gritted teeth.

I open the passenger door and for the first time, I notice that the seat is quite high which will require some effort. Normally I'm just jumping in and out but now I am conscious of every time I will have to use my stomach muscles. It's a bit like how whenever you cut your finger you then start stubbing it on lots of things while going about your daily business.

I grab hold of the handle above the door to heave myself up before sliding into the seat. I am just waiting to feel a tearing sensation as the superglue holding me together starts coming apart. Once I'm in I feel like I'm going to puke up. Norts jumps in the driver seat, takes one look at me, and says, "Fuck me, you've gone a bit white in the old fizzog[55]." Her laughing finally becomes a bit restrained.

On the short drive back to the compound Norts manages to find and drive through every pothole and so it starts again.

"Argh."

"Sorry."

"Argh."

"Sorry."

I ask her to drop me off at the medical centre and wait, as the 100-metre walk back to the accommodation would take the effort of a long forced route march right now. I shuffle through the door, and the medic remembers me from yesterday. "Ah, Staff, you're back?!" he says with surprise. "I'll let the doctor know you're here."

I strain myself to get into the plastic chair. The doc appears and beckons me into his office. I mutter a profanity under my breath as I strain once again to get up.

"So, Staff, I bet you feel pretty rough right now?"

"Just a tad."

---

55   Fizzog: face.

"Can I have a look?" he enquires.

I strain myself onto his examination table and pull up my top. He peels back the dressing, which by now has more blood on it and is losing its adhesiveness.

"Oooh," he exclaims, "they glued you up, I see. That'll leave a less impressive scar." This comment makes me think that, if he had done it, for a more convincing appearance he would have sealed me up with some hairy rope or the huge staples from the type of stapler with which your teacher used to pin your artwork to the wall.

"It works for me," I add. I ask when I can be expected to be evacuated back to the UK, and he updates me that, because I was operated on in a properish hospital, which is a sterile location and not a dusty old tent that's a field hospital, then there's no need to evacuate me. I am somewhat relieved and disappointed at the same time by this news. I'm relieved that I will not have to worry about the logistics of getting my stuff back and to see the end of the tour through with the team. I'm disappointed that I'll have to recover a long way from home in not the best of environments.

Again, he states the bloody obvious that I need to take it easy for a few days and not do any heavy lifting. I can't wait to take it easy and stop all this standing up and sitting down.

He gives me some more painkillers and tells me to come back in a few days.

As I strain for one last time, I finally get to lie down on my bed and give a big sigh of relief as I can relax. Still wearing my uniform, I unbutton my shirt and unzip my trousers further down so that there is no pressure anywhere around my stomach. I pull up my T-shirt, exposing the thick bloodied dressing, and, ensuring that it's still in place, I finally relax while the pain from the morning's straining slowly wanes. The experiences of the last 24 hours replay through my head and I think to myself, "Did that just actually happen?" I start to drift off to sleep. I am not aware that I'm asleep until I am disturbed by a noise outside, as the daily routine on camp carries on. Again, I drift off only to be woken, again, by another noise, and the cycle continues. This carries on for a while, then the rocket alarm sounds, and this time I come up from a deep comatose state to a high level of consciousness and make an outburst that would be worthy of an award.

"Oh, just fuck off, will you?!"

I look to my body armour on the floor across the room and think that trying to put that on would count as heavy lifting. I decide to remain on my bed because by the time I would have managed to get myself up and across the room the rockets would have found their targets and it would have all been a complete waste of bloody time and effort.

I continue to sleep lightly until the late afternoon. I hear my door open a few times throughout the day but I am feeling too exhausted to open my eyes and crank my head up to see who it is. I presume it's Norts, Joe, or someone else checking up on me, and I am grateful for whoever left a bottle of water next to me. I must have looked a right sight laying on my bed with my boots still on, trousers unzipped, shirt open, T-shirt pulled up to my chest and a big, thick, white cotton dressing on my stomach.

I start to feel a chill as day turns to night, and, after a lot of straining, pain, sweating, swearing, and resting, I manage to take my boots and uniform off. I slip under the lovely warm covers and continue to sleep.

Wednesday 2nd

I'm awakened by a noise, not otherwise specified, and as I opened my eyes I notice that it was now morning. The sun is breaking through the gaps in the bent and missing slats of the dusty Venetian blind that hang over my window like an unfurled impromptu protest banner dangling from an occupied government office. The shards of light are very visible in the exceedingly dusty air, and, by the steep angle that the rays are pointing towards the floor, I know it's late in the morning.

I start to stretch, and straight away the searing pain hits me as I feel the glue and my cut wanting to tear open. The big morning stretch will have to wait for another day. I pop a pill to take my mind off the pain.

As I lie there thinking, "Now what?" Norts, as if she has been waiting, knocks on the door and comes in. "Morning, Staff." She has in her hand a Styrofoam box and polystyrene cup that I know will hold some disappointment. "I thought you might be hungry, so I brought you some grub."

I realise that in the last few days I have hardly eaten and, as if my brain has suddenly appreciated this, it sends a message to my belly to switch on the starving desires.

"Norts, you're a star," I say chirpily to her.

"A mon-star," comes her quick reply.

"Nope, because you're best viewed through thick dark glasses from a few million miles away."

She laughs, hands me the box, and adds, "I gobbed on your toast by the way." As I munch on the exquisite cold toast, washed down with some tepid cofftea, I ask her if there has been any trouble at t'mill while I was away. Unsurprisingly, the British Army's operations in Afghanistan have continued to function during my absence. She informed the chain of command of my medical predicament and I could hear the

271

laughing all the way to Bastion, back to the UK, and then outwards to all the Mover detachments around the world. It was comforting knowing that the Movement detachment in the Falkland Islands were aware of my suffering.

I have to hobble to the shower for a much-needed de-gunge, as I'm feeling a bit grotty. Feeling clean again perks me up a bit as I can wash away all the smells of the hospital. The doc gave me some waterproof dressings for use in the shower, which I apply over the cut. These have industrial-strength adhesive and pulling them off, even with my shaved belly, brings a tear to my eye

I spend the day in bed looking at the ceiling and reading the few books that I have. I concentrate on the multitude of sounds from around the camp as it buzzes with life and constant expansion. Through this relentless din, I can make out people singing, and the man still repeatedly hitting the metal pipe with his hammer. I try a stretch and stop instantly when I feel the pain rising. It's a long day, only broken up by when Norts brings me more disappointment. This time it's cold noodles, with a cheese and ham toastie that has been toasted by a hairdryer. The light outside fades and the noises changes from the concoction of every racket ever devised by humans to the gentle low hum of the generators powering the hairdryers in the cookhouse. The pipe-hitting man is still at it, though. The overwhelming urge to stretch is constant, as my body feels like it has been compressed but every time the pain puts a stop to it.

Hamish and Tosh turn up just to laugh at me.

"You're a twat," adds Hamish, devoid of sympathy.

"You're a twat, too," I reply quickly.

"Get well soon, my little hero," says Tosh.

"Go and catch some criminals," I shout at them as they

leave, "and I hope your next shit is a hedgehog."

The door slams and I can hear them giggling as they walk down the corridor.

Thursday 3rd

I wake early, Joe arrives with the daily disappointment, he leaves, I continue to sleep, read, stare at the ceiling, and think about getting out of the Army and what life will be like after all of this. The day drags as I keep staring at my watch, which, in turn, makes the minutes grind by at an even slower rate. I close my eyes and again my concentration turns to the sounds outside. Today I can make out some birdsong through the unceasing racket. The evening's excitement is the rocket alarm going off followed by a couple of crump sounds in the distance. I don't react, as it's just far too much effort.

Friday 4th

I wake just as the man whose job it is to hit the metal pipe with his hammer constantly for the next twelve hours starts his shift. Dawn is breaking and I feel like I am on the mend at long last. I try a stretch with the trepidation of tearing myself open. To my utter delight, I can. It's the best feeling in the world. I lie on my bed with my hands above my head and, with a bearable amount of pain, I can enjoy stretching out my body and uncompressing all of my stiff joints. I roll to one side and arch my back and, with my eyes closed in sheer bliss, I give out a long satisfying moan.

I have to get out of this room for my sanity so I declare myself fit enough to undertake a walk to the office. It's a lot easier to get dressed now but I'm still a bit too tender to be able to do up my trousers just yet. Thankfully, by leaving my shirt untucked, I can hide this while keeping up the scruffy appearance. I pick up my gun and pause with the words of the doc about no heavy lifting ringing through my head. I decide that I have to take it, not because the alert state is high and I may be required to wield my awesome amount of firepower, in the shape of thirty rounds, down on some naughty local, but more likely because someone will ask me where my gun is.

Gingerly, I make my way outside and start walking a bit more carefully than usual, as today I don't want to trip up over something and go rolling around in the dirt. Approaching the small downwards embankment that has caused me problems in the dark, I momentarily stop. In the light of day, this is now a potential major problem. Instinctively, I start walking down it taking tiny baby steps to ensure my boots are getting a good grip on the loose soil. To anyone watching, I mustn't look right in the head.

Finally, I'm at the door to the building, and it's a pretty stiff one to get open initially. Not wanting to overstrain myself, I turn around and lean backwards on the door using my weight to get it moving. If anyone had at that moment been coming out of the building via that door I would have gone straight onto my arse. The office door is a lot easier to open, and as I do so, I am met by the sight of Joe at the desk clicking on the computer while Hamish and Tosh are sitting in the comfy chairs, doing some synchronised magazine reading. As they all look up to see who has entered their domain they give out a simultaneous cheer.

"He has risen, praise the Lord!" shouts Hamish.

"Bloody hell, he's alive," says Norts.

"Aww, my little hero," adds Tosh, which makes Norts laugh out loud.

My response contains the words in no particular order, "yourselves", "go", and a third one that rhymes with "duck".

274

Tosh suggests that because it's Friday night we should take a drive down to the Boardwalk. After all, he does have a handful of Green Bean free coffee vouchers burning a hole in his pocket. We all cram into the coppers' pick-up. I get to ride shotgun because of my medical state. Tosh does the driving, and for some reason, doesn't manage to hit or drive through any potholes whatsoever.

"I see your superior RAF driving skills are managing to keep us out of the potholes," I point out and then say, "Argh," just in case anyway.

He turns to me and says, "What's up with you?"

"I'm conditioned to say it now, like Pavlov's dog."

"I'll find you some potholes if you want?"

"I'll find you some fist-induced pain if you want?"

With coffees donated by the generous but unaware American public, we find a spot to sit and watch the military procession of soldiers walking around and around the covered wooden walkway. It's mainly US soldiers with their M16s slung low on their backs. Two Spanish Military Policemen, both over six feet, saunter past, followed by a rabble of excited scruffy-looking soldiers talking in a Slavic-sounding accent. I notice the Bulgarian flag on their uniform. After the coffee, I start to feel a bit rough. My stomach is starting to hurt and not only where they operated on me but all over. As we head back to our compound in the dark I'm thinking that I may have to go and knock up the medics. I make it back to my room and by now I'm sweating a little. Before I take a trip to find a medic, I decide to pop to the toilet.

Fifteen minutes later I arise like a new man with the pain in my stomach completely gone. I'm several pounds lighter, and I now remember the doc mentioning constipation and then realise that I haven't had a crap in the last five days.

Saturday 5th

Tosh is departing for home in a few days, so we go for the first of several farewell coffees at various establishments. Each time he pleads poverty citing that because he's leaving he has spent all his US dollars.

A few days earlier we had helped our Australian counterpart by getting one of her high-ranking officers up to Kabul. The conversation had gone something like this:

— "Hi, guys, I'm really in need of a favour. Can you help me in getting someone really really important up to Kabul today?"

— "Yeah, no worries."

As a reward for pulling out all the stops, bending over backwards, and going beyond the call of duty she invites us all to the Australian compound that evening as they are having a bit of a knees-up.

It's a full house in the office this evening as Paul is back from his R&R and just about take over the night shift from Joe

As the complete ATLO KAF detachment are leaving the office, Tosh says, from his usual position of reading a paper while sitting down with his feet on the table, "Where are you losers off to?"

"You should already know. I thought you were a switched-on copper?" says Norts.

"I am. I'm just waiting for my secret informant to tell me," his gaze turns to Joe

"You've not paid me this month," he says, straight away.

"We've been invited to a party at the Aussie compound," I say to him.

"Were you not going to invite me?" he asks, with a sad look on his face.

"The invite says 'Strictly no twats,' I'm afraid."

We all look at him, sitting there on his own with his dated newspaper crumpled up on his lap, and It's quite sad.

"Awww, look at him, old Billy No Mates, sitting there all on his lonesome," says Paul.

"Oh come on, then," I say, feeling sorry for him and beckoning him to get up.

The compound is just a short walk for us, so we decide to take in the evening ambience, which is mainly jumping out the way of large armoured vehicles while coughing our guts up on their diesel fumes. We arrive at the compound, which is surrounded by the usual high concrete blast walls, with just one way in and one way out. There's no guard, gate, or barrier so we just wander on in. There's a bend around to the left on the dusty track, which is also lined with the same high blast walls. These block any views into the compound by anyone who may be passing on the road. We round the corner and are greeted with a sea of green grass. It's more than just an unkempt grassy patch, it's a square lawn about the size of a tennis court. Time and effort has been spent creating and looking after it. Its surface is flat, it's been lovingly mown, and the edges are trimmed and straight.

"Well, I didn't expect that," says Paul.

All over the well-manicured lawn are soldiers, in their unique Australian light green camouflage pattern uniforms, lying about in groups chatting. I can't help but notice that some are drinking what could be beer from cans. On the far side of the lawn someone with a pistol in a holster is playing about with a microphone stand, trying to get the correct height for an unseen singer. Behind him is a guitar leaning against an amplifier with some wires trailing off through a window of a small shed-like structure, which is the source of power.

We see our Aussie friend and wave to her. She waves back as she hurries over to us. "Hey, I'm so glad you could all make it," she says excitedly. "You guys really helped me out in getting my important passenger up to Kabul today."

"Well it wasn't easy but we like to try and help out where we can," I say pulling a face looking at Joe, Paul, and Norts. They all look at the floor to hide their giggling smiles at the disproportionate heaps of praise and party invite for literally putting one person on an empty 55-seat Herc.

"You guys fancy a drink?" she asks us.

"Hell, yeah," is Joe's reply and from the speed of it, I suspect he saw the same as me which I hoped to be beer.

"We've no beer, I'm afraid," she adds pulling a face that sort of has an apologetic theme about it. Joe gives out a disappointed sigh that the Taliban could have sensed from several kilometres away.

She scurries off and returns minutes later with an assortment of soft drinks in cans that are freezing cold and painfully hard to hold on to.

"Come and have a sit on the grass," she says to us, "it's so much better in bare feet."

I notice that she's wearing flip-flops and she takes them off as she steps on to the grass.

We all remove our boots, crunch up our sweaty slightly smelly socks into balls and place them in the tops of our boots.

As our feet make contact with the soft grass we make sounds such as "oooh," and "ahhhhh."

Our Aussie host smiles and says, "It's lovely, isn't it?"

After months of boots, flip-flops, dusty plastic floors and general dirt, it's like a soothing medicine. We find a place to sit ready to listen to the guitarist while drinking our super-cooled soft drinks.

"What do you use this grassed area for?" asks Norts.

"Sitting on, mainly," replies the Aussie. "Sometimes barefoot meetings, maybe a bit of light sport."

"It's a brilliant idea," announces Norts. "We have a patch of flooded dirt," as she strokes the grass still in a state of amazement.

The armed roadie unexpectedly turns out to also be the artiste, as he picks up the guitar and welcomes everyone to the evening's entertainment with the classic line of "One, two, one, two, one, two, can everyone hear me OK?"

Without waiting for a reply, he launches into an acoustic version of Wonderwall. He is clearly an Oasis fan as every other song is one of theirs and he even has the mic set a bit too high so that he has the same straining-to-reach-the-mic pose as Liam Gallagher.

He finishes his set with Don't Look Back In Anger and, as the last notes, fade there's a mild round of applause followed by a massive burp from Tosh.

"These drinks are killing me," he says, as we all burst out laughing.

"You dirty little creature," I say to him. I then turn to our host. "I must apologise for our uncouth colleague," I say, "but he's RAF and can't help it. He's only just out of nappies."

Tosh lays down and stretches out letting out another loud burp.

"Oh, dear God," says Joe.

Tuesday 8th

Today is a great day, as our replacements will be arriving later on in the evening. And the even better news is that our flights from Bastion have been confirmed for Tuesday 15th at 0030. We get busy getting things in place for their arrival, which mainly means that anything we are not too sure about gets hidden in the bottom drawer. I try not to do too much, as I know Geordie, and he will make his empire from day one by changing things about for the sake of changing things.

Tosh's last day arrives and expectedly he is excited as a fat kid with a tray of cupcakes to himself. His tour complete, he now starts the process that will see him taken physically and administratively out of theatre. He will hopefully be back at home in just under a week.

He comes into the office smiling and waving a bit of white paper at us like it's a promise from Herr Hitler.

"Well, that was painless," he announces, wanting us to quiz him on what the bit of paper is, even though we all know that it's his clearance chit that is part of the Get Out Of Dodge process.

"Tosh," I say to him, collapsing into one of the chairs, crossing my legs, placing my hands together, and interlocking my fingers.

"Yes, Staff," he says, still waving his paper about.

"You know," I pause for effect, "that during this tour," I pause again, "the ATLO detachment has come to know you as..."

"A fucking massive knob," suddenly shouts Joe, as he grabs the paper from his clutches. He does that trick where he blows on the paper while pretending to tear it in half thus making the sound of ripping paper.

It doesn't have the desired effect as Tosh just exclaims that he'll go and get another one from the shiny arses.[56]

Joe holds the chit in front of himself at arm's length and starts to read it out aloud.

"Corporal Lines has no known sexually transmitted dis-

---

56   Clerks. It's implied that they spend most of their time sitting down so that their arses become shiny.

eases due to him being a virgin." Norts peers over Joe's shoulder. "It says here that you will buy all the Movers a coffee and doughnuts."

"Dream on, dickheads," he sighs and goes to grab the paper from Joe, who instinctively pulls back away from his grasping hand.

Joe crumples up the chit into a small ball and throws it at Tosh like a dart player. It bounces off his head, and I shout at the top of my voice. "One hundred and eighttttttty."

We allow Tosh the privilege of not queuing with the masses and take him in the pick-up direct to the back of the Herc that will, in turn, take him to Bastion for more slow death by administrative procedure. Joe is at the wheel, with Tosh in shotgun, while I am lying down in the back with my eyes closed and my feet perched on the lip of the window. I'm enjoying the sun, as it streams through the back window warming up the front of my uniform. I feel very relaxed as I rock gently, as Joe drives the pick-up at a slow speed along the smooth taxiway. But there's a bit of a sombre mood in the pick-up on that final journey with Tosh.

Joe enquires "So, Tosh, what will be the first thing you do when you get home?"

"Dunno, really,"

"Me neither," says Joe. "It's always a bit of a disappointment getting home, almost confusing."

"I'm gonna drink some expensive Champagne and eat Brie," I declare from the back. I can detect them looking at one another pulling confused faces.

"Why Brie?" says Tosh.

"I haven't had any for ages."

"That's a bit weird," says Joe.

"What's weird about wanting to eat Brie?"

281

"Dunno really, just seems a bit strange, if you ask me."

"I am asking you. It was a question."

All I can hear is silence from the front, but again I can sense the face-pulling.

We pull up to the back of the Herc and do our Mover stuff, letting the loadmaster know the passenger numbers and that we have one on the pick-up. The bus turns up and, after a short wait, the loadmaster gives us the thumbs-up for the passengers to file up the ramp disappearing into the dark.

Tosh is the last one on to the Herc and on the back ramp, Joe attempts to inflict one last bit of pain on him before he takes his seat.

"Take care, copper," he adds, breaking away from the minor scuffle, jumping off the ramp, and walking towards the pick-up.

We shake hands.

"Mate, it's been a good laugh having you along for the ride," I say.

"Yeah, it's been one of the better tours. Try not to get killed in the next week."

"I'll try. Keep in touch and we'll meet for a beer sometime soon."[57]

We park up in our usual place to watch the Herc climb away to disappear into the blue sky.

I look at my watch and announce "Right, Joe, it's time to take the pick-up to the garage for its service."

The pick-up was due a service and its annual check a month before Geordie's appearance. I had also instructed Joe,

---

57   That 'sometime soon' was six years later in a pub in Kent and I had to pay for the beers, as he was still tighter than a duck's arse.

Paul and Norts to report all faults to me so that I could compile a list. I had been receiving requests from KBR in the internal mail asking for us to drop it off for its service. I threw it in the bin and received another one a week later and promptly ignored that one too. I repeated this until I received a personal visit from one of the KBR staff asking why we were ignoring their requests to drop the vehicle off for its annual service. I wholeheartedly apologised saying that I had not received anything in the post but I would drop the vehicle off for its service promptly at 3pm on May 8th.

We drive through the gates to the vehicle maintenance compound at ten to three. We park the pick-up and go looking for someone. There's a door that looks promising and, after parting the beads with my hands to poke my head inside, I see a young guy sitting at a desk in a pair of blue overalls.

"Hi," I say to him.

"Hello, sir," he replies in an Indian accent. "How may I help you today?"

"We are here to drop off our vehicle for a service."

"No problems, sir, do you have the keys?"

Joe passes him the keys.

"Would you be kind enough to look at a couple of faults that have recently appeared?" I say, passing him my list of faults.

"Oh dear," he says, shaking his head, looking at the long list in his hand. "It's due a major service anyway, so we will have to keep the vehicle in for a few days."

"Keep it as long as you need, my dear friend," I reply, smiling. "No rush at all."

"Would you like a replacement?"

"No, no, thank you, we'll be able to get about by other means."

We both head back out through the hanging beads into the sunshine. The maintenance compound is, for me, a mildly painful ten-minute walk from our office. Being deficient of an appendix wasn't part of my grand plan when I cooked it up last month.

The plane containing Geordie's team is due in early that evening. As it's a momentous event, we all decide to meet them off the Herc over at Whiskey Ramp. On the walk down to the CATO terminal in the cool of the evening, there's a slight buzz of excitement among us. Upon opening the doors into the terminal, Joe loudly announces, "The fucking Movers are here and all Ramp flights are cancelled until further notice."

There is a mass sigh from all the passengers in earshot, and a confused Bogdan pops his head up from behind the counter saying something in Romanian that is a rude word.

"Only joking, Bogdan," I say to calm his fears.

"What are you all doing here?" he enquires.

"Tonight, Boggers, my old baldy Romanian friend, our replacements turn up." "Oh," is all that he says, as his bald head disappears back behind the counter.

We all clamber on to the big empty orange bendy bus that's not going to Bremen Mitte but to Whiskey Ramp and collectively decide to sit right down the back like a bunch of teenagers.

"OK, driver," shouts Norts at the top of her voice, "let's go."

The pneumatic door hisses shut and we start moving.

We all have seats to ourselves and with our backs to the windows we put our feet up. "It's like coming back home after a night on the piss," says Joe.

"Except we're sober," says Norts.

"And we're the only idiots on the bus," I add.

"I suddenly fancy a kebab," says Joe, licking his lips.

"Fight, anyone?" enquires Paul.

As we approach Whiskey Ramp, we can see that the Herc is just taxiing to its parking spot. The bus parks up in its usual place, close to the blast wall on the edge of the ramp. We wander down the length of the bus as Norts shouts, "Door, please, driver."

The Herc engines are still going at full whack, as the crew are busy inside doing their shut-down checks. The back ramp is open, and I can see the faint dim red glow of a light somewhere the down the front of the plane. Expectedly, the propellers start to slow as the whine of the turbines continues. As they stop spinning, the tone of the turbines then begins to reduce. The main bright white lights of the interior flicker on, revealing a cargo of humans.

Paul walks slowly forward with his arm up waiting for the nod from the loadmaster, who is preoccupied looking at technical things around the back ramp. Paul manages to get his attention and then receives the "OK to approach" thumbs-up and his pace quickens. They momentarily chat and the loadmaster predictably hands Paul the passenger manifests in an envelope.

Geordie appears from inside the Herc. He stops briefly on the back ramp as if he is surveying his new home for the next six months, and then stumbles as he misjudges the step off the ramp to the concrete floor. I walk towards him as he wobbles towards me. I put my hand out to him to shake his hand and just as I am about to welcome him to KAF he says...

"Fucking hell, man, it fucking stinks here."

Wednesday 9th

I stand in the hot morning sun and I can feel the first beads of sweat running down my back. Geordie's words from last night make me aware that my nostrils are again being assaulted by the smell from the Poo Pond. After breathing in the molecules of shit for six months I wouldn't have been surprised that if, upon my return to the UK, I had undergone a chest X-ray, the doc would have announced that I had a medium-sized turd in my lungs.

I have arranged to meet Geordie and his team outside the accommodation at 10am. It was already 10 past and I remember how exhausted I had felt as I stepped off the back of the Herc almost six months to the day. As I wait, I start recounting my horrendous journey from Brize Norton to Kandahar with the memories of travelling, endless boring briefings with sleep deprivation, and broken-down planes thrown in for good measure. I'm sure the whole deployment process was designed by pilots and chefs in collaboration to ensure that you are far too fatigued to complain to either of them about the unpunctual service or out-of-date sausage rolls on your arrival in country. I shudder and say, "Uurgh."

Just as I decide to go inside to give them all a wake-up call, they all appear at the door, squinting in the bright morning sun. Trying to protect their eyes with one hand and with the other fishing around in the countless pockets on their uniform for either a hat or a pair of sunglasses, they look like an urban dance group who couldn't afford a choreographer.

I can't help but smile, as I know I now have five days to show Geordie and his team the ropes. Regardless of the outcome, soon we will be on one of those planes out of here and, hopefully, a functional one. There will be no more dust or smells, no more Spams asking if I know Prince Harry, no more being woken by the rocket alarm, no more listening to the man hitting the metal pipe with his hammer, no more meeting interesting people, no more gazing at the sun setting over the mountains far off on the horizon.

"Morning, all," I say excitedly, rubbing my hands together to try to get them all motivated. "Did we sleep well?"

My question is answered with nodding heads and grunts and looks of bemusement.

"Was that a rocket attack we had last night, Staff?" asks one of the younger members of Geordie's team. I sense some fear in his question. Naturally trying to quell his fear I say, "Yeah, but don't worry, they are fucking useless at actually hitting anything." I possibly should have stopped there but I added, "In six months they have only managed to kill two people."

"Uh, OK." was his unconvinced reply.

Trying to back-pedal a bit, I go on, "Look at it like this, there are 30,000 of us here on KAF. There's more chance of you having a heart attack, being run over, or dying of food poisoning than of one of those things landing on your head."

"Aww, divvn't werry, lad, we'll be canny," pipes up Geordie in his high-pitched accent, spoken like a true leader.

Now is my time to strike.

"Err, the pick-up is in for servicing unfortunately, so we are using Shanks's pony everywhere for the next few days."

"Aww, shite, man," says the future KAF ATLO, somehow a whole octave higher. I wonder that, if I give him some more bad news, his next response will be a frequency higher and make the stray dogs start howling.

"Come on, then," I say, as I set off walking. I'm still in slight discomfort from my operation, but the pain will be worth it to see the chubby bugger suffer in the hot sun.

I take them all to the DFAC for their first meal and their spirits seem to lift a little. They all chatter excitedly amongst themselves as they scoff down their first breakfast. With my usual cup of cofftea, in the finest Styrofoam that money can buy, I gaze across the dining area at all the different nationalities sitting at the tables in groups, all hunched over their food chatting away.

Now and again someone laughs out loud. Lying on the floor is an assortment of weapons from around the world that would give a gun-loving gangsta a proper hard-on. Most are on their side while some of the heavier weapons are held up on their tripods. I'm thinking about how quickly you can get used to being surrounded by foreigners with weapons when Geordie starts telling me about his journey out here.

It's almost a carbon copy of my experience, except someone in charge has now introduced a 24-hour admin period upon arrival in Bastion to allow a period of adjustment. The word "admin" is always used instead of "sleeping" or "doing nothing", as it implies that at least something is being done, when it's blatantly obvious that it's not. I imagine that the briefing teams got fed up of constantly having to talk louder than 300 snoring soldiers. As they drain the last of their coffteas I look at them all in turn and pose the question, "All done?"

I pick up my weapon from the floor, stand up, and point to the exit with my head and the words, "This way."

They follow me towards the exit with their plastic trays loaded with the remnants of their breakfast, and they obediently dump the leftovers into the bin, as politely requested by one of the many signs. I slip my sunglasses on before I push the door open to let them all outside, whereupon they are all instantly blinded by the sudden transition from the dull DFAC to the late morning sun.

I walk quickly over to the office to start the same process that we went through back in November with Bev. Geordie is already starting to look a bit red in the face.

After going over what was in the office I take him down to the CATO terminal which is about half a mile away. It's starting to get hotter as the sun is now high in the sky. I put a fair old pace on and I can feel my scar starting to burn, but I can see in my peripheral vision Geordie struggling to keep up. His stubby legs are going so fast that they are almost a blur. He must be taking at least three steps for every one of mine. We arrive at the terminal and I announce that we are here. I open the door and go inside, he follows me inside out of the heat of the sun. By the rate at which he is panting it's obvious that his pre-deployment training didn't involve much physical activity. I start introducing him to various members of CATO staff. I can see that the sweat is now dripping off his nose all over the floor.

We assist with all the admin and start showing Geordie and his team the ropes while batting off a constant barrage of questions. We have been breathing and sleeping the job for so long now that we could actually do it in our sleep, and sometimes I find myself hurrying an explanation as my enthusiasm is draining by the hour.

One of the first things his team does is tailor their bush hats, as the Chain of Command still hasn't been able to stamp out this fashion.

KAF ATLO SITREP
week ending 09/05/2012

▶ Staff Sergeant Tucker's team have arrived and we will start the handover process in the morning, *i.e.* hiding all our mistakes.

▶ Staff Sergeant Lee is feeling better after his operation. Please feel free to pass on his thanks to all those who sent messages of get well soon.

▶ NAAFI continue to attempt to sell over-priced goods and out-of-date magazines to unsuspecting soldiers.

▶ From the KAF ATLO team and myself, it's been a blast. We are flying down to Bastion on Monday so we will see you then and make sure the kettle is on.

Sunday 13th

By mid-afternoon, I have covered everything that I can think of. "Have you any more questions?" I ask Geordie one last time.

"Nah, man, I think that's aboot it," which means that the official handover process is done and he's now in charge of the ATLO KAF detachment. I feel a huge sense of world-off-my-shoulders-style relief as the responsibility is now his alone.

"I'm off to do a few things," I say to him as I leave the office to go and meet up with Joe, Paul, and Norts for a coffee at a pre-arranged time. It's a pain suddenly not being able to communicate with one another by text, as we have handed over the Nokia phones. I end up waiting on my own sipping my coffee for half an hour before they turn up. I hear them before I see them. Spirits are high, as they have also handed over to their counterparts, and we are all now free of our responsibilities. We sit on a bench in the sun drinking coffee, feeling good about ourselves, laughing and chatting. We are now starting the process that will see us slowly freed from the administrative shackles of this operational tour, and It's one of those moments that will remain crystal clear in my mind for years to come.

I have to go back to the office to pick up something that I've forgotten. At first, I think I've inadvertently gone through the wrong door as it looks totally different from how I remembered it a few hours earlier. I see a smiling Geordie wrestling a filing cabinet into the corner while puffing and panting, which makes me realise that I am in fact in the right office. He has predictably rearranged everything to make his mark at the start of his new empire.

Monday 14th

We book ourselves onto the first Herc out of KAF this morning, which means a very early start for us all. With the excitement of our impending departure, I hardly sleep at all and am wide awake even before my alarm went off. The Taliban had one final go during the night with a rocket attack, that's the last one I will ever experience. I'm straight on the floor with my hands over my head. The last few hours here aren't the time to take any chances. I hear Geordie follow my end-of-tour and over-cautious reaction as he crashes onto the floor muttering something that sounds like, "Fucking hell, man."

Just as I walk out of the room for my shower my alarm clock goes off. I leave it beeping, just to annoy Geordie one last time. As an after-thought, I pop back in and flick the fluorescent lights on. The alarm clock and lights are off when I come back into the room. I flick the lights back on and I can see the lump that is Geordie in his bed but I can't tell if he's asleep or awake. I had packed up most of my gear the night before so once I'm dressed it's just a case of dragging it outside as noisy as I can be while saying, "Sorry, Geordie."

I pop back in one last time to say goodbye to him.

"Take care, buddy, and I'll see you around."

He looks up from his bed with a pair of eyes that look like he's gone twelve rounds with Mike Tyson, his hand appears, and he says, "Aye, see yer aboot, man."[58]

We arrange to meet at 5am outside the accommodation, and, as I drag my gear outside ten minutes early, I am greeted by Paul, Joe, and Norts already waiting for me, sitting on their gear.

"Cutting it a bit fine there, Staff," says Joe, looking at his watch and tutting.

"I like living on the edge."

In the clear cool morning blue sky, there is a Reaper drone circling overhead at a lower than normal altitude.

I look up at it and say, "What have you done, Joe?"

"I hope it's one of ours," says Norts.

"There's more chance of it taking us out if it belongs to the Spams," adds Joe.

It continues to circle and we continue to watch it.

"You know we might be on a big TV screen in the Pentagon while some generals debate if they should vaporise the four scruffy-looking targets looking back at them," I say.

"Maybe it's had one of those badly timed annoying messages telling you Windows is updating and is going to re-start," adds Paul.

It eventually stops circling and as it flies off into the distance Joe sings, "Da da doo da," which we recognise as a bad version of the Windows shut-down tune.

---

58   That was the last time I ever saw him, as our paths never crossed again. He left the Army a year after me and I heard he started a career in organising First Aid courses for civilian companies.

Because the pick-up is still away for repairs as planned, I've had to bribe Hamish with all my leftover Green Bean free coffee vouchers to give us a lift to the terminal. Because it's our end of tour, dragging our belongings all the way to the terminal just wasn't going to happen. He appears at the door of the accommodation, rubbing his eyes, and looking more asleep than awake.

"You're a bunch of cunts," is all he can manage, as he wanders off to get the RAF pick-up.

As he pulls up on the side of the road, we chuck all our gear into the back of the pick-up and pile in. Three minutes later we pull up at the deserted terminal, pile out, and chuck all of our gear back out of the pick-up. We shake hands with Hamish in turn, while bidding him our farewells. He just grunts at us all as he just wants to go back to bed.

For our last flight, we decide to do the full passenger experience and not abuse our position to bypass the tedious process of check-in. Forty minutes later we have our bags checked-in and we are all waiting in the upstairs departure prison cell, bored stiff.

"We should have just arranged to go straight to the Herc," I say.

We are squashed into the Herc by the loadmaster, as it's a fairly full flight but we manage to get to sit together. As usual, it's a flight of being with your own thoughts once the ear defenders are put in your lugholes to mask out the ear drum-destroying din. I realise that this will be my last ever flight on a Herc and take time to look about. I can see all the internal workings, made up of wiring looms, rods, cables, quilted insulation panels, and piping. It really is a complex piece of machinery that has to work well together to keep us in the air.

The sound of the reducing engine power signals the start of

our descent into Bastion. Even though it does have a few small round windows, you can never see anything out of them, as the bright light streaming in is just too great for your eyes to adjust to because of the darkness inside. I feel the pressure in my ears, as the descent is probably steeper than your normal Ryanair jet into Magaluf. The Herc changes direction several times and the sun's rays streaming through the small window slowly move about. The power is eventually reduced even further and I feel the nose rise and we level off which indicates that we are about to touch down. You can hear the runway below, rushing by before we even bump onto it. As soon as the wheels make full contact with the tarmac the power is increased to full with the propellers in reverse to assist with the pilot's heavy braking. I have already braced for this to lessen my arse sliding along the net webbing seat.

Our entrance into the new arrival lounge, that, for once, isn't a tent, isn't much to write home about. Nick meets us with the comforting words, "Fucking hell, here's the Regimental skivers at last."

"Blah, blah, blah," is all I can think of as a comeback.

We retrieve our bags, and the same clunky pick-up that took us all to the departure tent six months earlier takes us all to another tent that is used for recreation. The day is spent lounging about, drinking too much coffee, wandering about, and catching up with people we haven't seen for a while. Nick and most of his team are still busy handing over to their counterparts, and I don't see again him again until later that evening.

"Right, I'm all done now, so time for a brew," Nick says, physically looking better now that his burden of responsibility is passed on.

"You have to hear this," he adds, while filling up his cup

with hot water from the boiler.

"You know Staff Sergeant 'Jo' King?"

Jo wasn't her first name but this is what she'd been christened when joining the military and nobody had a clue what her first name was.

"Yeah, I know her."

"Well she's taken over from me, and, during the handover, she says that she's got a bet going with Geordie Tucker as to who can lose the most weight on this tour."

"I'm sure you should be fit and ready to deploy at the beginning and not seeing it as an opportunity to treat it like a personal Slimming World," I say.

"I had to pop back to the office, and as I open the door I catch her necking a whole packet of Haribo sweets out of the bag like someone who hasn't eaten for a month. I say to her, 'Fucking hell, Jo, you ain't gonna win the bet doing that'.

"As she wipes the excess sugar from her gob she tells me that the bet doesn't start until we've all fucked off."

"Getting that last sugar hit in," I say, laughing.

Tuesday 15th

It's just gone midnight, and we are all waiting outside, sitting on a picnic bench, with all hope of the 0030 departure fading, as we know it's impossible to load the C-17 and take off in 30 minutes. There was never any hope really, as this is an RAF plane, so it was a foregone conclusion that it was going to be late anyway. The hope was just that it wasn't going to be too late.

Dave Davidson is on the end, chain-smoking his way through as many fags as physically possible to try to elevate his nicotine levels to compensate for the impending ciggy-free two-hour flight.

"You should try two at a time?" I suggest.

"Don't be daft," he says, putting a new one in his mouth with his left hand, while stubbing the last one out with his right hand.

Nick is doing an impression of a passenger who thinks he's forgotten his helmet for a flight.

"Me helmet, me helmet, I've lost me fucking helmet, oh bollocks, I'm in the shite now," in a deep Scouse accent. He then says, "Errr, it's on yer 'ead, Staff."

"Oh, yeah, err, thanks for that," he carries on as his over-active imagination continues to run riot and another performance starts.

"Imagine that there was a red and blue button that we had to press in times of emergency and I had briefed Jo King to press the red one."

"Ok," I say, confused as to exactly where his latest act is going.

"Just as I'm getting onto the back of the plane I suddenly remember that I briefed her wrong and it's actually the blue button she should press in times of emergency. I look back to Jo King as I'm being herded onto the back of the plane and start shouting to her but she can't hear me above the noise of the engines."

He stands up and starts shouting in the direction of an imaginary Jo King, "It's the blue button, the blue button, press the blue one, not the red one, the fucking blue one."

It's a performance worthy of an award for something as he is surrounded by 40 soldiers all looking at him in total silence. Some are looking in the direction he was shouting thoroughly confused as to what they are actually experiencing.

We finally depart Bastion at 0200 hours, late, all crammed into the back of a C-17 that will take us to Al Minhad to meet up with a more comfortable plane that will eventually take us on to Cyprus. My knees are pressing against the seat in front, but, as I have an end seat, I am able to stretch my legs out at an angle, giving some needed relief. It's really dark in the bowels of the plane, apart from a red light that is high up in the ceiling down towards the front. I briefly fall asleep, and wake to feel my feet pinned down by something heavy. Through the darkness, I can just make out that someone has given up trying to sleep in their seat and has lay down in the narrow space between the seats and the side of the fuselage. He is using my feet as a pillow. I'm worried that if I move my feet that in his relaxed state he might crack his head open on the hard aluminium floor.

I have no option but to remain there and I slowly feel the pins and needles creep across both of my feet. I try to ignore it but, in time, my legs are numb from the knees downwards. He stirs, briefly raises his head from my feet which I use to retrieve them. His head drops back down and, without my pillowy feet there for his noggin to rest on, it continues to fall all the way down towards the aluminium floor and makes hard contact. I feel the contact through my seat and wince at the violence of it. He sits up rubbing the side of his head and looking about in the darkness wondering what just happened. As the blood starts filling my numb legs I get the pain I get every time I try to move them as the blood flows back into them.

I'm relieved when the aircraft finally pulls up to a stop on the ground at Al Minhad. There's just a bit more waiting to be done to make the pain of being squashed in the metal tube for the last few hours an experience that will stay with you for just that little bit longer. Finally, we are allowed to get up and get the blood flowing back to our numb limbs, as we all congregate in the aisles that are down the sides of the cabin and not the middle. I disembark from the dim interior of the aircraft into the artificial sodium light of the brightly-lit apron. There is a noticeable increase in the temperature. I follow in line as we are all pointed in the direction of a collection of Portakabins. It's 0430, and I have a horrible taste in my mouth comparable to having smoked several cigars, but really it's due to having been up most of the night drinking cheap cofftea. Apart from the short power snooze before being woken by the in-flight entertainment that was the pillow clown, I've been awake for over 24 hours. The room we are directed into is just as bright inside as outside, except that the lights are markedly whiter. There are lots of comfy-looking seats placed around small coffee-style tables that are covered in reading material. I see Nick and Joe waving at me to beckon me over to their claimed little cluster of seats. I pick up a newspaper as I sit down and look at the date.

"Fucking hell, this paper is yesterday's," I exclaim.

Joe leans forward and picks up a *Runner's World* magazine. "It's this month's copy!"

"So this is where the up-to-date reading material supply chain stops, eh," adds Nick, "the sneaky bastards."

I try to read the paper for a few minutes, but my eyes won't stay open. I put it down, lay my head back and close my eyes...

Instantly I am shaken awake by Nick with his elbow in my ribs and the words, "Come on, lad, it's time to go."

"How long was I asleep?"

"About an hour, Rip Van Lazy Git."

I wipe the dribble from the side of my mouth and stand up, still not quite awake, with only one eye functioning. The direction is all in reverse now, as we file back out of the door in the direction of a passenger jet that wasn't there an hour ago. The sodium lights have been switched off and the sky is a light orange as the sun is just peeking its head over the horizon. I shuffle slowly in line to the bottom of the steps, where the shuffling becomes even slower. I start my way up the steps one at a time. One step, wait, another step, wait. I see the door to the plane as my final exit from this part of the world. Once I have gone through it there's no going back and I am home and dry. The queue becomes even slower. Another step, long wait, one foot on the next step, wait. The door is tantalisingly close but we are not moving. At the speed of a tortoise with four broken legs, I finally make it to the door, and I am greeted by a slim lady in her blue cabin crew uniform who looks very out of place surrounded by all of us in our military fatigues.

"Welcome on board, sir," she says in an NOS Eastern European accent.

"Thank you," I reply with a smile.

I continue to shuffle down the aisle behind Nick to the first available seats. We place our helmets, body armour, and daysacks into the overhead luggage and slide into our seats.

In his Scouse accent, and with an elbow in my ribs, he says, "Where's yer helmet. Staff?"

He starts to giggle, closes his eyes, and in his own world says, "The blue button, it's the blue one, the fucking blue one."

I manage to stay awake while the cabin crew rush around doing what cabin crew do. The engines slowly start to wind up and after some 'bings' and 'bongs' and unintelligible mutterings on the PA system, we start to move. The plastic fittings in the cabin rattle as we slowly bump our way along the sea of white concrete towards the runway. As the plane approaches at an angle, I can see all the way down the runway, and it's so long that it disappears over the horizon. As it lines up on the runway, the plane comes to a halt for a brief second before the engines go to full power. The pilot releases the brakes and we are off. I am pressed into my seat slightly as we gather speed. There is some motion from side to side as the pilot uses the rudder to keep the aircraft travelling in the general direction of the runway. The nose rises and the wings bite into the cool morning air lifting us from the ground. I am just about to say something significant to Nick when I hear someone behind me say, "Ooh look there's the Bur, the Burj, the Bergerac, the Bergerac Kal." Unable to pronounce it, they eventually settle with, "It's that fucking massive skyscraper."

I look out of the window and even though it's a long way off his description is pretty accurate, as it is a fucking massive skyscraper.[59]

Like nearly everyone else on the plane, I try to sleep most of the way to Cyprus, but it's not the restful type of sleep. I keep waking as my head falls every time my neck muscles relax. It's a relatively short flight to RAF Akrotiri, and before long we are descending over Lebanon. I can see all the way up the coast towards Turkey and the whiter-than-white snow-topped peaks of the Mount Lebanon range. As we near touchdown, I make out Limassol's beach front, which is already filling up with holidaymakers starting their day of sunbathing.

The aircraft thuds onto the runway and, as the reverse power and brakes are applied, there's that same motion from side to side as we slow down. Before long the plane has parked up and we are shuffling down the aisle towards the back door. The same lady who greeted me a few hours earlier bids me farewell, and, as I step onto the metal stairs, I instantly feel the relief of the cool wind on my skin. It's like feeling you are home as the oppressive heat of the foreign land is now just a memory. We file across the apron towards the terminal. It's the only logical place to walk to, but we are being directed by

---

59   The Burj Khalifa is, indeed, fucking massive.

hi-vis vest-wearing persons, just in case we suddenly forget how to follow the line and decide to go our own way. On the left of the terminal is a large balcony, and I can see the heads of those soldiers who arrived yesterday and will soon be getting on the aircraft that we have just vacated and which will take them back to the UK. Into the terminal we go, across the shiny well-polished floor, up some stairs, and straight back out of the terminal, through the automatic glass sliding doors, and onto waiting coaches. They are brand-new looking posh coaches, and are adorned in an unreadable Greek script and not the German that I had become quite used to seeing. We put all our gear in the underneath luggage compartment then board the coach for 20 minutes of waiting, while the RAF Akrotiri movements staff mill about, scratching their heads over a problem that they have encountered. The coaches set off one at a time and, 200 metres from the terminal, they park up one at a time outside a building. A very young hi-vis vest-wearing RAF Mover with a two-way radio climbs up the steps onto the coach to make a well-practised announcement.

"Ladies and gents, welcome to RAF Akrotiri. Shortly you will be taken into the transit building, where you will be able to have a shower. On your way in please collect a laundry bag and a name tag. Place your uniform inside the laundry bag and write your name on the tag."

Simultaneously everyone on the coach places their hands on their chest to feel if they have a pen on them in one of their breast pockets.

The young Mover, expecting this, continues with his performance, "There are pens inside the building."

The self-patting down stops immediately.

"You will get your clean laundry back later this evening. After your shower, you can change into your civilian clothes that you were told to pack in your daysacks."

"I'm glad he clarified that," says Nick. "I wasn't looking forward to the next 24 hours bollock naked."

He rabbits on, "You'll then be taken to the cookhouse for a free breakfast." The 'Save As You Starve' policy had found its way to Cyprus.

"I'm glad that he clarified that too, as I didn't have time to get any Sterling from the fucking Bureau de Change back at Kandahar," I say to Nick.

"You will then be briefed on the day's coming activities. On conclusion of the day's activities you will be taken to your accommodation for the evening. Thank you for your time." He disappears down the steps just as quickly as he arrived.

The few women on the flight wander off to the female door, while in the male side it's pandemonium, as two hundred soldiers try to use the five pens and ten shower cubicles available. I give up and go back outside to escape the madness. Spotting some breeze blocks that are neatly piled up by some bushes, I park my backside on them. I can hear the high-spirited chaos inside the building as the British Army's finest laugh, scream, cheer, and shout swearwords. Dave Davidson wanders over from his hiding place behind a coach trailing a cloud of smoke like he's actually on fire. He's just restoring his nicotine levels to off-the-scale after the morning's cigarette-free flight.

"Alright?" he says, in-between breathing in the filth like a scuba diver who has just surfaced after running out of air.

"Are those fags the ones from Kandahar?" I enquire.

"Aye," he says, in the brief second that the cigarette isn't glued to his lips. Doing some quick maths in my head, and knowing how many he smokes in a day, I say, "I only sent you down 2,000 a few months back."

"I got Paul to send me some down every week."

"They're probably banned here, you know?" He shrugs his shoulders, and, from behind the smoke, I hear, "I don't give a shit." The level of bedlam coming from inside the shower block sounds like it's reducing, so I mooch off for a shower leaving Dave Davidson to finish his current pack of 20 cancer sticks.

The turmoil that is most of the passengers transforming from their dusty military kit into laddish holidaymaker outfits has now moved outside the building leaving me to shower in relative calm. I bag and tag my kit and throw it onto the pile of laundry bags in the corner of the room not expecting to see it again. I make that slapping noise that you can only make when flipping and flopping across a smooth tiled floor in flip-flops which means you won't be able to sneak up on anyone. Slap, slap, slap, slap, I go, as I slowly make my way outside towards the noise. Everyone has formed into small groups of their own units and I see the tribe that is the Movers hanging about under the shade of a tree. As I slowly make my way over to them the slap, slap of my flip-flops changes tone as I step onto the rough tarmac floor.

A short tubby moustachioed ginger-haired sergeant in a hi-vis vest, who looks like he's from the 1970s, is holding a clipboard in one hand, which gives him total authoritarian rule amongst us flip-flopped rabble. He begins....

"Ladies and gentlemen, if I could have your attention for the next few minutes. My name is Sergeant York."

"You reckon he was christened Sergeant York?" asks Nick.

"I am in charge of the team," he pauses, his left arm that is holding the clipboard makes a movement to highlight the line of 20-plus bored-looking soldiers, all in hi-vis vests, that are his team and not some random hi-vis vest-wearing soldiers who just happened to be standing next to him at that time.

"They will be looking after you for the next 24 hours."

"Do they do massages?" shouts someone from the back, setting the crowd off giggling.

"If you have any questions please feel free to approach my team or me."

"What's the capital of Switzerland?" calls a different voice, followed by an outbreak of laughter.

Sergeant York looks defeated already.

"I think Sergeant York was volunteered for this task and doesn't want to be here," says Nick.

"You will be escorted from here to the cookhouse for breakfast."

"Escorted?" says Nick, "Are we under arrest?"

I had been through the decompression process after a previous tour of Iraq. On that one, we were taken to an exclusive military beach near the Episkopi Garrison called Tunnel Beach. It was named so imaginatively because it was only accessible via a tunnel.

We were dumped on the beach for the entire day to swim and get sunburnt to our heart's content. I fell off the big rubber banana inflatable that was being towed by a speedboat and cracked a rib on some random Captain's bald head who had been sitting in front of me. I doubt if he had any hair it would have cushioned the blow. Later that evening we were taken to our accommodation for a barbecue of Greek food and all the beer we could consume. On the flight out the next day, I was doubled up in pain from my rib, hobbling because I had sunburnt my feet and had a hangover from hell. I was in serious need of some more decompression. "I can't wait to have a swim in the sea," I say to Nick, thinking of the healing properties that the sea would have on my scar.

"Unfortunately, Tunnel Beach is shut due to maintenance

on the tunnel," announces the tubby Sergeant York.

"You're fucking kidding me," is all I can come up with.

Sergeant York continues, "Alternative exciting activities on offer for you today will be go-karting and swimming in the garrison pool."

"I can't swim and I don't have my driving licence with me," shouts another voice.

"I blame the government cutbacks," says Nick. "Last time I was on decompression we had water skiing, quad bike off-roading, magic shows, massages, zorbing, and sightseeing trips over the Med to see the pyramids."

"Really?" I say unconvinced.

"Yeah, we did, I swear."

"When was this?"

"Err, actually no. I think I dreamt it."

We are herded off to breakfast in a long line, with our hi-vis vest guards escorting us. They look like they are ready to pounce on anyone who might try to make a break for it. At the entrance to the cookhouse, I see an A4 piece of paper stuck on the glass door expressly forbidding the wearing of flip-flops inside the cookhouse.

"We're in the shit already," says Nick. "Go and polish your toenails ready for CO's orders."

"I fucking bet it's one sausage, one egg, one rasher of bacon, one small spoonful of beans, and one piece of shit bread."

Our merry band of Movers claim a table of our own and all stare quietly at the paltry breakfast that is exactly as I have described above.

"This is what happens when you turn the fucking shithouse into a profit-making company," says one of the young privates sitting on the end.

Some big-looking bloke is having an argument with one of

the staff because he wants two sausages. The civilian chef is having none of it, while the hi-vis vest guard is trying to calm the situation down by placing himself in-between the two. He gives up and displays his displeasure by muttering on top of his breath, so the chef can hear him, "Fucking civvy cunts."

He continues to rant, and I know everyone in the cookhouse is agreeing with him.

"All they can afford is £1.59 per soldier on the biggest operational budget. I'd rather steal a Land Rover and drive down to McDonald's."

This threat of car crime gets the hi-vis vest guard's attention, and they are all quite uneasy after his announcement.

After breakfast we mill around a small garden out the front of the cookhouse waiting for the slow eaters to finish their hearty breakfast. Dave Davidson is creating his version of a smoking volcano as he burns his way through another pack of 20 climate changers.

"You know why the breakfast was so small, don't you?" Nick says to me. I don't reply, as I know it's going to be one of his stupid answers.

"So we don't drown when we go swimming in the garrison pool. It's common knowledge that if you don't wait four hours before swimming you'll get cramp and die."

Sergeant York makes an appearance again with his clipboard and starts calling out units.

He shouts, "29 Regiment RLC."

"Here," shouts Nick back to him. "Well, it's not the entire Regiment as the majority are in the UK. but it's OK, as they got a note from their Mum excusing them from operational tours."

The fortunate units that he calls out are off for a morning's go-karting down at the garrison go-kart club, and we are directed to a waiting convoy of minibuses. At the go-kart club we are given green overalls and white crash helmets that are all sized for someone with a Mekon-sized[60] head. On the club veranda appears a tanned and upbeat guy in a pair of shorts, a Hawaiian shirt, and deck shoes. He starts to brief us and he's far too jolly for the crowd.

"This guy looks like he has spent his entire career in Cyprus," says Nick.

"Hi, guys, welcome to the Akrotiri go-kart club. I'm Corporal Smudge Smith and I'll be running the go-karting today. I see you're all kitted out and I bet you're raring to go?"

Silence is all he gets as appreciation for his pun.

We are suitably kitted out, apart from lack of foot protection, as we are still wearing our flip-flops. I suspect a few toes might be detached during the non-contact racing that's about to start.

"When you're out there today, please try not to crash into one another or I'll send you to the naughty step."

A big angry-looking Scottish guy who's more tattoo than soldier says, "I'm not fucking five years old, pal."

"Errrr," he stumbles, as the comment has put him off his usual cheery patter, "please follow the instructions of the marshals and, err, enjoy yourselves." He reels the last bit off at a breakneck speed so that he can disappear back into the safety of his office.

We take turns causing mayhem on the track, mainly crashing into one another or trying to make others crash. It's actually tremendous fun, and soon we are all laughing so much that our heads hurt. In my case, my side hurts, as, even though the Doc didn't forbid go-karting, I'm sure it's not good for me. As one go-kart comes in, someone else takes the seat, and then

---

60   The Mekon was the super-intelligent alien with a massive green head who was the arch-enemy of Dan Dare in the 2000AD comics that I read as a kid.

rushes down the pit lane as fast as its lawnmower engine will let it go. One of our hi-vis vest guards, who was watching us from the veranda, was getting bored, so he asks if he could have a go. Within 10 minutes we have all come in for a break, and we are now watching all the guards race the go-karts from the veranda.

"I'm glad they're enjoying our fucking decompression," says the angry Scottish guy. Soon the convoy of minibuses is back, and it's now our turn to go swimming. The hi-vis vest guards park up and hand in their helmets. I had served in Cyprus a few years earlier and lived on Akrotiri. My old house is just around the corner from the pool and I am interested to have a quick look. As we pull up, I can see it in the distance down the road. Wanting to get a better look for old times' sake, I wander around the minibus and across the road, much to one of the guard's surprise. Out the corner of my eye, I see him suddenly leaping into action. He rushes my way with his arms out wide as if he's about to rugby tackle me. He continues towards me and, still with his arms out, he manoeuvres himself around the front of me. I am expecting him to say, 'Nothing to see here'.

"Fucking hell, mate, calm down, I'm not about to go AWOL."

I'm truly shocked by his over-the-top reaction. Must be contaminated and kept away at all cost from the garrison's inhabitants, who are going about their daily business.

"You need to go back over the road, sir."

He calls me "sir" because he doesn't know who he's dealing with here, as my leisurely attire doesn't give away my rank.

"I used to live in that house over there. I'm just having a look, Mr Mackay."[61] I look at him and he's still looking uneasy

---

61   The tough and austere Scottish prison warden from the 70's sitcom Porridge, played by Fulton Mackay.

and ready to tackle me to the ground.

"Do you think I'm gonna make a..." I pause, as I realise whatever I say will fall on deaf ears.

He's not going to relax until I head back over the road. I am beaten by this strange response so I turn around and walk back over the road muttering "Un-fucking-glaublich."[62]

I say it in German so not to cause offence.

The rest of the afternoon is spent floating around the pool, reading books, and helping ourselves to the big never-ending selection of ice creams and fizzy drinks from a bored-looking lifeguard. I enjoy relaxing in the pool and run my hands over my scar which is still pronounced. I was looking forward to the healing properties, even if they had been psychological, that I would have got from a dip in the big blue. I find a book by Buzz Aldrin about his experiences on the Apollo mission to the moon, which keeps me entertained for the rest of the afternoon.

About 4pm, Sergeant York returns to grace us with his presence, and proclaims, in a tone that's been repeated a thousand times, that we will be taken to the transit camp near Episkopi, where the evening activities will be a barbecue and a comedian.

We gather our stuff together and, wanting to see if Buzz's mission to the moon was a failure or success, I slip the book into my bag. Our hi-vis vest guards start herding us towards the door and the waiting coaches parked up on the road outside. I see the hi-vis vest guard from earlier and make eye contact with him. He looks back at me and smiles sarcastically. I start to walk off in a direction away from the coach while keeping eye contact with him and he continues to smile. I keep walking off, waiting for his smile to show signs of di-

---

62   Unbelievable.

minishing. As soon as I see a reaction I turn around and start walking back towards him. As soon as I see his smile return, I turn around again and continue away from him. It's all bloody childish but I am enjoying annoying him. I keep this up for about five minutes, which is enough time to start see his face turning red, and not from the sun.

I park my arse next to Nick on the coach, and he says to me, "What was that all about?"

"Just annoying the SS guards."

The journey to the transit camp takes me past familiar places... Akrotiri village with its excellent kebab shops, the aerial farm, which was a collection of different styles of aerials covering a few square kilometres of open space, and which I think was used for eavesdropping, the salt lake with its pink flamingos, the rows of apple and lemon orchards either sides of the road, the strawberry fields where I often bought my children cartons of big succulent strawberries in December.

The coach struggles up the small, steep, winding track which leads to the transit camp that is hidden away from all habitation. In normal times, it's used for visiting units from the UK or Germany who are taking part in a battle camp so that they can get to practice infantry skills in a different environment. The coaches all pull up in a neat line, and, once again, a hi-vis vest guard climbs up the steps to give us another brief.

"Welcome to Radio Sonde transit camp," he says this, as if it's a luxury resort complex, and not just a collection of concrete buildings surrounded by rocky barren scrubland in the arse end of nowhere.

"Your accommodation is ready and your laundry is here."

"I bet I have some tiny person's laundry," says Nick, doubting the administrative capabilities of our hosts.

"This evening there is a barbecue laid on for you, and entertainment in the form of a comedian."

"I do like Peter Kay," shouts someone from the back.

"It's not Peter Kay, I'm afraid," replies the hi-vis vest guards in a serious tone.

There's a collective "awwww" from everyone.

Briefing over, we pile off the coach and go looking for our accommodation that has been allocated by unit. Everyone is walking about, checking the bit of A4 paper stuck to the door to see if it's their unit's accommodation.

"I'm gonna sit this one out," says Nick, as we wait by the coach, "because I'm a forward thinker I let everyone go forward and do the work for me."

I hear someone shout in the distance, "29 Regiment is over here,"

"See that," he says winking at me, "I didn't have to move an inch."

We both head in the direction of our newfound accommodation, making the flipping and flopping noise as we go.

It's cool in the accommodation blocks and, in typical transit style, it's quantity over quality. Even the bunk beds are slim-lined to get a few more into the small space. In total, there must be beds for about 30 people. We all choose a bed by chucking our gear on it and then go looking through the pile of laundry bags.

Before I even get close to the pile a laundry bag hits me on the side of the head followed by the words of Joe, "There you go, Staff,"

The next hour is taken up by a shower, some sorting of the little kit that I have, and a realisation that I'm feeling really tired. "I do like a bit of Cypriot food, you know," I say to Nick, as I'm starting to feel hungry.

"I don't think I've ever had any," he replies, "Is it like kebabs and stuff?"

"They do afelia, sheftalia, halloumi cheese, souvla and souvlakia," I say naming a few of the things I remember from my time here.

"Never heard of any of them," says the Neanderthal. "I had pitta bread once, isn't that Cypriot?"

"You need to get out more."

We hear the announcement that the barbecued dinner is ready for serving and a huge cheer goes up from everyone. In good old fashioned British Army leadership, we let the junior ranks go first. In due course, it's our turn to join the queue as we file towards the chefs dishing out the grub. As I get closer to getting served I see that, instead of the Cypriot delicacies I was expecting, that it's going to be a burger and big sausage that wouldn't be out of place on a roadside cafe on the A1. Other gastronomic delights on offer are chicken legs and breasts, and several gallons of mayonnaise-soaked coleslaw in a large oblong stainless steel container.

I load up the paper plate with the meat selections and a hefty dollop of mayonnaise cabbage hell. I have to balance it on the palm of my hand with my fingers outstretched to give some support to the flimsy plate as it struggles under the weight of the food. I follow the queue, where I am further burdened with bread, a bottle of water, plastic cutlery, and napkins. Then the act starts of trying to get to a table without dropping anything. At that moment, any table will do, but I'd still prefer one surrounded by friends. Spotting them all huddled on a wooden picnic bench, I slowly shuffle in their direction, just on the edge of balancing and dropping the lot on the floor. I ask Joe to take some of the stuff off me before I just drop it all on the table. He chooses that moment to pretend to be deaf so I just let go of the lot to a round of laughter. My sausage rolls off onto the floor, the chicken breast makes a dash across the table, but the flat burger stays put. I pick up the water bottle and slap it down in the coleslaw. I was hoping for it to just make a bit of a mess, but, due to the watery viscosity, it goes all over the place. Everyone is covered in white mayonnaise spots on their clothes, face, sunglasses, and hair. Joe has some dripping off his nose.

"Fucking hell," he says using a napkin to clean it off.

"Fucking hell, Staff," I emphasise.

"Fucking hell, Staff," he corrects his lack of discipline.

Nick arrives in the same precarious balancing state as I did just seconds before and sees the coleslaw carnage.

"Fucking hell, did they manage to fire a rocket all the way over here?"

"The coleslaw took a hit for us," says Norts.

I pick my sausage off the floor, give it a blow, wipe it on Joe's top, and put it back on my plate.

"Will you fuck off?" says Joe, recoiling from the greasy sausage that's leaving grease marks.

"Will you fuck off, Staff?"

"I'm gonna shove that sausage up your arse, Staff."

Everyone breaks out in howls of laughter.

After dinner, the bar is opened, but there is strict rationing in force. Not because there isn't enough booze but because "enough booze" wouldn't be enough for us after six months of being on the wagon. Our entitlement is either four cans of lager or one bottle of wine. Within seconds the bar is ten-deep and in the scrum everyone pushes, elbows, and bumps one another to get to the front for their first alcohol hit in months.

In time, the mass brawl diminishes, and Nick and I can walk unmolested to the bar. We give our names to the hi-vis vest-wearing disinterested barman, who was one of our hi-vis vest guards earlier in the day.

He enters a state of deep concentration as he looks down a list on his clipboard. I am half-expecting him to say, "Sorry, lads, your names aren't down, so you ain't coming in," but instead he says, "Aha!" as he finds our names, highlights them to denote that we have had our ration, and duly passes us each four cans of a local Cypriot beer.[63] "Can we not just get one now, otherwise the others will go bastard warm," says Nick.

"Sorry lads, you have to have your four beers together," says the hi-vis vest barman. "It's the rules."

"You mean it's easier to highlight my name than put one tick against it you fucking little sh...?" says a tired and argumentative Nick, as I drag him away.

With our prize, we go in search of somewhere to sit. Moving in the opposite direction to the crowds, who are making their way to the makeshift stage to wait for the comedian, we find a couple of old garden chairs behind one of the buildings that has a view across Episkopi Bay and the Akrotiri peninsula. The sun is low in the sky off to our right, the sea is a deep blue, and some smoke, either from a house on fire or someone burning their garbage, rises straight up in the calm conditions.

We arrange the chairs so that we can soak up the view and park our arses. "This isn't too bad," says Nick. "Some people pay good money for this." He takes a drink from his can, pulls a face, and says, "The view, I mean, not this cat's piss."

"It's scientifically proven that things taste better when they are free," I say optimistically. I take a swig from my beer, and, like a reflex action, my face scrunches up from the unusual taste. "I suppose, as taxpayers, we are technically paying for

---

63   I once heard someone claim that the beer in question was akin to armpit sweat.

this beer." I take further mouthfuls, and my palate starts to adjust to the odd taste. "Maybe it is free," I say, looking at the can in detail.

We hear the comedian start his act with a round of applause from the crowd. His voice is muffled in the distance but I can tell from the pace and modulation when the punchlines are due. There's a slight delay before I hear the corresponding laughter. By the time we finish our fourth warm can, it's getting dark. "I dunno about you, Nick, but I'm feeling pretty cream crackered."

"It has been a couple of strange days," he replies.

"It's always weird coming back. It's undeniably harder than the deploying bit I think. When you deploy you are mentally ready for it. The change in daily life, the increase in work, and the fact that your arse belongs to the Army just that bit more. But when you get back it's a massive anti-climax. You expect the world, but the world has continued to move on and didn't wait for you."

"Fuckin' hell, Staff, that's a bit deep for this time of the day. I'll get back tomorrow, walk through the door, and the missus will say..." He puts on a high-pitched whiny voice, "'Where have you been?' or 'The fucking sink is leaking again.'"

"Well, that's enough philosophy and shit warm beer for one evening," I say, as I get up. "I'm gonna hit the sack."

We flip-flop our way back to the block in search of our beds.

Wednesday 16th

The sun is streaming through one of the tiny windows and it's right in my face. At first I think that someone has put the light on, but, as I realise it's the sun, I roll over. Before I open my eyes I can feel that my tongue has become a sandbag and dried my mouth out. I open one eye and stare across the room at the green lumps on their beds, and I can hear the calm breathing from everyone. Struggling to keep my eye open I blindly send my hand in search of a bottle of water that I hope I left automatically on the floor the night before. As I feel about on the cold tiles for a plastic bottle, I clumsily knock one over with the back of my hand. With the mental picture of what's happening in my head, I grab the fallen bottle, pop the top off and pour the instant liquid relief into my mouth. I remain prone on my back, with my eyes shut, and some water dribbling down my cheeks, and my mind goes through the events of the day before. Departing KAF, the hours spent in Bastion, the flights, the stopover in Al Minhad and what we got up to in Cyprus. Although all that happened in the last few days, it feels like months ago already. I think of the barbecue and chatting to Nick and the last thing I can remember was walking back to the block. I think I had fallen asleep before I made it to bed. I didn't even dream, as dreaming was far too much like having to do something in my exhausted state. I start to think about the coming day and that tonight I will be back in Cirencester and how extraordinary that thought feels.

Standing In front of the mirror with my toothbrush in my mouth, I see someone looking back at me. It's like a bad copy of me, that has been dragged through a hedge backwards, put on numerous uncomfortable flights at all hours of the day, and made to wait a lot. My eyes are only half-open, and the white toothpaste all over my chin makes me look like I'm foaming from the mouth. After a shower and a shave, I start to feel a little bit better and the clean uniform helps in my regeneration back into something that feels normal.

After breakfast, there's an air of excitement, as everyone is busy packing up their kit and putting it into neat little piles outside each of the accommodation blocks in anticipation of the coaches arriving. Once we think everyone is out of the blocks, Nick does a quick counting of heads to ensure that we haven't left anyone sleeping in their bed. It would be slightly embarrassing should we leave someone behind. The hi-vis vest guards make an appearance the same time as the coaches' drive through the gate, which is timed well as the serene atmosphere suddenly erupts into the-last-helicopter-out-of-Saigon style chaos. The hi-vis vest guards enter the coaches, and turf the few that made it on back off. Sergeant York makes his last appearance in front of us. His job will start again with the arrival of the next batch of end-of-tour soldiers, who will be arriving on the plane that will take us home today. He requests that we all fall in for the departure briefing.

"I do hope Sturmbannführer York isn't going to give us any bad news this morning," says Nick.

"Good morning, ladies and gents, I do hope you all had a good evening and enjoyed the entertainment," says Sergeant York with a painful looking smile.

"It's bad news..." says Nick.

"Unfortunately," says Sturmbannführer York, pausing for a brief second.

"I fucking knew it," says Nick in a hushed voice "I fucking bet you any amount of money that it's a TriStar, and the piece of crap broke down."

"Your flight," Sergeant York continues to drag out the news, "has been slightly delayed."

"There was a technical issue with the aircraft last night."

"Yep, it's a bastard TriStar," shouts Nick.

I don't know it at the moment, but this is to be my last ever flight onboard an RAF aircraft, and, just like my first one back in 1990, it's going to be late.

Sturmbannführer York continues to talk about some other stuff, but by now he's lost the attention of the crowd, as the mutterings of disappointment spread like a petrol-fuelled fire in dry Cypriot grass.

The decompression staff don't want us hanging around the transit camp, so we are told to get on the coaches as we will wait for the plane down at the terminal in Akrotiri. We chuck our meagre belongings in the belly of the coaches and line up to get on. The hi-vis vest guards are doing their last head-count to make sure no one has escaped. Just as I put my foot on the first step one of the hi-vis vest guards says, "Good luck."

"Thank you," I say back to him smiling, as we have just recreated the scene from The Great Escape, where Gordon Jackson is caught out by the Gestapo.

Hours later, the TriStar finally turns up, and we are all out on the balcony, watching it taxi towards the terminal. "About time, yer fucking tardy bastards," shouts the angry Scot.

As soon as it comes to a halt on the empty pan, the steps are moved into position by the doors. The passengers start disembarking, and today it's our turn to watch them walk towards the terminal.

"Oh they're in for a treat," says Nick. "I bet they can't wait to watch the decompression staff on the go-karts."

Laughter breaks out around Nick from those who hear his comment. "Aye, the cheeky bastards," says a guy shaking his head, "I never had a go."

The first thing I notice out of the window, as we pop out of the clouds somewhere over Oxfordshire, is the greenness of the countryside below. It's not like it's become any greener, but it's like trying something sweet after months of abstinence. There's such a wealth of different types of green spread out - light greens, dark greens, mild greens, green greens, and eat your greens. Even from up here, my eyes can sense the freshness of Spring and I am quite excited about it. As the TriStar turns and weaves on its path into Brize Norton my eyes are glued to the outside soaking up the colour. I continue to gaze outside even after landing. Only after the plane comes to a halt and the seatbelt sign pings do I look back inside.

The minibus pulls up outside the cookhouse and, as I was the last one on, I'm the first one off.

"Welcome back, Staff," says a Major, holding the cookhouse door open for us. I've no idea who he is so I just smile and nod as I pass him. As I walk inside I am confronted with a wall of families made up of wives, young children, mums, dads, aunts, uncles, and grumpy looking teenagers who all start clapping and cheering. I can't help but feel a bit embarrassed and I don't know where to look.

"Welcome back, Staff," says a smiling Private, as he hands me a can of cheap lager. "Bacon butties are on their way."

I hurriedly duck out of the limelight and to the side where the wall of families starts. I turn around, put down my can, and start clapping as the rest of the soldiers walk in as if I am trying to blend in. Some of the young children and wives are too excited to wait and break out from the wall running forward to hug their loved ones. I feel that what I am experiencing is quite personal, and that I shouldn't be privy to this.

I see Nick come through the door, and I grab his attention as he is handed his shitty can of welcome-home lager.

"Fucking cheapskate bastards," he says, rolling the can around in his hand examining it carefully and pulling a face. "They could have at least forked out for some wife-beater.[64]"

"Your missus not here?" I enquire.

"Nah, she's still at work," he opens his can, takes a swig,

---

64   Wife-beater: Stella Artois.

and starts patting me on the back.

"Well done, Staff, you're looking good. How was your tour? Kill anyone?" He starts giggling at himself, and carries on laughing at his own monologue.

"As a token of your Government's appreciation, we'd like to give you this can of shitty lager for your service over the last six months. Without people like you the world would be a more chaotic but safer place," he says, as we raise our cans.

"Go on, lad, get it down your neck," he adds, still patting me on the back and encouraging me.

"To the Taliban," I say, raising my can again, "and their bloody awful aim."

We are passed a bacon roll each by a chef who looks like he'd rather be somewhere else.

"Red and brown sauces are over there," he says in a monotone voice, as he moves onto the next unfortunate customer repeating himself like a robot. They are individually wrapped in tin foil and comfortingly warm. The uninterested chef probably made them earlier in the day in anticipation of our early return and then hastily reheated them upon an excited telephone call from the guardroom to the cookhouse as we drove through the main gate.

I open mine up, take a bite, and, as I pull my full mouth away from the soggy roll, all of the boiled bacon, including the rind, is pulled from in-between the unbuttered roll.

"Furr fuff's safe," I say with my baconless roll in one hand, can of beer in the other, and a load of stringy bacon hanging from my mouth like a meaty beard. Like a helicopter carrying an underslung load, I attempt to guide the bacon back onto the empty roll that's still in the tinfoil with my head. When it's on target I let it go with my mouth. The boiled fatty cargo looks like a falling curtain and folds itself up on top of the roll with a mouth-sized bit missing. Placing my beer down I compact it all up into the foil and leave it on the side.

"Unfortunately, Staff," Nick announces in his official voice of the government, "due to the amount of money we pissed up the wall sending you all to Afghanistan we've had to let the professional chef go."

I take over with the announcement.

"Your bacon rolls were made today by Tommy, who works at the sewage plant, but is doing some unpaid community work for a slight misdemeanour involving a dog, a pigeon, and YouTube."

"I think it is the dog," says Nick, poking at it suspiciously with his little finger, before he closes it and places it on the side next to mine.

Troopy Evans wanders over and nods at us both in turn. "Staff, Staff," she says in her Welsh accent, "it's not a bad welcome back party, is it?"

"The welcome back fund must be pretty depleted now," says Nick, with just enough of a sarcastic tone that Troopy's Sandhurst training doesn't pick up on it.

"What have you both got planned for the rest of the day then?" she asks us.

"I'm gonna get out of this garbage," referring to my uniform, "get some lovely smooth-but-a-bit-musty civvies on. Then I'm gonna get on my bike, enjoy this weather, and cycle to Tesco's for some expensive Champagne and a massive wedge of Brie,"

"Brie?" she says, surprised, "that's a bit weird."

"You're not the first person to say that, which I find a bit weird."

"Are you not able to get home tonight?" she says.

"Nah, my family are down in Kent so I'm gonna have to

wait until we wind everything up on Friday. My car probably won't start anyway and I'll take a few days to get used to travelling faster than 20mph."

It was normal to have a few days back in camp after a tour just to let everyone come down a gear or two. The last thing we wanted was all of our soldiers tearing up the motorways at 100mph and killing themselves needlessly in a traffic accident. It was in reality lots of sitting about with a few games of football and early knock offs that was all done under the guise of admin. "What about you, Ma'am?" I enquire.

"If I can get my car started I'm heading off to Wales as my best friend from Uni is getting married at the weekend."

"That's a bit weird," I add.

"Why's that a bit weird?"

"Why's eating Brie weird?"

She shakes her head and ignoring my comment she turns to Nick.

"What have you got planned, Staff Number Two?"

"The troop commander has just called you to a turd, Nick," I giggle at him, "do you want me to be your material witness?"

"I'm just off home to get moaned at." he says, with a face like thunder.

The cookhouse starts to empty as the families begin making their way home for a more private reunion. I wish Troopy Evans a good leave and make arrangements to meet Nick in the Sergeants' Mess bar later on that evening. I have one remaining task to complete. I go looking for Joe, Paul, and Norts to bid them farewell before they disappear off on their leave. Paul is with his family being led by his two young and exceedingly excited children towards the exit. Not wanting to invade too much I catch him before he reaches the door, pat him on the shoulder and say, "Paul, thanks very much for all your hard work over the last six months. If I don't see you tomorrow have a good leave and I'll catch you in a few weeks, pal."

"You too, Staff," is all he manages to say over his shoulder as his children continue to drag him away with the thrilled cries of, "Come on, Daddy."

I find Joe and Norts mixing with their peers gulping their beer as if closing time is just about to be announced.

"So what are the plans, troops?" I enquire.

"It's the all-ranks bar tonight for us, then we are going to hit town," says Norts.

"Well I didn't expect that," I say, rolling my eyes. "I'd be contacting the Padre if you weren't going to get plastered tonight. I actually meant what are your plans for leave?"

"Dunno," replies Joe. "Maybe book a week's holiday with the missus, carry on house hunting, sit about getting bored counting down the days to the next tour?"

"Quality," I reply.

"I'm gonna go and see my Dad," says Norts, "then I'm not too sure. Probably just catch up with friends. I'll find something to do, I always do."

"Well don't go too mad tonight, will you? I don't want to be down the cop shop in the morning explaining to the Rozzers that wearing traffic cones on your head while climbing a statue is totally out of character. I'll see you about, but if I don't make sure you have a good leave."

I shake their hands and add, "Thanks for all your hard work though, you all made it a good tour and ,who knows, maybe one day I'll write a book about the last six months and make you all sound like a bunch of tossers."

As I make my way outside I hear Norts shout.

"We'll see you in court."

My gear is lying on the pavement at the front door to the accommodation block. The appendix scar starts to itch at the thought of straining under the weight of my kit. I manage to 'voluntell' the help of a couple of passing soldiers to drag my gorilla box back up the stairs. Just like six months previously, it makes a considerable thump on every step, which is amplified by the all-metal construction of the stairwell, and even more so by the cheap flimsy walls that is the Sergeants' Mess accommodation block. I stop outside the door to my room, tell them to just dump it there, and thank them for their help. I push my way in. Straight away the expected musty smell hits my nostrils. It's not very overpowering as I did remember to leave the window open just a bit for some ventilation. Nonetheless, my desk now looks like the window sill to a cheap hotel, as it has more than a few dead flies now decorating it. I drop my bag and go back out into the corridor to pick up my other bag and push the plastic gorilla box in with my foot at the same time. As I give the box one final push, it slides clear of the door, which I let slam shut behind me. I take off my jacket, throw it on the floor, and walk to my bed that is stripped bare. I sit down on the end of it, let out a sigh and say...

"What the fuck was that all about?"

British casualties for the month of May
5 killed & 23 wounded

Total British casualties during the six months
32 killed & 111 wounded[65]

Total civilian Afghani casualties
Unknown

65   https://www.gov.uk/government/statistics/op-herrick-casualty-and-fatality-tables-released-in-2012

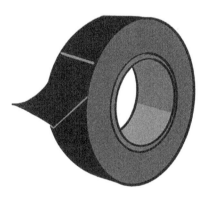

Epilogue

I LEFT THE Army on 5th August 2013, exactly 24 years to the day that I walked through the gates to report for my basic training at Buller Barracks in Aldershot. My final act of military exertion was the handing in of my ID card to a bored clerk in the Regimental Headquarters. He couldn't even manage a smile that morning, which I presumed was because he was jealous of me with his years ahead of him. I walked outside, got in my car and unceremoniously drove out through the gates of 29 Regiment never to return again. The brass band, clapping crowds, and company organising the firework display had obviously got stuck in traffic that morning.

I had started the transition process that would take me from serving soldier to Mr Civilian earlier that year. It involved such exercises as CV writing, interview techniques, and meetings with people like my old school career advisers who were as uninterested in doing their job now as much as way back then. The new professions that they would suggest for me, with my logistical background, were in exciting areas (their words not mine) such as Warehouse or Project Management, Health and Safety or other generally dull sounding jobs. I was dying inside little by little every time they made a suggestion, as this was supposed to be an exciting time with the reboot of life that would see me getting out of the military rut that I had unintentionally settled into. I really just found it all rather depressing. I have always been a great believer in things happening for a reason, and tried to convince myself that something would turn up eventually.

As a treat for the depression caused by the switch process, I headed off to Cotswold Airport one day to start an ambition

327

that I had had since I was a child. I had always had a desire to fly but this was barred to me due to cost. Now in the twilight of my military career I found myself in the fortunate situation of having the prerequisite requirements to gain my pilots licence. Time and money.

A few months later, I somehow managed to pass the skills test and gained my Private Pilot's Licence. With high-octane careers in Project Management and Health & Safety not quite enticing me, I decided to start the training towards my Commercial Pilot's Licence. After even more time and money - the hardest period being six months in a classroom with a load of straight-out-of-school 18-year-olds learning the theoretical knowledge to pass the Civil Aviation Authority exams - I passed my Commercial Pilots Licence on 26th November 2015. I became a flying instructor the following year and started my own company which I named Buddy's Aviation. Buddy was my dad's nickname and I always wanted to be the CEO of BA. Getting into flying late meant I had to catch up, and, after a year of honing my flying skills instructing at a school in Essex, I started to venture into organising and taking pilots on trips over to the continent. This has proved quite popular and, as my business has flourished, my logbook has filled up with more and more exciting destinations. It would be the fairy tale ending if I weren't writing this last bit of my book while working at a COVID-19 testing facility.

But that's another story.